'Powerful and absorbing, S... ...., painstakingly documents the gross injustices facing women around the world. Some of the stories made headlines, many passed unnoticed and too many occurred much closer to home than we might realize. Elaine has done us a great service in not only describing what is happening, but also seeking to understand why it happens – and what needs to be done to tackle this worldwide problem. This is not an easy book to read, but it is a necessary book. I hope the stories she shares and facts she brings before us will encourage us all to pray – and to join in the work of bringing healing and an end to gender-based violence.'

Jackie Harris, Editor, Woman Alive

'This is a courageous and a terrifying book. We all know that acts of violence against women are a problem, but never have we realized the scale of the problem is so huge. Where others would be cautious to speak out for fear of offending the sensibilities of other cultures, Elaine Storkey is clear and fearless, inspired by true compassion. Scrupulously researched and documented, illustrated with both statistics and personal stories, this is a book that changes perceptions and could play a substantive role in achieving change.'

Margaret Hebblethwaite

'Elaine Storkey's book is well researched and deeply moving. She captures most vividly for her readers the way in which patriarchy, religious and cultural traditions, complications in the law, lack of education (not always) and isolation can combine and lead to women being abused, being permanently disfigured or their untimely death. This violation of the human rights of girls and women is indeed a "deep scar" across humanity. The collusion that perpetuates the deepening of this scar will only cease when there is true respect given to girls and women in societies throughout our world. Reading this book can be the first step to breaking that collusion.'

The Revd Rose Hudson-Wilkin, Chaplain to the Speaker of the House of Commons

'This is a timely book, emerging as the world awakes, too slowly, to the problem of violence against women and girls. Elaine Storkey examines this issue through her characteristic twin lenses of clarity of thought and kindness of heart, carefully building up a mosaic of facts, figures and testimonies of those who have suffered in many different settings. I challenge anyone to read this book and emerge unchanged.'

Baroness Maeve Sherlock, House of Lords

Elaine Storkey is a philosopher, sociologist and theologian who has held university posts at King's College, London; Stirling; Oxford; Calvin College, USA; and the Open University. A Fellow of Aberystwyth University, former Director of the London Institute for Contemporary Christianity and high-table member of Newnham College, Cambridge, she has also lectured in Africa, Asia and Haiti. Her presidency of Tearfund, the aid and development agency, spanned 17 years. A broadcaster and author, she has been a passionate advocate for justice and gender issues for 30 years, implementing many changes for women through 28 years on the General Synod of the Church of England.

SCARS ACROSS HUMANITY

Understanding and overcoming violence against women

Elaine Storkey

CASCADE *Books* · Eugene, Oregon

Pickwick Publications
An Imprint of Wipf and Stock Publishers
199 W. 8th Ave., Suite 3
Eugene, OR 97401

www.wipfandstock.com

ISBN 13: 978-1-4982-8232-1

In grateful memory of my father,
James Thomas Lively

Contents

Acknowledgements

I am grateful to all those women who have let me into their lives and shared their stories with me. I want to thank Tearfund for planning and arranging my trips during my 17 years as President, and for all those colleagues who travelled with me. My admiration for the international partners and their relentless work for the alleviation of poverty and injustice has never abated. I shall always be in the debt of those who hosted my visits, negotiated with officials, and kept me safe when stopped by armed militia at checkpoints. Thank you to Peter Grant and Mandy Marshall of Restored, who share the deep concerns of this book, and work hard themselves to end violence against women. Natalie Collins of Spark has been a wonderful encouragement, and her energy spurs me on. Christina Rees, Kate Coleman and Cham Kaur Mann have been supportive of the project from the beginning. I have appreciated Rose Hudson-Wilkin's involvement and I cannot overestimate the encouragement of Carolyn Armitage, who read the uncompleted manuscript and gave invaluable advice.

The tireless work of Heal Africa in Goma, Democratic Republic of the Congo (DRC), has been an enormous inspiration. The wonderful Lyn Lusi, who died far too early, but lives on in the healed lives of others, showed me the level of commitment needed if violence against women is ever going to be eradicated. Catherine Clark Kroeger, my friend and mentor over many years, shared the vision of this project, and would have loved to see its outcome. I am grateful to Mary Evans for her long friendship, and for arranging my lectures in Ethiopia, and to Lauren Bethel and the International Christian Alliance on Prostitution for all they have taught me. The time I have spent with the groups they partner has been moving and enriching.

I want to thank the team at SPCK for their enthusiasm for this book, and for all their help. Their scrupulous attention to detail has been gratifying. And, as always, I have relied on the support, commitment, love and insights of Alan, who has urged me on and endured my absences overseas. His partnership in marriage these many years has been total. Finally, thank you to Zadok, Torin, Kieran, Elijah, Iona and Ezekiel for keeping me sane.

Introduction: naming the problem

There is one universal truth, applicable to all countries, cultures and communities: violence against women is never acceptable, never excusable, never tolerable.
United Nations Secretary-General Ban Ki-moon

On 25 November 1960 in a sugarcane field in the Dominican Republic, three sisters were brutally assassinated. They had been tortured, strangled and clubbed to death. They were three of the four Mirabal sisters who had spent many years highlighting the corruption and injustice of Rafael Trujillo, the infamous Dominican dictator, whose cruel and despotic regime brought death to more than 50,000 of his own people. The women were persistent in their defiance. Their husbands had been incarcerated for political opposition, and they themselves had spent much time in jail. One night, as three of them were driving home from visiting the isolated prison which held their husbands, their jeep was intercepted on a remote mountain road. They were dragged out of the vehicle, taken to a lonely field, and savagely murdered. The jeep they had been travelling in was then thrown over the cliff, with their bodies inside, so that the world would think it an accident. But no one was fooled. There were cries of outrage from the Dominican Catholic Church, already in conflict with Trujillo, and this was followed by international condemnation. The despot's rule was never to recover. Within a year his regime would be finished, and he himself assassinated.

Nearly 40 years later, in 1999, a representative from the Dominican Republic brought a resolution to the General Assembly of the United Nations that 25 November should be known as the International Day for the Elimination of Violence against Women. This day had long been remembered in Latin America and now it was the United Nations' turn. The resolution was adopted. Not only would the bravery of the Mirabal sisters never be forgotten, but

1

the brutality meted out to them would stand as a marker for all violence inflicted on women, along with the call for its elimination. What had begun as a protest by four courageous Catholic women against a vicious tyrant now became a justice call for women across the globe who suffered at the hands of tyrants, whether that tyranny was political, military, economic, structural or domestic.

Yet there is a paradox here, of course. The Mirabal sisters were well-connected, highly educated, fluent, popular and influential. They had once moved in elitist circles, were articulate as women in the public sphere. The injustice their family received was visible and recognized; their murder was open to scrutiny and its outcome had far-reaching consequences. Yet few of the women with whom they now share this day will also share these characteristics. Far more often these women will be unidentified, silent, out of public view, hidden behind a veneer of normality, or suffering in isolation. Their deaths will not make the headlines; their names may never be known. But they are ever present, and exist in their millions. As the statistics calmly tell us, acts of violence to women aged between 15 and 44 across the globe produce more deaths, disability and mutilation than cancer, malaria and traffic accidents combined.

The truth is that violence on such a scale could not exist were it not structured in some way into the very fabric of societies and cultures themselves. It could not continue if it were not some-how supported by deep assumptions about the value of women, or some justification of the use of power. In many cultures such assumptions are reiterated every day in the absence of legal protec-tion for women, or indifference towards issues of human rights. Even in advanced democratic societies, where women play a signifi-cant part in public life, the level of domestic violence and sexual abuse suggests that these assumptions remain powerful and effective, even though they are concealed behind closed doors.

So what is it about human societies that tolerates the kind of animosity and violence towards women which is greater than that found in animal communities? What is it about some human cultures and tradition which makes it normal for women to undergo rape, beatings, cutting, molestation, infanticide, trafficking, bride burning, child prostitution and sexual slavery? It seems ambitious to hope that we can find an answer to these questions. But if violence to women is ever to be eliminated, we need to know what it is that we are up against.

My wish is that this book will be a contribution to that search. It has been eight years in the writing, begun after a trip to Africa brought me in contact with women whose sufferings from war were heart-wrenching. My conviction has grown that the power we are up against is destructive. I am just daring to hope that this effort might add its own weight to changing the structures and extinguishing the brutality which have harmed and destroyed far too many women.

1

A global pandemic

One in three women may suffer from abuse and violence in her lifetime. This is an appalling human rights violation, yet it remains one of the invisible and under-recognized pandemics of our time.

Nicole Kidman

Reflecting on the vast crowd of Egyptians who gathered in Tahrir Square in 2011, Mark LeVine suggested:

> What made Tahrir truly revolutionary . . . was that in the Square you could see, *feel*, the possibility of a new Egypt, a different Egypt, an Egypt that could fulfill the dreams of the majority of its inhabitants. Young and old, rich and poor, Muslim and Copt, metalhead and Sufi, everyone radiated '*silmiyya*' – peacefulness – even as they screamed at the top of their lungs . . .[1]

Two years later, on the second anniversary, the mood of the crowd in Tahrir Square was very different. Mixed in with mob anger and frustration at the feared political impasse were seemingly gratuitous assaults on women. The fact that these occurred in a public place in broad daylight was no deterrent. The incidents even seemed orchestrated. Testimonies from victims and their rescuers painted a horrifying picture of tens or even hundreds of men, grabbing the women protesters, dragging them along the ground, tearing off clothes and veils and seizing their breasts and thighs. Women activists, co-ordinating rescue attempts of women under attack, were readily admitted by men into the centre of the crowd and then became subject themselves to brutal physical and sexual assaults. The same place where, two years earlier, women stood on what they believed was equal footing with men to protest for greater freedom now became the place where they were singled out for violence and harassment.

A report in 2014 presented over 250 cases, from November 2012 and January 2014, in which women protesters were sexually assaulted, often raped, by mobs of men.[2] The eruption reflected long-term problems within Egyptian society. According to Egyptian journalist and commentator Dr Nervana Mahmood, 'Egypt is ranked the worst country around the world in terms of violence on women. Eight out [of ten] women are harassed in Egypt every day.'[3] Diana Eltahawy, Egypt researcher for Amnesty International, reported on Amnesty's blog Livewire: 'Almost every girl and woman – regardless of age, social status or choice of attire – who has walked the streets or taken public transport in Cairo, has experienced some form of verbal or physical sexual harassment.' She went on to describe a 'culture of denial, inaction and in some cases complicity by law-enforcement officials, who not only fail to protect women from sexual harassment and assault, but also fail to properly investigate allegations and bring perpetrators to justice'.[4]

There is more to attacks on Egyptian women, however, than mob rule or 'stranger-violence'. Some of it is much closer to home. Two mothers living in Cairo – 32-year-old Nour and 36-year-old Zeinab – were among the victims of domestic abuse identified in 2012 in Egypt's independent English-language newspaper, *Daily News Egypt*. Their stories of rape, torture and brutality at the hands of abusive husbands are horrifying but not unique. Nor is the failure to gain help from relatives, or ask for a divorce.[5] A study carried out in 2009, by the Egyptian centre for the rehabilitation of torture victims, *El Nadim*, found that 79 per cent of the 1,261 women they surveyed said they had been exposed to domestic violence. In over half of the cases reported (55 per cent), the perpetrator was the husband. Most of the remaining cases were carried out by fathers (20 per cent), brothers (12 per cent) and the husband's family. Even though there were some marginal differences related to the level of women's education and income, the report saw these as not very significant. Its message was clear: 'women subjected to domestic violence in this research cut across all social and educational statuses.'[6] Violence against women is not criminalized in Egypt and the present regime does not give this issue any high priority. With so little protection from the law, the current outlook is very bleak. We might well conclude that this is indeed a society where women are particularly vulnerable. We might be thankful that this level of assault and disregard for women's safety rarely happens in other countries.

Unfortunately, we would be wrong. Reports from across the world and endorsed by the United Nations tell a much more shocking story. They are quite categorical that violence against women is not confined to a specific culture, region or country, or even to particular groups of women within a society. Rather, in all societies, women and girls are subjected to forms of physical, sexual and psychological abuse. Violence against women is carefully identified as a manifestation of the historically unequal power relations between women and men, a process which cuts across lines of income, class and culture. As the Secretary-General's study put it:

> Women are subjected to violence in a wide range of settings, including the family, the community, state custody, and armed conflict and its aftermath. Violence constitutes a continuum across the lifespan of women, from before birth to old age. It cuts across both the public and the private spheres.[7]

Many factors contribute to this violence. There is the impact of traditional and customary practices – the lower status many women have in the family, workplace and society. Social pressure can exacerbate the problem, especially when women feel isolated by fear of stigma, so find it difficult to give an account of their experience. Yet, even if these women did speak of the brutality they endured, in many countries the lack of legal protection leaves them further exposed. The dearth of laws or courts, the absence of legal aid, the requirement of witness corroboration, and the likelihood that offenders will go unpunished mean that in so many areas of the world women do, literally, suffer in silence. Reports from the United Nations draw their conclusion: 'Gender-based violence is perhaps the most widespread and socially tolerated of human rights violations . . . It both reflects and reinforces inequities between men and women and compromises the health, dignity, security and autonomy of its victims.'[8]

Virtually every minute of every day, there are incidents, somewhere, of domestic abuse, rape, honour killings, sexual violence, harassment, acid attacks, bride burning, femicide, mutilation or violation of trafficked women. In some countries, violence is actually an outcome of actions by the state – sometimes by torture, more often by omission, or lack of legal redress. The high incidence of violence against women in armed conflict, particularly where rape is used as a weapon of war, is now very evident. Military fighting men, brutalized by combat, can turn their savagery even on their own village women and leave them damaged for life. The extent of violence against women cannot be underestimated, nor can its consequences. The impact ripples through every area of society; it affects women, children, families, neighbourhoods, men, lawmakers, law-enforcers, health providers and so many of our social institutions. It does indeed leave scars on the face of humanity.

The worldwide problem of violence against women does not mean, of course, that women's personal experiences of violence are the same across the world. Cultural differences are very significant. Culture powerfully influences the kind of violence women are exposed to, and the ways in which it is manifest. We could give a huge list of factors which play into the experiences women endure – factors such as ethnicity, nationality, class, age, marriage patterns, work, economic circumstances, disability or religion. These in themselves can make it difficult to have a single united response to gender violence. But they present a bigger danger also; they can cloak the reality of abuse as it masquerades as local custom, or hides behind religious protocol.

Confronting the problem has been made more difficult because many cultures have had a persistent history of denial about violence against women, even when it occurs daily in their midst. Both nationally and locally, the problem has been shrugged away, with government officials, senior police and military personnel very reluctant to admit that women are in any sense in danger from attack in their region.

'No problem here!' Living with denial in the Congo

My experiences some years ago, in the eastern provinces of the Democratic Republic of the Congo, brought this home to me. In

2005, in a lull in the long-term bloody conflict, I was asked to meet with some senior military officers. They wanted to thank me, as President of Tearfund, for the work our non-governmental organization (NGO) had done in resourcing an education project on HIV & AIDS prevention for their soldiers. They were courteous and hospitable, fulsome in their appraisal of the benefits of the programme. We ate and drank together, joked about English footballers, and they generously offered to answer any questions I might have in appraising the success of the initiative. I took courage and, as calmly as I could, asked if they thought there might be a link between the spread of HIV in that province and the high incidence of sexual violence against women. I was neither assertive nor judgemental, yet the atmosphere changed abruptly. They looked annoyed, grim-faced and offended. My question met instant repudiation. There was no violence to women, they assured me emphatically. I had been misled. Women were lying to me in order to get sympathy and money. Their advice was that I should simply ignore the women's claims.

Pursuing my theme as cautiously as I could, I assembled evidence, offering descriptions of what I had seen on my visits to clinics and hospitals, assuring them that, as a woman, I could recognize sexual damage when it confronted me. Eventually, the men admitted, slowly and reluctantly, that some gender violence in the Kivu Provinces of the Congo might exist, but that these attacks on women were carried out by soldiers from Rwanda and Burundi, not from the Congo. So they concluded with: 'Go and speak to the authorities there!'

Accepting that this might well be a problem in Burundi or Rwanda, I probed whether it could really be true that no Congolese soldier ever raped a woman. Eventually, with enormous reluctance, they conceded that perhaps in 'small isolated pockets' Congolese soldiers raped women (though there were mitigating circumstances, and the women were not without blame!). When I then asked how many soldiers had been convicted and sentenced, however, there was complete silence. It became chillingly evident that there was no legal protection for women against appalling acts of violence. There were no laws, no cases brought to court, no judges to try such cases, and no reparation for the women who had been assaulted and severely damaged. In legal, political and military terms, the problem, quite simply, did not exist. The Congo's well-attested reputation as a 'rape capital' of the world was laid before me. We shook hands solemnly and parted. I was to find it would take many months of advocacy, pressure and prayer within the country before anyone was brought to justice for those crimes.

'There should be laws against it!'

An example from the Congo, in 2005, might be thought of as extreme. In terms of legal provisions, it is not. In spite of the huge size of the problem globally, few countries considered violence against women as needing special prohibitive legislation until the last decades of the twentieth century. In 1979 the General Assembly of the United Nations adopted the Convention on the Elimination of All Forms of Discrimination Against Women (CEDAW) – often referred to as the international bill of women's human rights. The text of the Convention had been prepared by working groups for three years, and its crucial importance was reflected by the speed with which it entered into force – on 3 September 1981, faster than any previous human rights convention. By 2014 it had been ratified by 187 United Nations (UN) member states; the seven states not to have ratified it included South Sudan, Iran and the USA. Under CEDAW, states are required to eliminate gender-based discrimination, not only by making sure that there are no existing discriminatory laws that leave women exposed to violence, but also by ensuring all necessary steps to allow women to experience actual equality in their lives.

Related to CEDAW, violence against women was acknowledged to be a human rights concern in June 1993 by the UN World Conference on Human Rights in Vienna. Seven thousand participants attended this gathering, most of the international human rights community, along with government delegates from 171 states. It broke new ground in addressing gender-based violence, creating a Special Rapporteur on Violence Against Women mandated to carry out country visits. The resulting 'Declaration on the Elimination of Violence Against Women' was a powerful statement of intent, giving a voice to many, long silenced. The immediate focus was to bring protection for women within the framework of international law, introducing terminology to name wrongs, and pushing through the boundaries of gender-blindness in legislation.

Individual countries were also making their own provisions. In the USA, advocates joined professionals from the courts, law-enforcement agencies, victim services and women's movements to highlight domestic and sexual assault, urging Congress to make it unlawful. The result was the pivotal Violence Against Women Act (VAWA) of 1994. (It later added date assault and stalking to the original law on domestic violence and sexual assault.) On the twentieth anniversary of the VAWA in 2012, Vice President Joe Biden announced that annual rates of violence against women had now dropped by 64 per cent. The US Senate had strengthened and re-authorized the Violence Against Women Act in February 2013 despite persistent opposition from a group of conservative Republicans. One provision had given Tribal Nations the right to prosecute non-Tribal members who commit acts of violence on Tribal land, which helped address the particularly high level of violence towards Native American women (though only a third of them reported incidents).

By the end of 2005, 89 countries had some legislation on domestic violence, and a growing number of countries had instituted national plans of action. This was verified in the UN Secretary-General's comprehensive report. Marital rape was a prosecutable offence in at least 104 states, and 90 countries had laws on sexual harassment. However, gaps remained in a large number of societies. In 102 nations there were no specific legal provisions against domestic violence, and no one could be prosecuted for marital rape in at least 53.[9]

Since then, progress in legislation has been marked and rapid. A campaign in Europe from 2006 to 2008, initiated by its leading human rights organization, the Council of Europe (founded in May 1949), pressed for comprehensive standards for the protection of women against violence. The result was the 'Istanbul Convention' (The Convention on Preventing and Combating Violence Against Women and Domestic Violence) adopted by all 47 member states at a meeting in Istanbul and opened for signatures on 11 May

2011. As the first legally binding initiative in Europe to create a comprehensive legal framework to protect women against all forms of violence, it was a landmark treaty. Countries swiftly embraced it. By October, after Poland and Croatia had added their signatures, the Convention had been signed by 26 member states of the Council of Europe. By May 2015, 18 European countries had *ratified* the Istanbul Convention, committing resources for its implementation. The UK was not among them.

Britain's record on legal redress has not been good. Even though all political parties publicly supported the elimination of violence against women, only Scotland had seen proper measures for implementation,[10] allocating £10.3 million to frontline services for victims for 2012–15. Scottish local authorities had commissioned specialist services critical to prevention and early intervention.[11] Yet research published by the European Union (EU) Agency for Fundamental Rights (FRA) in that year showed that the UK as a whole ranked among the worst countries in Europe in relation to high reporting levels of domestic violence.[12] Since then, there have been persistent calls for Britain to ratify the Convention and tackle the root causes of violence against women. Only if the UK commits itself to providing the necessary resources can it demonstrate zero tolerance towards gender-based violence.

Beyond Europe and North America legal changes were racing through other countries. Many desperately needed them. Afghanistan passed its law eliminating violence against women in August 2009, criminalizing child marriage, the selling and buying of women to settle disputes, assault, and more than a dozen other acts of violence and abuse. In 2008 Guatemala made history by passing its 'Law Against Femicide and Other Forms of Violence Against Women'. By the end of 2012 other Latin American countries had followed suit, including Puerto Rico, Bolivia, Peru, Argentina, Uruguay, Mexico and Nicaragua. The level of domestic and sexual violence in Nicaragua had been particularly high; with only six million inhabitants, it actually recorded 37,000 women victims of violence in 2011: 80 women a year were known to have been killed by their partners. In the Philippines the incidence of violence against women noticeably dropped after strict protective laws came into force in 2010.[13] After the United Nations General Assembly created 'UN Women' in July 2010, the monitoring of initiatives in gender equality and the empowerment of women has shown encouraging results.

By mid-2013, the Executive Director of UN Women reported that 160 countries now had legislation which addressed violence against women. The vision behind CEDAW in 1979 had become widely recognized and accepted, forming part of the legislative structure of many countries. Having laws on the statute books is significant. It helps a country to redefine the issue, identifying the violation of women as a crime, and acknowledging their right to peace. It makes a vital commitment to procuring their freedom from danger of assault.

But then we need implementation . . .

It would be good if the story could end there. But sadly, the truth is that real progress has been patchy. In some countries, both the introduction of laws and their implementation has been hampered by inertia. In others, the presence of law has not produced any identifiable change in behaviour. As the UN *Handbook for Legislation* reported:

> Significant gaps in legal frameworks remain. States throughout the world are still failing to live up to their international obligations and commitments to prevent and address violence against women. Too many perpetrators are not held accountable. Impunity persists. Women continue to be re-victimized through the legal process.[14]

Afghanistan is a case in point. Over a 12-month period, the UN collected information from 22 of Afghanistan's 34 provinces. It reported in 2012 that although a rising number of incidents of violence against women were being reported, and courts were issuing more convictions, the overall use of the law remained low. Cultural restraints, social norms, customs, religious beliefs, discrimination against women, acceptance of violence, fear, social stigma threats and exclusion meant that incidents of violence were still under-reported. The report's conclusion was that there was still a long way to go before women and girls in Afghanistan were to be fully protected from violence through the law.[15] This became bitterly evident in May 2013, when parliament was again asked to endorse the Law on the Elimination of Violence Against Women. Conservatives decreed many parts of the law to be un-Islamic – not least the veto against girl-child marriage – and, after two hours of argument, no endorsement was given.[16] A new law the following year banned relatives of accused persons from testifying against them, effectively silencing victims and undoing years of progress.[17]

After the Taliban were toppled in Afghanistan, girls had at least won back the right to be educated there. But even education was brought to the fore in Pakistan through the appalling case of 14-year-old Malala Yousafzai. Shot in the head by the Pakistan Taliban for daring to persist in her advocacy for girls' education, she became a symbol of the fight against gender oppression. Her unarmed bravery was a beacon of light against the cowardly acts of militia, whose repressive ideology turned a child's desire to be a doctor into a threat against their power: a graphic illustration of the way in which internal conflict negatively impacts women. It also powerfully highlighted the issue of violence against women, and the actions of the Taliban received international condemnation. A tweet by Pakistani progressive Nadeem F. Paracha summed up the disgust at such bullying: 'Come on, brothers, be REAL MEN. Kill a schoolgirl.'[18] Yet, although a worldwide groundswell of protest followed against Malala Yousafzai's treatment, and she herself has since occupied an international stage, it is probably also true that the violent attack has been a setback for girls in Pakistan. Brought for medical treatment and refuge to the UK, Malala has been able to mount a global campaign for girls to be educated. But back in her own country, it still needs, even more, to materialize.

Why is change so slow?

There are two simple answers to that question. The first is that many cultures resist legislation. The second is that, even when it happens, legislation is not enough. At the end of the Commission on the Status of Women, in New York in March 2013, one writer pointed to the chasm between legal reform and actual emerging change. Despite a massive increase in the number of laws, many women around the world still have no knowledge of their rights and even less of how to lay claim to them.[19] This is largely because there has not been an accompanying shift in attitudes and culture. The problem is that violence and discrimination becomes effectively sanctioned by the state, especially when it is 'significantly tied to cultural and social norms that pervade a nation, which are then used to justify, excuse or tolerate violence against women and girls'.[20] Many of the later chapters will be looking at this question, especially at the force of culture and tradition.

It is in the name of such cultural and social norms that there is current resistance to a global implementation plan. Some women's groups are concerned that it is in the very countries where it is most needed that the plan is least likely to be adopted. They look with some concern at the way authorities within some African countries and the Organisation of Islamic Cooperation (formerly the Organisation of the Islamic Conference) are conflating the drive to end violence against women with an attack on traditional and religious culture. 'Honour killings' and female genital mutilation widely persist, despite the fact that they are unlawful, demonstrating that the resistance is not easily overcome. Especially in patriarchal societies, links with wealthy Western countries can have a negative effect on women's freedom. This is especially true in times of economic downturn. Yasmeen Hassan, Global Executive Director of Equality Now (a US group), explains that '[the authorities in such patriarchal societies] feel more and more bullied by the west. The recession has made things worse, they have less control over their economies but at least they can control women.'[21] Several studies have also pointed to 'worsening economic conditions, persistent environmental degradation, internal conflict and wars', and documented their impact on attitudes towards women in poorer countries.[22]

The constant need for vigilance

I have just been focusing on cultures where there is a constant struggle to maintain effective legislation to eliminate violence against women. It seems that a great gulf separates those societies which respect women enough to punish those who violate them, and those which reinterpret violation in cultural terms. Yet I do not want to leave the impression that in those cultures which do have strong protective laws the problems are solved. They are not. Very often, the issues of safeguarding simply move up a notch. The danger here is that the presence of laws on the statute book can lull people into believing that the problems are solved, and society simply pays lip-service to the issue. When laws and policies limit women's freedoms or even deem women as 'complementary' instead of 'equal' to men, this trickles down to public perception of women and girls and their role in society.[23] To take seriously the reality of gendered violence means rethinking the way we plan our cities, our transport, street lighting, building construction. It needs to seep into all the provisions we make for those who are vulnerable to attack.

These needs are reflected in random examples. They came to the fore, for example, in an incident in Baltimore, Maryland, USA. A woman psychiatric patient was murdered in the Clifton T. Perkins Hospital Center by another patient – a man with a long history of sexual violence against women. Appallingly, he had been placed in a hospital unit which housed both women and men and, with unbelievable ease, he simply took the opportunity to enter this woman's room and strangle her.[24] Her death opened up the need for planners and policy-makers in the state of Maryland and beyond to recognize the assumptions behind their own policies, and to accept the need to address the potential for violence against women inside their own institutions and places of care.

More regular examples of risk are found among women health workers, as was evident from an incident in a hospital in Middles-brough, UK. A nurse was helping a male patient in the shower, and as she turned her back to allow him privacy, he grabbed her indecently and subjected her to a sexual attack. The patient had a history of assault, but the health worker was not warned and was left alone with the man. The hospital admitted liability and she was compensated, but years later, she still suffers from flashbacks due to the shock of the incident. The frequency of such attacks on care workers was pointed out by a union spokesperson, who reiterated the need for better communication and procedures to be put in place.[25]

The multiple errors involved in incidents of this type all remind us that laws are not enough. When, according to UN Women, up to seven in ten women are targeted for physical or sexual violence in their lifetime, there needs to be ongoing vigilance and seriousness about the problem, and the onus for safeguarding simply cannot be left to women themselves.

Conclusion

As a UN report reminds us, 'Violence constitutes a continuum across the lifespan of women, from before birth to old age. It cuts across both the public and the private spheres.'[26] It also takes many forms – physical, sexual, psychological and economic – which are interrelated yet which remain largely hidden, suppressed by silence. Intimate-partner violence is very widespread, and sometimes leads to death. Harmful and violent cultural practices, including early and forced marriage and female genital mutilation/cutting, are also pervasive. Traditional communities still somehow hide the insidiousness of femicide (gender-based murder of women), sexual violence, sexual harassment and trafficking. Even violence perpetrated by the state, through omission of protection, torture, public agents or public policy is persistent, along with the high incidence of violence against women in armed conflict, particularly rape. So we can begin to understand the all-encompassing nature of the problem on a global scale: that one in three women has either been beaten, coerced into sex or abused in some other way – most often by someone she knows.

In spite of all this, we have to recognize that cultural history is not on our side. Violence against women has actually been celebrated in dance and traditional rituals; it has been glorified in art, literature, film and music. In the history of even Western culture, male aggression has been described or depicted without censor, and woman's suffering re-presented as somehow beautiful or part of her journey to refinement. Legends such as 'The Rape of the Sabine Women', an act said to have been carried out by men of ancient Rome in 750 BC, have excited far too many painters – from Nicolas Poussin (1635), Peter Paul Rubens (1635), Jacques Louis David (1799) and Pablo Picasso (1963) to the 'light-hearted' reference in the BBC comedy *To the Manor Born* about parting one's spinach and finding the rape of the Sabine women on the plate underneath. It found its way into the happy 1954 musical film *Seven Brides for Seven Brothers*. William Shakespeare's play *The Taming of the Shrew* is still being debated with respect to its misogyny.[27] Today rape and gender violence is being treated as a source of humour by misogynous stand-up comedians in sleazy gigs.

Yet, whatever its history, and however artists try to justify their material, it should be blatantly evident to all that violence against women has far-reaching consequences for women, their children and society. Without doubt, it violates human rights, undermines development, generates instability and makes peace harder to achieve.[28] The unmitigated tragedy is that despite the fact that they are widely outlawed across nations, so many different forms of violence are able to persist. Passive sympathy for those who suffer is not enough. Elimination of such injustice takes commitment, perseverance and concerted global action. And it needs each one of us.

2

Violence begins before birth: selective abortion and infanticide

————◆•◆•◆————

Having a girl is to plant a seed in someone else's garden.

Hindi saying

In India, where female infanticide has existed for centuries, now female feticide has joined the fray . . .[1]

Dr Sabu George, a Delhi-based researcher, has spent the past quarter-century exposing what he calls 'the worst kind of violence' in Indian history – the elimination of millions of unborn girls. He regards it as nothing less than 'genocide', and describes the first few months in the womb as 'the riskiest part of a woman's life cycle in India'. An incident reported in a newspaper article illustrates the problem:

> Earlier this month, police arrested two people after the discovery of 400 pieces of bones believed to be of female foetuses in the town of Ratlam, Madhya Pradesh. Last September, the remains of dozens of babies were exhumed from a pit outside an abortion clinic in Punjab. According to investigators, that clinic was run by an untrained, unqualified retired soldier and his wife. To dispose of the evidence, acid was used to melt the flesh and then the bones were hammered to smithereens . . .[2]

The writers of this article go on to describe an Indian documentary series on television, in which two undercover television journalists identified 100 doctors in private and government hospitals who were prepared to carry out illegal sex-selective abortions. Unaware that they were being filmed, these doctors calmly discussed the ease with which foetal remains could be disposed of. If they were too

18

bulky to be thrown into rivers, or buried in fields, street sweepers could be hired to clear them away.

It is an alarming picture of mass termination: prenatal offspring, aborted for no other reason than they happen to be female. During some years the toll has involved as many as two million foetuses, according to a UN report,[3] with some regions of India faring particularly badly. Although accurate figures are very difficult to compile, estimates suggest that 'among the stock of women that could potentially be alive in India today, over 25 million are "missing".[4]

Not all of that is the result of abortion. Female babies who do not fall victim to prenatal selection and elimination are not guaranteed survival after birth. Age-old methods of eradicating them are still in evidence.

> Last summer, a farmer in southern India discovered a tiny human hand poking from the ground. A two-day-old baby girl had been buried alive. The reason? Much of Indian culture favours males over females, sometimes brutally so. Against odds, this baby survived. Her grandfather confessed to attempting murder because his family already had too many females; keeping this one would be too costly.[5]

The disposal of newborn girls seems to be commonplace; 'it happens without any hindrance' said a father whose wife had killed their two baby daughters.[6] Some tiny infants become victims of 'poisoning, throat splitting, starvation, smothering and drowning'.[7] Others are left outside police stations, in bus depots, crowded fairgrounds, or in railway toilets. Most abandoned babies are found too late to save their lives. And although, technically, these discarded offspring die of neglect and exposure rather than deliberate killing, it is still difficult to argue that this is anything other than infanticide. The lucky ones are left outside orphanages, placed in wicker cradles in purpose-built alcoves where the weight of the baby triggers an internal alarm; the babies are taken in and fed, and the orphanage staff struggle to know what to do with another unwanted offspring. The growth of these orphanages is partly a government response to a desperate situation.

The practices of female infanticide and foeticide are a powerful depiction of the institutionalization of violence against women.

There could hardly be any clearer statement of the low value and disposability of girls and women than when, all over the country, 'the elimination of girl children, either through sex-selective abortion or infanticide, goes largely uncensored, undetected, unpunished and unmourned'.[8] These procedures are now woven into the fabric of much of Indian culture, sitting menacingly alongside sexual violence, domestic abuse and rape, and anticipating the brutalities experienced by women in other contexts.

Despite the orphanages, it is evident that there is an uneasy collusion between the state and society in relation to the issue. The shared ideology goes deep into Indian tradition as the very authorities charged with safeguarding the life of the girl child are themselves steeped in an ethos that reinforces the preference for a son and sees the birth of a girl as a disappointment. Substantial social and economic forces come into play: the process of arranged marriages, the patrilocal system where girls are removed from their birth family to the family of their husbands, the pressure on brides from their mothers-in-law who want male heirs, and the huge financial advantage for any family in having sons.

Yet, for more than 40 years, the law has officially offered protection for unborn girls. The Medical Termination of Pregnancy Act, passed in 1971, allows abortion in India only under very strict conditions. It must take place within 12 weeks of conception, there must be grave risks of injury or ill health to the mother, or there must be substantial risks to the child of severe abnormality and impairment.[9] In effect, this means that:

> Indian laws do not, under any circumstance, allow sex determination tests to be undertaken with the intent to terminate the life of a fetus developing in the mother's womb . . . Any act causing the termination of the pregnancy of a normal fetus would amount to feticide, and in addition to rendering the physician criminal[ly] liable, is considered professional misconduct on his part, leading to his penal erasure.[10]

Despite the strongly worded prohibition, the practice continued to grow. Innovative technology made sex selection easier. The cost became affordable by many families and by the mid-1990s clinics were advertising their services of terminating girls as 'spend 3,000 now and save 300,000 later'.[11] So, further regulations became necessary to control the use of these technologies and prevent misuse for sex-selective abortions. The Pre-natal Diagnostic Techniques (Regulation and Prevention of Misuse) Act was passed in 1994, and tightened in 2002. This put sex-selective abortions very firmly and publicly outside the law.

Although the procedures have remained illegal, the laws against selective abortion have had little obvious impact on actual practice. Sabu George and Brinda Karat pointed out in 2012 that, in spite of millions of crimes which take place every year in relation to sex selection and sex-selective abortions, since 1994 when the Prohibition of Sex Selection was passed, there have only been 93 convictions.[12] So the relentless loss of girl children continued. The lethal cocktail of patriarchal traditions, technological development, financial incentives, ruthless corruption and legal indifference has meant that the law has simply failed to protect unborn girl babies.

Technology, clinics and regulation

Indian patriarchal tradition on its own could never have produced the problem as it exists today. Technology continues to play a substantial part. Ultrasound equipment to determine the sex of an unborn child was initially introduced into India in 1979. India has about 35,000 ultrasound clinics, but the proliferation of unregistered clinics, the widespread sale of scanners and the collusion of doctors in expediting sex-selective abortions has compounded the threat to girl babies. There are guaranteed earnings for those whose business is to identify the sex of a child, and, with developments in technology, the growth in mobile ultrasound machines has mushroomed. These machines, which can be operated outside medical centres, are now available in every part of the country. According to one technician, 'You will find an ultrasound machine even in a village which has a road over which only a bullock cart can go, and electricity to run the machine and nothing else.'[13]

The expanded law, forbidding the sale of scanners to unregistered clinics and quack doctors, was aimed to curtail this expansion. Each ultrasound machine must be officially registered under the name of the doctor who is to use it. Yet the widespread abuse of the regulation is glaringly evident. One ministry official reported, 'We recently found 21 ultrasound machines registered under a single doctor. This means these clinics have been individually opened with one single radiologist manning it. How can one doctor operate 21 machines at the same time?'[14] In fact, it is estimated that more than 16 million illegal ultrasound scans have been conducted since the law restricting sales was introduced, illustrating what Sabu George calls a widespread 'indifference of ethics'. He sees the General Electric (GE) company which provides the machines, and those who sell them, as sharing the moral accountability for this: 'How many more millions of girls will have to disappear from India before companies such as GE will recognize their responsibility?'[15]

The responsibility is shared also by doctors and clinics. Brinda Karat and Sabu George argue this, clearly: 'The strong links between sections of a powerful medical fraternity who make profits through the use of sex-selection technologies and politicians and bureaucrats has made a mockery of the legal provisions.'[16] But, in many other quarters, tunnel vision seems to operate in failing to recognize the contribution and collusion of all these participants. Some argue that such agents cannot be held to blame, since they are only providing what the family wants. Sometimes, the blame is even placed on the women themselves – either arguing that this is what women want, or framed in terms of discrimination meted out by women against other women (mothers-in-law against daughters-in-law). The power of patriarchy, greed, indifference or corruption is thus ignored with the result that 'it is women ... who end up getting criminalized, with doctors invariably let off the hook'.[17]

Ultimately, it is governments which have the responsibility to uphold legislation and ensure justice for their citizens, even for the most vulnerable who have no voice of their own. Activists, like Sabu George, feel that for the law to have any teeth the government must be far more proactive. One example stands out:

Although the law expressly bans advertisements of sex selective technologies, Google has been advertising sex selection for the last three years after giving a commitment to honour Indian laws. Even though this has been brought to the attention of the government and raised in Parliament, the government has failed to act.[18]

It is an indictment indeed.

A problem rooted in tradition – the dowry

India's government is only too aware of the power of tradition, and we cannot understand the problem of sex-selective abortion without grasping the importance of that tradition's deep-seated preference for sons over daughters. A welter of factors continues to make males more socially and economically valuable than females. Only sons carry out certain functions under religious and cultural traditions; inheritance and land rights pass through male heirs; elderly parents depend on support from sons in the absence of national security schemes; greater male participation in the workforce enables them to bring in more family income. Women, on the other hand, provide no economic support for their natal family after marriage. Traditional concepts such as *paraya dhan* dictate that a girl is not seen as a permanent member of her birth family, and so if she is given a share in its assets or property, the family will lose out. Not only that; because of the dowry which goes to the bridegroom's family, she will cost the family a great deal of money when she marries.[19] This makes daughters an unproductive investment.

The dowry affects all sections of Indian society. For the rich, it symbolizes status, power and prestige. For the poorer sections, it carries with it a sense of honour. They may not be able to afford the opulent weddings of the rich, but they still need to show they can provide a decent nuptial and dowry. It has been suggested that 80 per cent of bank loans in India are taken to meet the costs of these, and that a spate of suicides among farmers in Vidarbha (in the state of Maharashtra) was linked with failure to repay loans used for marrying their daughters instead of for their farms.[20]

All this is barely surprising, considering what burden a dowry requirement now imposes. It has grown with affluence. 'Decades ago, a wealthy bride's father would have been expected to give gold bracelets. Today it is jewellery, fridges, cars and foreign holidays – and the bride's family may end up paying the bill for the rest of their lives.'[21] It is hardly surprising, either, that the culture of the dowry has many strong critics. The writer Priya Virmani is one:

> A shift in India's attitude towards weddings is urgently due. Bluntly put, dowry equates to a family paying a man to take their daughter's hand in marriage. And the man, with his family, works to extract the maximum price for 'taking' the woman, in ways that can scar lives and damage the institution of marriage. A practice that conflates its women with gold, silver and furniture is absolutely reprehensible. Simply having anti-dowry laws has proved hugely inadequate – urgent emphasis needs to be put on enforcement.[22]

Virmani also outlines the even darker side of the dowry. In extreme cases, the newly wed bride can be murdered by her in-laws or driven to commit suicide because their dowry demands have not been fully met. In 2012, 8,233 dowry deaths were reported, but it is estimated that one woman in India dies every hour in a dowry-related case.[23]

The issue of selective abortion used to be seen as a problem of poverty, where parents of large families could not afford more children, and so they aborted the less economically productive. But it is now clearly as much a problem of affluence as poverty. It is educated parents who plan their families and seek to identify the sex of their child, and often more affluent parents who are willing to pay the fees from clinics, radiologists and doctors. Development and globalization have brought many people more money and a decrease in family size, but they have not erased traditional patriarchal values. Wealthier – and better-educated – Indians still want sons. One survey revealed that female foeticide was highest among women with university degrees. They are only too aware of the impending demand of the groom's family in relation to any daughter they might have. Priya Virmani observes ruefully: 'India's economic liberalisation in the 1990s has seen a proportionate rise in levels of greed, and a bride is perceived by her in-laws as a potential cash cow.'[24] In 2015, an educated woman's fight in Delhi against her affluent in-laws made headlines. Dr Mitu Khurana had been harassed by her husband's family for a Honda city car as a dowry and they then allegedly forced a sex determination test on her. She refused to have an abortion and filed a complaint against them. Her marriage ended but she sought the help of her own parents, and gave birth to twin girls.[25]

Distorted sex ratio

The demographic consequences of mass female foeticide can be seen throughout most of India, but especially in its most developed parts. In most countries and under normal circumstances, the sex ratio at birth usually ranges from 102 to 106 live male births per 100 live female births. This levels out as boys are biologically more likely to suffer child mortality, so in adult populations (i.e. those of 15–64 years) the ratio of men to women is often around 101 to 100. In the USA and much of Europe it is equal.[26]

It is usual for states to have strict regulations on birth registrations, and to publish statistics on sex ratios at birth – part of effective governance. But the Indian census does not publish data on sex ratios at birth. Instead it publishes the child sex ratios – the ratio of girls per thousand boys under the age of seven.[27] Yet even these figures point to a deteriorating situation. Figures for females to males under seven from the last four census surveys show rapidly increasing disparities. The 1981 census figure was 962 girls to 1,000 boys; in 1991 this had dropped to 945; in 2001 it had was only 927, and in the 2011 census the ratio had decreased further, to 914.[28]

These figures are for the whole of India, and so mask the considerable regional variation. Kerala, for example, is an exception – the only state where females are 1,058 per 1,000 males.[29] South India has normal sex ratios. This in itself is important, for the status of women in parts of South India is higher than in the rest of the subcontinent, and women and their families there seem less motivated to abort their daughters because of a preference for sons. But these higher figures mean that there are other parts of India where the ratios of girls to boys are extremely low, most significantly in the more economically developed states. An article in 2007 reported that in Delhi, one of the richest cities in India, there were just 827 girls born per 1,000 boys.[30] The 2011 census showed a steep fall in the child sex ratio across states like Punjab, Haryana, Gujarat and Maharashtra, along with the union territories of Delhi and Chandigarh. In Punjab, for example, there are only 846 girls per 1,000 males. In Haryana there are only 830, dropping down as far as to 774 in the rapidly developing, cattle-wealthy district of Jhajjar.[31]

What is clear is that the declining sex ratio cannot be simply viewed as a medical or legal issue. K. S. Jacob sees it as very firmly embedded within the social construction of patriarchy and reinforced by tradition, culture and religion. For him, there is a whole set of subtle and blatant discriminatory practices against girls and women under various pretexts, and '[f]emale foeticide and infanticide are just the tip of the iceberg. It is this large base of discrimination against women that supports the declining sex ratio.'[32] Affluence has not challenged foeticide. It has simply made it easier.

Missing girls – shortage of brides

It is in a society's interest to have equal sex ratios, for heavily lopsided ratios will eventually bring many serious dysfunctions to social order. The most crucial one is that there will be a shortage of women of marriageable age. In their book *Bare Branches*, Valerie M. Hudson and Andrea den Boer note that a generation of men unable to find wives has already emerged, men who will never marry and have children. They argue that it is these men who are already largely responsible for social unrest in areas where women are scarce.[33] A report in 2015 suggested that even if India's sex ratio at birth were to return to normal and stay there, by 2050 the country would still have 30 per cent more single men hoping to marry than single women.[34]

The present shortage of brides is so acute in Punjab and Haryana that the problem has seeped into politics. Candidates standing for office in local elections promise they will 'help provide girls' if they are returned to power. There are reports of village leaders being asked by unmarried men to find them brides. The likelihood of girl kidnapping and coerced marriages is on the increase, and there is worrying evidence of the trafficking of under-age girls, even into polyandry. Bought by families for marriage, they are then treated as bonded labour and sex slaves. In 2005, the United Nations Population Fund had predicted this outcome, suggesting that:

> A shortage of females does not necessarily translate into improved prospects for those who remain. Indeed, a small pool of marriageable women may only increase demand for trafficked women, both for the purposes of marriage and prostitution, and could force many girls to cut short their education in order to wed and bear children – all to meet an insatiable demand for marriageable young women.[35]

Groups like Shakti Vahini ('Power brigade') work with the police to rescue trafficked brides but feel overwhelmed by the size of the task. Its executive director, Ravi Kant, says, 'We're losing the battle. It is in every village. The police are saying these families are doing nothing wrong. There's collusion between the law and the politicians, and it's destroying the whole social fabric.'

It is now becoming evident that the impact of India's missing girls on everyday life in many parts of the country is dramatic and alarming. It is simply not healthy to have a large cohort of young, single men, angry that they are unmarried in a culture where being a father and head of the family confers status. The anger becomes directed, as so often before, at the vulnerability of women. In 2005, the UN Population Fund had anticipated a link between the high number of males in the population and increased crime and violence. Seven years later the whole world saw what this meant. The gang rape and murder of a young woman medical student on a bus threw the problems of misogyny in India into sharp relief. And as hundreds of thousands took to the streets in protest, it was sadly evident to all the activists who had fought long and hard against female foeticide that the depths of the problem had finally, and tragically, hit home.

The future for Indian girl babies

India owes an enormous debt of gratitude to the tireless activists who have not let this issue drop off the national agenda. Many of these advocates have also been responsible for changes in the law. Early examples are the citizens' campaigns in Maharashtra which brought about the first legislation against sex selection in the country back in 1987[36] and the public interest litigation filed by Sabu George, and two NGOs (Masum and Cehat), which led to Supreme Court directives to state governments to implement the Prohibition of Sex Selection Act in 2001. More recently, concerted campaigns from a number of groups have forced some of the states to back down on their 'two child' norm, which disqualified candidates for office if they had more than two children. But much more remains to be done. It must start with the recognition of the violation of fundamental human rights – that today women are being denied the right to be born.

A much fuller implementation of the laws that already exist is also needed which can recognize and punish the complicity of all the agents involved in this 'genocide'. For '[b]y only targeting communication to families and ignoring mass crimes committed by unethical doctors and remaining silent on the vested interests of the ultrasound companies, India is unlikely to stop the ongoing genocide against the next generation of women'.[37] As reported rapes in New Delhi soared from 306 during six months in 2012 to over 1,000 in the same period in 2014, and molestation cases rose sixfold, the desperate need is clearly for a whole paradigm shift.[38] In the words of Bijayalaxmi Nanda:

> The State and civil society need to move beyond statist and patriarchal notions of marriage, reproduction and gender relations. This means more than just celebrating brave mothers who have saved their daughters or focusing on 'poor men', who have no women to marry. This means accepting women as equals and as individuals with needs, dreams, desires and rights, including the right to exercise control over their bodies. And this is the truth that we as a country are still not ready to accept.[39]

Deep-seated cultural attitudes have merged with contemporary materialism to produce a system which can devalue, degrade and control women in every stage of their development. Campaigners tell us that India has the power to change this, but needs the will to do so. The challenge is for civil society, educators, faith leaders, media, churches and legislators to join in developing and implementing a greater vision of equality. Only when girls are valued and cherished, across the whole culture, does violence against women at the very beginnings of life stand any chance of being eradicated.

3

Cut for purity: female genital mutilation

————•◦•————

The pain of circumcision is like a heavy burden I always carry with me. It is like darkness in my life, in my chest. You can never forget it.[1]

Up to 140 million women worldwide have undergone female genital mutilation/cutting (FGM/C). That equates to more than twice the entire population of the UK. Women who have endured this process assure me that it is something that stays forever in the memory, and it often revisits them without warning. A Sudanese writer recalls her own experience of being cut at the age of six:

> Despite the passage of twelve years, the scene still remains vivid in my memory. From the moment the horrendous experience has begun, and until the last day of your life, it will never cease to torment you. I will never forget the faint sound of the scissor cutting my flesh four times, the stitching four times or relative hideous pain in urination or retention, the accompanying complications and the nightmares of vicious cycle of cutting-stitching-cutting and legacy of hereditary pain.[2]

Sudan ranks fifth worldwide among countries practising FGM and some 89 per cent of Sudanese women are circumcised – around 14 million women and girls.[3] In spite of many testimonies like this one, three million girls across the world are estimated to be at risk from genital cutting every year. Most of the practice is concentrated in 26 African nations, but with migration the practice occurs now in every part of the globe. Even in North America, Australasia and Europe, it takes place in clandestine forms. A report on FGM issued by the UK government in 2014 suggested that around 140,000 women in England and Wales are living with the consequences of FGM and around 10,000 girls under the age of 15 are likely to undergo cutting.[4]

Female genital mutilation has no known health benefits, in any of its forms. On the contrary, it is known to be harmful to girls and women in many ways and is extremely painful and traumatic. The procedure involves cutting off the clitoris, and, depending on the extent of the process, other parts of the external genitals may also be excised. Three main forms of FGM are practised. The least invasive form, 'clitoridectomy' (often referred to as 'sunna' by Muslim women), involves the removal of the hood and part of the clitoris. 'Excision' involves the removal of the clitoris and adjacent labia, while 'infibulation' (often referred to as the Pharaonic or Sudanese type) is the most extensive form of cutting away and stitching, removing much of the tissue in the genital area. Around 15 per cent of all FGM cases are estimated to be of this very invasive form. With infibulations, the entrance to the vagina is commonly sewn almost completely shut, allowing only a small gap for urine and menstrual blood to pass through.

In cutting the girl, often no anaesthesia is used. The procedure is performed with razor blades, sharp rocks, knives and, sometimes, scalpels. The genital area is covered with egg yolk and herbs to control bleeding, and afterwards the girl's legs are tied together for several days. Infection, excessive bleeding, septic shock and difficulty in passing urine are common immediate effects; scarring, excruciating intercourse, kidney impairment, infertility, fistulas and almost unbearable pain are subsequent problems. Many girls die in the aftermath of the procedure. With the most invasive process women are 'opened' after marriage, and for delivery of a child. Because of the nature of the wound, many women are re-stitched after each childbirth.

The medical problems do not clear up quickly, and, indeed, in cases of the most dramatic form of cutting they may never clear up. The removal of normal genital tissue interferes with the natural functioning of the body in both childhood and adolescence. It produces immediate damage and causes long-term health consequences throughout adulthood. Childbirth becomes complicated with risks to mother and child. Maternal mortality is higher and babies born to women who have undergone female genital mutilation suffer a higher rate of neonatal death compared with babies born to women who have not undergone the procedure. In one study in Sierra Leone by the World Health Organization (WHO), 40 per cent of the girls who had undergone FGM were likely to see their babies die.[5]

The considerable emotional effects are less readily recognized, especially where FGM is culturally constructed as beneficial to the girl. In those cultures, it is not uncommon to find blanket denial of any negative impact. When the cutting takes place in early adolescence, it is supposed to herald the girl's entrance into mature womanhood, so she is encouraged to see it as a positive asset. Beneath this veneer of acceptance, however, the real experience can be one of confusion, regret and frightening memories. When she was giving birth to her first child, a long way from her native land, Halima Mohammed experienced terrifying flashbacks of her earlier cutting which left her anxious and panic-stricken. She describes how traumatized she felt when she saw the doctor approaching her:

> Having seen a long needle with a curved head in his hand, my heart beat, pummelled with rapid great force, my breaths matched the rapidness of my heart's pounding and my face became soaked in sweat and tears. I was a prey to anxiety and stress and felt like shaking inside all over. Trauma memories of childhood experience came back to me. An image of Hajja Zeinab, the midwife who cut me, replaced the doctor.

In addition to the excruciating pain of childbirth, she also recounts the sense of degradation and humiliation she faced as a survivor of FGM:

> [The doctor] asked the nurse to hand him a needle. When she approached him, she had a look on my open wound. Her eyes popped wide open and lower jaw dropped in an aghast manner which she didn't even bother hiding. I could see it from behind her muzzle. I felt a deep rage, accompanied by anger, shame, grief, low self-esteem, depression, pain, and disgrace, but didn't utter a word. The horrified look on the nurse's face when she saw my open wound, had communicated an interrogative message to me: 'WHY?' – a question that I repeated helplessly for decades.[6]

Halima's story is not an isolated one. The legacy of FGM/C in childbirth and beyond is something she shares with millions of other women. Even in her own family it has had terrible consequences and she reflects sadly on the lives and deaths of her sisters and cousins:

> The image of some relatives' sufferings are still vivid in my mind: Salwa who had fistula following a hard late labor, Rugaya whose newborn had a brain damage that kept him crippled for life, three relatives who lost their lives during labor, two relatives were divorced because of their reduced sexuality, etc. 'How can I live with a cold woman whose vagina is like a leaked irrigation pipe?' said a man who divorced one of my relatives when asked about reasons for separation. FGM/C was responsible for threading their tragedies.[7]

History and culture

Little is known about the origin of this practice, or when it was first performed. Because infibulation in the Sudan is also known as *pharaonic circumcision* there is a persuasive assumption that FGM was present in Egypt under the Pharaohs. The Greek geographer Strabo mentions male circumcision and female excision after visiting Egypt around 25 BC.[8] Even further back, a Greek papyrus in the British Museum dated 163 BC appears to refer to cutting rites performed on girls at the age when they received their dowries. Charles Seligman, physician and ethnologist, suggested in 1913 that ceremonies performed by Hamito-Semitic people on the Red Sea coast were a likely source of the practice, and that it radiated from 'the shore of the Red Sea westwards and southwards across Africa with ever diminishing intensity'.[9]

Much more is known about the cultural reasons for the practice, and why it has persisted so long. Despite an ongoing condemnation of it from the World Health Organization, and other international bodies, female genital mutilation is often believed, by those who practise it, to offer an impressive array of health benefits. It is supposed to prevent many sicknesses, including cancer and jaundice, and prevent offensive vaginal discharges and parasites. It is said to make conception and childbearing easier. It is even believed that it will purify a mother's milk. These myths persist because the cultures which hold them rarely engage with the kind of medical discourse now accessible to ordinary lay people in many other societies. In some traditions, it is even maintained that an un-excised clitoris will grow as long as a male penis and dangle between the legs – a prospect understandably viewed with revulsion by women and men alike! Because clitoridectomy is so widespread in these cultures, evidence to the contrary is not easily available.

There are strong sociological pressures also which keep the practice alive. In those societies where it is the norm, it is a means for women to earn respectability, gain a degree of mobility and move into an acceptable social status.[10] Not circumcising a daughter is seen in some communities as condemning her to a life of isolation, shaming her and her entire family.[11] The age at which it is carried out varies considerably, and reflects local traditions, but when performed on adolescent girls, genital cutting is seen as a rite of passage – the transition from childhood into female adulthood. Girls enter a new gendered society, which they share together as they face their future as wives and mothers.

> By allowing your genitals to be removed [it is perceived that] you are heightened to another level of pure motherhood – a motherhood not tainted by sexuality – and that is why the woman gives it away to become the matron, respected by everyone.[12]

Being a wife or mother will now be purified because circumcision, and specifically infibulation, is believed to reduce the sex drive in women. It also diminishes any likelihood of sex outside marriage and separates them from uncircumcised girls who are often considered to be unclean and promiscuous.

Women are in charge of the procedures of circumcision, and so it is often seen as perpetuated by women themselves. And women are often involved in the negotiation about when, where and how it should be performed. For some women, indeed, their expertise in FGM provides them with a livelihood. Yet, despite women's intrinsic 'ownership' of the actual process, at a deeper level they are not the ones in control. Effectively, these women are upholding the assumptions of patriarchal authority: maintaining its powerful command over female sexuality and fertility. For even though traditional African societies make little requirement of male chastity, virginity in girls is seen as essential. Loss of virginity may make it impossible for a girl's family to arrange her marriage and negotiate a bride price. That is why in some cultures, in Somalia for example, mothers regularly check their daughters to make sure they are still 'closed', and a prospective husband's family may even have the right to inspect the bride's body prior to marriage.[13] Enforcing and regulating the purity of the girl is seen as giving proper respect to the bridegroom. But it is also an efficient way to enforce the double standard of sexual morality. Even though genital mutilation does nothing to reduce a woman's sex drive, sewing up most of the entrance to the vagina certainly does discourage women's sexual activity outside marriage.

Coping with cultural alienation

Women may suffer silently within their own society as a result of infibulation, but struggles with the legacy of FGM take on a new dimension for women who travel abroad to live in a new country. It is difficult enough for immigrant women to assimilate to new surroundings and cope with changes in language, transport, lifestyle and relationship. But for those who have gone through invasive forms of genital cutting, the sense of being different from other women is accentuated. A study among African women in the UK highlights this. Forward, the Foundation for Women's Health, Research and Development – an organization led by African Diaspora women – used an innovative, qualitative research method to learn about the experiences of Sudanese and Somalian women in Bristol. The Bristol Participatory Ethnographic Evaluation and Research (PEER) study, published in 2010, gives us some key insights into the women's beliefs and perceptions. Through sensitive listening from those who knew these issues themselves, the women in the study were able to describe, in their own voices, the kinds of struggle and isolation that many experience in the UK.

One key area of concern to the women was their relationship with the health service and health officials. Well-women's clinics are a beneficial asset to women across the country, as they provide safe, confidential areas where women can undergo tests of a very private nature. For these African women, however, such benefits were always double-edged. Self-consciousness about their 'difference' made them hesitant to visit a doctor's surgery.

> When I go to the health centre I feel I am different from other women. It bothers me when people ask me questions, especially when I have not met the person before. I can't be happy to talk about this type of FGM as it makes you different than the other women.

Even routine tests became emotional issues which dredged up past suffering.

> Because our women have their private parts looking different from the majority of patients, they are reluctant and put back appointments such as the smear-test. They worry about what the doctor will think, especially if they are cut, so they prefer not to be tested at all. It affects our life and makes us suffer a lot during the period, because the space they left is so small. In the wedding night we suffer for more than one week from the scars.[14]

The impact on their marital relations was something that many of the women expressed concern about. Inevitably, the ordeal starts the night they are married.

> The big night or the wedding night is supposed to be the happiest night in the woman's life. But for a woman who has had FGM it becomes the worst night of her life.

The sensitivity of the listeners brought not just frank disclosures, but tears of anger and regret from the women who shared their feelings with them.

> I have the friend who I did the interview with, when she started talking with me, especially on how much she had suffered, and still is with her intimate relationship with her husband; she cried so much and it was tears of real anger. She was telling me how she had returned back from her honeymoon feeling so unhappy. She felt that no one considered her feelings and they were all waiting to hear her experience. She felt that her husband was really so considerate of her feelings and the pain she went through.[15]

Several of the other women also told of their husband's distress at causing them such pain when they 'opened them up' for intercourse. Others, however, felt their suffering was not taken seriously.

> The night of marriage is a nightmare for those circumcised pharonic-ally. Some suffer for such a long time. You can find that men do not respond to the request of the wife to stop. As some men think that women naturally exaggerate. They keep pushing without mercy. They can end up seeking medical attention instead of enjoying the tourist areas and hotels.[16]

Now that they were in a culture where FGM is both unlawful and highly discouraged, the women were more open to recognizing the harm that had been done to them. Yet they also acknowledged that laws prohibiting the practice in their new country did not in themselves prevent families from persisting with it. This fact has been borne out in evidence from different kinds of agencies in the UK. Forward estimates that 6,500 girls in the UK are at risk of FGM every year. Reports abound of girls being returned to their home countries at puberty for the cutting to be done, and then brought back to the UK. This is despite the 2003 law in the UK, which created a prison sentence of up to 14 years for anyone carrying out FGM on a UK citizen abroad. No one has yet been convicted under this law. There are also pockets of evidence that it is being carried out, away from the public gaze, in Britain itself. In May 2012, undercover investigators from the *Sunday Times* filmed medical professionals in the UK offering to perform female genital mutilation on girls as young as ten. Although it was a shocking revelation for the paper's readers, for women from the African Diaspora it was hardly news. One of the women in the Bristol Peer Report summed up the attitude in her community: 'We know that in 1985 the UK passed a law against FGM but no one has ever been prosecuted. It goes underground.'[17]

She is clearly right. Although almost 160 incidents of FGM were recorded in the 2008–9 British Crime Survey, there have been no convictions since it was criminalized in 1985. And although FGM is incorporated into child protection, there seems to be no collection of data on the number or type of social-work cases which have been involved in it.

None of this would surprise the campaigner, Nimco Ali. One of the founders of Daughters of Eve, a non-profit campaigning organization set up in 2010 by three British survivors of FGM, she was in little doubt that it takes place within the UK. The reluctance of local people to interfere in the cultures of immigrant communities often allowed the process to persist. Ali did insist, however, that the appropriate response was not to leave Somalian, Sudanese or other African communities to sort the issues out for themselves. That was, for her, an abnegation of public responsibility. As with every other issue which puts vulnerable people at risk, proper involvement and law enforcement by public authorities was essential.

> There needs to be a commitment by the police, social services and others that it's high on their priorities, not just something that they pay lip service to. FGM is a safeguarding issue and needs to be treated as such, not passed back to communities affected by it.[18]

Voices of the campaigners have been heeded. From September 2014, a mandated collection of data on women treated for FGM conditions was introduced, and figures released in January 2015 by the Health and Social Care Information Centre gave witness to its ongoing recurrence in the UK. Researchers identified 1,946 new cases of FGM from September to December 2014, with 558 cases in December alone. This was an increase in the ability to identify women who have undergone FGM.[19]

A very different story follows the tougher safeguarding measures in France. FGM was defined as a crime under French law in 1983 with the threat of ten years in prison, or up to 20 years for cutting a girl under the age of 15. The law is rigorously enforced and little girls are examined routinely for genitalia abuse. With dozens of trials, many convictions, and people serving long prison sentences for their involvement in FGM, the incidence in that country has begun to decline; some say these are linked.[20]

Historic opposition to female cutting

Many of the campaigns today against FGM are led by women and medical practitioners who have first-hand experience of treating patients. But public opposition to it has been around for more than a hundred years. The problem has been that resistance in former times came, initially, from outside those societies; it was often accompanied by clashes of culture which sadly resulted in the practice being reinforced rather than eradicated. This was the case early in the last century, when female circumcision, as it was then called, became a sharp point of tension between traditional tribal life and the growing indigenous Christian churches in Kenya.

A case study: Christian opposition in Kenya

The unease had been fermenting since 1906. From early after their arrival, Christian missionaries from the Church of Scotland, and the Africa Inland Mission, had led an attack on the practice of female circumcision. Their biblical conviction – that it was incompatible with a Christian vision for human relations – found its way into church teaching and spiritual discipline. There was a united voice of opposition from church leaders, and by the 1920s it was a condition of Kenyan church membership that daughters should not be subject to such cutting. Strong penalties were imposed on baptized members who broke this rule; they could find themselves brought before church elders, and their membership suspended. Unfortunately, this became a powerful tool for Kenyan nationalists who saw it as an unwarranted intrusion on their culture, and a heavy-handed imposition of colonialism. It may have been heavy-handed, but colonial imposition was certainly not the motivation. The women missionaries were familiar with the appalling consequences that genital cutting left for women, not least in childbirth and its aftermath, and saw nothing to commend it. From a medical point of view, they believed it to be sheer mutilation. They also felt the sexualized rituals which then went along with the practice were degrading for human relations, and especially for women.

The efforts of the missionaries were not without success. By the end of the 1920s, there was a large body of opposition to the practice among Kikuyu converts. These African Christians rejected the idea that they were copying Western values, and became keen to claim that their resistance came from authentic, Christian-Kikuyu freedom, not colonial pressure. A group from Kiambu articulated this clearly: 'We find it our duty to take up our stand on the matter, and show that it is not Europeans that make the law against circumcision of women, but we Kikuyu ourselves.'[21]

It was a brave stand, yet the strength of feeling in the culture as a whole was largely against them. Older women, traditionally given authority as overseers of the practice, were reluctant to give it up. And because so much status hung on this essential rite of passage for girls, even church elders could not always prevent their wives and daughters from carrying it out.

So intense was the battle over cutting that the period in Kenya between 1929 and 1931 has become known as the 'female circumcision controversy'. Recognizing that they had a major fight on their hands, the missionaries tried to gain support from women's rights groups and humanitarians in London, as well as from the colonial government. Encouragement came from the Africans themselves, where, at the United Native Conference of all Protestant missions in Kikuyuland, the African delegates voted unanimously that 'female circumcision was evil and should be abandoned by all Christians'.[22] As the issue increasingly divided Kenyans, it also became a test of loyalty, either to the Christian churches or to the Kikuyu Central Association. The temperature rose amid church suspensions and physical conflict, and led to suspected murder. The beaten body of 63-year-old Hulda Kumpf, an American missionary opponent of female circumcision, who had lived and worked peacefully in Kenya for 23 years, was found at the Africa Inland Mission station in January 1930.[23] Her assailant was unknown, but the evidence pointed to the fact that she had been martyred for her opposition. The unrest fuelled political resistance and the issue became a focal point of the Kikuyu independence movement. Even Jomo Kenyatta (1894–1978), who became Kenya's first prime minister in 1963, defended the practice on grounds of tribal identity. He wrote in 1930:

> The real argument lies not in the defense of the general surgical operation or its details, but in the understanding of a very important fact in the tribal psychology of the Kikuyu – namely, that this operation is still regarded as the essence of an institution which

has enormous educational, social, moral and religious implications, quite apart from the operation itself. For the present it is impossible for a member of the tribe to imagine an initiation without clito-ridoctomy (*sic*). Therefore the . . . abolition of the surgical element in this custom means . . . the abolition of the whole institution . . .[24]

Decades passed until, under pressure from the British, the council of male elders in Meru, Kenya, issued a ban on clitoridectomy in 1956. But prohibition strengthened tribal resistance to the British and probably further inflamed the Mau Mau Uprising which had begun in 1952. It certainly provoked a violent reaction from young women, around 2,000 of whom carried out the procedure on each other, both in defiance of the colonial authorities and in protest against denying women the right to make decisions about their rituals. The stand-off became entrenched. The earlier refusal of the Nyeri Native District Council to accept the abandonment of female cutting had become set in stone.

You white men came among us and we seeing that you were good men welcomed you with both hands; we readily do all you wish us to do . . . you impose taxes upon us and we pay without a murmur; when your taxes become more than we can pay we will come as suppliants and tell you so. But in this matter of our girls, we cannot see eye to eye to you, and we cannot agree to obey you, even if you attempt to coerce us.[25]

Today in Kenya the debate about FGM has passed down from those early years. The practice is still widespread in tribal areas, but there is increasing resistance from the younger generation throughout the country. In 2013, the UN reported a strong decline in FGM among the young: women aged 45–9 are three times more likely to have been cut than girls aged 15–19.[26] Even some tribal groups committed to retaining their culture have been moving away from its practice. Those early missionary women might have been gratified by African leadership in changing attitudes. For example, the Maasai Education Discovery (MED), an organization created and operated by Maasai to celebrate Maasai culture, has drawn on resources from educationalists, NGO and the churches to oppose FGM. Acknowledging the hold that the practice had on previous generations, one young Maasai speaks of her own indebtedness to African Christianity:

> My mum became a Christian about 10 years ago, and her attitude
> toward female circumcision changed. As a result, I was not circumcised. I am the new face of the Maasai girl and I will do all I can
> to help educate my community and my people positively and
> to ensure that I am a person who will be regarded as a source of
> hope in my community. Gradually we will be able to eliminate this
> outdated cultural practice.[27]

Thanks to so many Kenyan activists, there is optimism for the future.

Growth of public concern

Even though there was strong, widespread resistance to change in most cultures committed to FGM, the scale of the eruption over FGM in Kenya was not mirrored elsewhere. In fact, by the mid-century, a serious analysis was taking place on the international front about its benefits and dangers. The involvement of the United Nations became evident in 1952 when the UN Commission on Human Rights raised the issue for the first time. Six years later the World Health Organization was invited to begin a study of the 'persistence of customs subjecting girls to ritual operations' and to present subsequently its findings to the Commission on the Status of Women. That study continued for the next decades, and in 1979, backed by the UN, WHO organized a major seminar in Khartoum to address traditional practices affecting the health of women and children. This seminal gathering brought recommendations that governments should work to eliminate the practice. A formal statement from WHO to the UN Human Rights Commission in 1982 opposed the medicalization of FGM and strongly advised health workers not to perform FGM under any conditions. Their seriousness became even more evident when they indicated that they were both willing and ready to support national efforts towards the elimination of FGM.

Pressure now began to mount. When African women's organizations met in Dakar, Senegal, in 1984, to discuss Traditional Practices Affecting the Health of Women and Children, FGM was high on the

agenda. It was roundly condemned by the World Health Organization as a serious health hazard and a cause of quite unnecessary
human suffering. Out of this initiative came the Inter-African
Committee on Traditional Practices Affecting the Health of Women
and Children (IAC), which currently has committees in 26 African
countries. By 1994, a programme of action had been formulated
and adopted by the International Conference on Population and
Development. The language of human rights grew stronger and
the programme referred to female genital mutilation as a 'basic
rights violation' and urged governments to 'prohibit and urgently
stop the practice . . . wherever it exists'.[28] A year later, at the Fourth
World Conference on Women in Beijing, female genital mutilation
was given the global prominence it needed. It was very significant
that the drive to condemn the practice was now led by African
delegates. Describing it as both a threat to women's reproductive
health and a violation of their human rights, the Conference called
on governments to 'enact and enforce legislation against the perpetrators of practices and acts of violence against women, such as
female genital mutilation'.[29]

Citing genital mutilation as one of the acts of violence against
women has taken it on a journey from the category of culture to
the category of offences. It effectively acknowledged the practice
as a crucial issue of injustice to women, and a deprivation of their
freedom. This had long been the view of Nahid Toubia, health
rights activist, and the first woman surgeon in the Sudan. Calling
for global action on FGM as long ago as the early 1990s, she
saw it as both a considerable health threat and also part of the
social and economic injustice women faced the world over. Her
own principle was clear: 'If women are to be considered as equal
and responsible members of society, no aspect of their physical,
psychological or sexual integrity can be compromised.'[30]

Religious barriers

Although rejected by religion, female circumcision is often associated
with Islam, as it seems predominant in those countries where
Islam is the major religion. Yet it quite clearly predated Islam in

Africa by centuries. And neither the Qur'an, the primary source for Islamic law, the *sunna*, nor the *hadith* (collections of the sayings of the Prophet Muhammad), include a direct call for the practice. Oral histories are often cited to show that, when Muhammad was asked his opinion on female circumcision, he told his followers 'to circumcise, but not to destroy [the clitoris]', for its preservation would be 'better for the man and would make the woman's face glow'. This has been interpreted by many educated Muslims, particularly in those countries where Islam is not a major religion, as a call against female genital mutilation. Interpretations from certain Islamic clerics, however, suggest that this means that Islam should endorse clitoridectomy in post-pubescent girls, but not infibulation.

This is the view of Imam Afroz Ali, the founder and president of the Al-Ghazzali Centre for Islamic Sciences and Human Development, based in Sydney. His statements in December 2012 provoked rebuff and outrage among the Australian medical profession. Arguing that Western definitions about female circumcision are prejudicial and 'probably reflect a toeing of the line of secular and modern claims against some forms of such acts or against some religious practices in general', Ali tries to draw a line between FGM and female circumcision. In a paper he defines the latter as the partial removal of the clitoral hood and insists it is the 'divinely ordained right of a woman' under Islam. He adds that the 'choice to undertake the procedure is entirely upon the woman, upon her puberty, when she becomes aware of any sexually inhibiting or arousal conditions'.[31] Even though the imam believes the practice should only be performed on post-pubescent women, and argues it has the same status as genital cosmetic surgery (labiaplasty) – which is legal in Australia – his critics are not impressed. The response of Professor Ajay Rane, Vice President of the Royal Australian and New Zealand College of Obstetricians and Gynaecologists, was unequivocal. He said American, Australian and New Zealand colleges of obstetrics and gynaecology condemned all clitoral de-hooding operations, whether defined as legal labiaplasty or cultural female circumcision: 'there's no science behind them to support enhancement of sexual performance or feelings, and they can cause horrific complications.'[32]

Their view is echoed by many Islamic gynaecologists also, not least by the renowned Professor Hassan Hathout who died in 2009. A Muslim educated among Presbyterians in Scotland, and a close affiliate of the Vatican, he also studied Christian theology and ethics. He worked for many years in Kuwait, before going to the United States, and was a key figure in interfaith dialogue. Challenging the authenticity of *hadiths* which advocate female circumcision, he rejected also the idea that it was to curb sexual excitation and help Islamic girls remain chaste. 'To me this sounds like cutting a portion of the tongue and thinking this diminishes hunger. As an enlightened Muslim and as a gynaecologist, I have always advised against female circumcision.'[33]

Encouraged by his stand and that of others, the Muslim Women's League has, for the past 15 years, signified its own opposition to FGM. Their statement is very clear:

> Muslims are called upon by Allah (swt) to enjoin the doing of what is right and forbid the doing of what is wrong. Clearly, mutilating a woman's genitalia in the name of Islam violates the most sacred tenets of our faith. Therefore, we must oppose this practice.[34]

Facing attack 'for the sake of our daughters'

Although the view of the Muslim Women's League is now the predominant one, campaigners against FGM continue to face opposition, including from those who claim that Islam requires it. Vivian Froad, one of Egypt's anti-FGM campaigners, relates how, in villages where true information about the practice was being disseminated, 'men in their late teens got up on the podium and started shouting that what we were doing was against Islamic law'.[35] Rugiatu Turay, the founder of a campaigning group in Sierra Leone, has received death threats and been attacked by men armed with either magic or machetes. She tells of an occasion when more than a hundred people paraded a symbolic corpse outside her home. 'They came right in front of me, sharpening their cutlasses.'[36] Even in the UK, Efua Dorkenoo, a director at Equality Now, an international NGO set up 20 years ago to protect and promote the human rights of women and girls, says she regularly receives death threats aimed at stopping her campaigns against FGM. 'I'm told my offence in speaking out is greater than that of Salman Rushdie and that I should die.' She is in no doubt that others are also at risk. 'Any woman or girl who speaks out against FGM is in very serious danger from extended members of their family, their neighbours and from their community, especially from so-called gatekeepers of their community.'[37] The fact that these, and other activists, continue to press for an end to the practice indicates not just their bravery, but also their utter resolve to ensure the future protection of girls at risk. And the truth remains that no religion supports it.

The issue came to a head in Egypt during the massive unrest of 2013. While the world watched the political and military turmoil in that country, in a quiet clinic a long way from the capital, 13-year-old Soheir al Batea died on a June evening during an illegal operation to cut away her clitoris. The operation was at the request of her father and performed in a clinic where the doctor used anaesthetic, yet the child never recovered. There had been many casualties before in Egypt, of course, for despite a law in that country banning FGM in 2008, it is estimated that around 95 per cent of women aged 15–49 have undergone the process. Yet Soheir's death brought a fresh focus on both the danger and scale of the problem. The outcry was widespread. Equality Now pointed out how the loss of this precious young life 'tragically highlights FGM as a violation of the human rights of girls and women with serious health risks regardless of performance inside or outside a medical establishment'.[38] Along with UNICEF and many other voices in Egypt and across the globe, they called for a proper implementation of the 2008 law and the prosecution of the doctor.

Looking forward

According to the World Health Organization:

> Female genital mutilation is . . . a violation of the human rights of girls and women. It reflects deep-rooted inequality between the sexes, and constitutes an extreme form of discrimination against women. It is nearly always carried out on minors and is a violation

of the rights of children. The practice also violates a person's rights to health, security and physical integrity, the right to be free from torture and cruel, inhuman or degrading treatment, and the right to life when the procedure results in death.[39]

Nowhere has this view been more fully endorsed than in the landmark UN resolution passed in December 2012. Led by African countries, co-sponsored by two thirds of the General Assembly and adopted by consensus, the resolution called upon its 193 states to implement a worldwide ban on FGM. And although no one expected that this would happen overnight, or that countries like Indonesia would not defy the ban just two months later, it represented a 'paradigm shift'. As the campaigning group No Peace Without Justice declared, the adoption of the resolution was not an end in itself, but the beginning of a new chapter in the fight against this form of violence against women.

By 2015, campaigners against FGM had joined forces with those calling for an end to child marriage to unite voices across the world calling for the freedom of the girl child. The first ever global Girl Summit, held in July 2014 in London, saw young women speakers from Africa and Asia share their stories openly with delegates from international organizations. Issues, long hidden in layers of tradition and custom, were unwrapped and exposed to greater public scrutiny. One of the campaigners, Dr Ann-Marie Wilson of 28 Too Many, having listened to the stories of over 2,000 survivors, observed that not one girl was pleased she was cut. She presented a declaration to the UK government, signed by 350 faith leaders, that FGM was not supported by any faith.[40]

Yet the challenge of eradicating this destructive practice still remains. It requires enforcing legislation, monitoring the practice and supporting those who want change. Every citizen has a voice. We can stand alongside the women who know its effects to eliminate the threat for the next generation. The No Peace Without Justice team includes everyone in the task ahead. It is 'now up to all States and all of us to work together, so that the women and girls of tomorrow will be free from the threat of FGM'.[41] Amen to that!

4

Early and enforced marriage: child abuse by another name

———•◆•———

This is an issue about life, families, communities, broken dreams and shattered bodies. It is about girls at risk of marriage; just as much as it is about the millions of adolescent mothers and girls in marriage.
Nyaradzayi Gumbonzvanda

This is not marriage, but rather the selling and buying of young women.
Ahlam al-Obeidi, Iraq radio

Some mind-blowing statistics

Every three seconds a girl under the age of 18 is married somewhere across the world – usually without her consent and sometimes to a much older man.[1] The United Nations Population Fund suggests that, every day, 39,000 girls marry too young.[2] It is predicted that more than 140 million child brides will have entered marriage in the decade up to 2020, 18.5 million of them under the age of 15; if nothing changes, the annual figure will grow from 14.2 million in 2010 to 15.1 million in 2030.[3] As the General Secretary of the World Young Women's Christian Association (YWCA) observes, the number of children married under age is now higher than the total population of Zimbabwe![4]

Figures like these do indicate the massive numerical scale of the problem and the difficulties in eliminating it. But they do not unpack the human misery enfolded inside them. A moving exhibition mounted in 2014 by the United Nations in Geneva opened that up. Through very sober photographs and short, poignant narratives we came face to face with the wrecked hopes and tragic lives of survivors of child marriage. Ghulam had wanted to be a teacher, but was pulled out of school at 11 to marry a 40-year-old man; 14-year-old Afisha, in Ghana, was unable to be educated because of her father's poverty, and instead was sold as a bride for cola nuts and 60 *cedis* (about £25); Asia was ill and bleeding from childbirth at 14, as she cared for her two-year-old child and new-born baby; Tehani was only six when her 25-year-old husband muffled her screams with his hand over her mouth and raped her.[5] Many other stories, not in the exhibition, are equally horrifying. Elham Assi, 13, bled to death just days after she was married to a 23-year-old man in Yemen. She had extensive tearing around the vagina and rectum, having been tied down and repeatedly violated by him. Nujood Ali, also in Yemen, was ten when she fled her abusive, much older husband.[6] She bravely took a taxi to the courthouse in the city of Sanaa, becoming the centre of a landmark legal battle.[7] All these individual accounts might focus only on a tiny number of youngsters, but they reflect the lives of millions of girls whose names we may never know.

Those millions remain hidden in statistics, and I risk numbing you with figures, but they do tell their own story. Early and enforced marriage is found in pockets in Latin America and even in the more affluent Western world, yet levels in those areas do not begin to approach the rates found in African or Asian countries. A third of all girls there are married under 18 and one in seven under 15; some 'brides' are as young as five years old. But the country with the highest prevalence of child marriage in the world is Niger, where a staggering 75 per cent of all girls marry under 18, and 33 per cent under 15.[8] This is followed by Chad and Central African Republic (68 per cent), Guinea (63 per cent), Mozambique (56 per cent), Mali (55 per cent), Burkina Faso and South Sudan (52 per cent), Malawi (50 per cent), Ethiopia (49 per cent), Sierra Leone and Burkina Faso (48 per cent), Eritrea (47 per cent), Uganda (46 per cent), Somalia (45 per cent), Zambia (42 per cent), Congo, Madagascar and Senegal (39 per cent).[9] When the International Centre for Research on Women (ICRW) carried out an analysis of demographic and health data, they added Mali and Bangladesh to the countries with rates over 60 per cent, and Eritrea, Uganda, India, Nepal, Nicaragua and Tanzania to those with rates over 40 per cent. Unless figures in all these countries are brought rapidly down, gender-based poverty and violence against girls will stand no chance of being eliminated.

Children at risk

Early and enforced child marriage puts the girl child at risk more than almost any other practice. Health risks alone are frightening. Young girls are not yet physically mature, so early sexual activity brings many threats of damage for their developing bodies. They are also at risk from sexually transmitted infections from their older husbands. Because child brides know little about safe sex, and in any case are hardly in a position to negotiate contraceptive use in their marriage, they have little protection. In some cultures there is the belief among men that sex with a young girl will leave them inured to HIV & AIDS when, of course, what really happens is that they pass on the virus to the child. A young bride also has little defence against the force and roughness of an older male partner so intimate-partner violence is a frequent part of early and enforced marriage. Claudia Garcia-Moreno, a leading WHO medical expert, puts it starkly: 'Child marriage marks an abrupt and often violent introduction to sexual relations. The young girls are powerless to refuse sex and lack the resources or legal and social support to leave an abusive marriage.'[10]

Because sex often takes place with no contraception, girls become frequently pregnant, and this brings yet more dangers to under-age girls. With their pelvises still narrow, and their bodies immature, these youngsters are five times more likely to die during pregnancy or childbirth than women over 20. In fact, because of its multiple risk of complications, the Executive Director of the UN World Population Fund speaks of pregnancy as the leading cause of death among girls aged 15–19. Around 70,000 of them die each year during pregnancy or childbirth.[11] For girls who become pregnant younger, the risks are still greater. 'Child marriage is a silent health emergency in the sense that it's often overlooked as a root cause of maternal mortality and morbidity,' says Jeffrey Edmeades, social demographer with the Washington-based ICRW.[12]

Clinics treat many young mothers with fistulas; other girls often suffer in silence with incontinence and infection. Even if the mother does retain her health, her child may not do so. Stillborn rates are higher for babies of child brides, and children born alive are likely to be underweight, and prey to high infant mortality.

Second only to health risks are the communal and educational deprivations which child brides face. Girls can find themselves socially and psychologically isolated. Their friends may still be at school, but as brides-to-be they are likely to have dropped out of school in anticipation of their change of status. The widely held view is that a married girl has crossed the threshold into adulthood and adults do not need to be educated. Indeed, in places where the education of young daughters is not seen as a sound economic investment, the education of child wives is even less so. Early marriage, therefore, effectively ends the education of a girl, and her subsequent pregnancies and child-care can mean she never has the opportunity to return to any form of study. ('Learning' now might focus on how to relate to older wives within the neighbourhood – or even the same household if the husband is polygamous.) So, it comes as no surprise to find that levels of illiteracy are high, and development of vocational and life skills is low among girls who marry under age. These factors, in turn, increase dependency, and lower a girl's chances of educational fulfilment. They also make it very unlikely that she will build up economic resources of her own in the future. We can echo the concern expressed by Michelle Bachelet, then Executive Director of UN Women: 'No girl should be robbed of her childhood, her education and health, and her aspirations. Yet, today millions of girls are denied their rights each year when they are married as child brides.'[13]

Nyaradzayi Gumbonzvanda, who heads up the World YWCA, did not mince her words in her summary to the Human Rights Council in 2014:

> [C]hild, early and forced marriage is a confluence of the multiple violations of the rights of girls. It is about poverty, discrimination and exclusion; it is violence against women and girls, abuse, rape and exploitation. Forced [marriage] is abduction. It is illegal, immoral and an unacceptable harmful practice.[14]

So why do so many girls become child brides?

Stories from Niger, which tops the rate for child marriage, give many clues as to why early marriage persists. The country ranks lowest on the UN development index (187 out of 187) and has the world's highest birth rate. Poverty is endemic. One journalist observed: 'Every choice in this landscape is defined by the imperative of survival.'[15] Survival for individual families means decreasing the number of dependants. Take the northern Niger city of Agadez, where life reflects the daily struggle against hunger and poverty; early marriage means one less mouth to feed, and brings in much-needed finance. So daughters are married off to wealthier men from neighbouring Nigeria who might pay thousands of dollars for a Tuareg girl, depending on her beauty. Sadly, the money paid for her is no guarantee that she will be treated well. One mother had few delusions about the outcome for her daughter: 'there is no room for women to dream dreams.'[16] In Niger, poverty, illiteracy, social convention and religious conservatism all combine to make the problem of child marriage a hard one to defeat.

The impact of poverty can leave its mark anywhere. Economic pressures on poor families can be enormous, especially in the aftermath of natural disasters – floods, tsunamis, droughts. Wherever life is marked by the desperate scramble from debt or destitution, early marriage for a daughter might be a reluctant last resort. In some families it can even lessen the relentless ordeal of raising another child to adulthood. 'I was given to my husband when I was little,' explains Kanas from Ethiopia, now a teenager, 'and I don't even remember when I was given because I was so little. It is my husband who brought me up.'[17]

Poverty is not the only driving factor, however. In almost every country where it is prevalent, child marriage is also linked to systems of ownership and control, and to a low view of childhood. It's a disturbing consequence of gender inequality and oppression. In cultures where a girl's sexuality is under strong monitoring, early marriage, like FGM, ensures that her virginity is intact, thus making her a suitable wife and preserving the honour of her family. (There is no onus on her husband, however, to postpone his sexual activity until after marriage.) A girl's sexuality is transferred from being under the control of her parents to the ownership of her husband. In many societies, alliances between families – social and economic – are cemented by marriage, and children are often betrothed early – even before birth – with parents negotiating about when the marriage should be consummated. Yet, many recognize the consequences of using child marriage to bring in finance or build up family alliances. Marilyn Crawshaw, who works with an NGO in the Khyber Pakhtunkhwa region of Pakistan, is convinced it puts girls' welfare at risk. 'If you see children as some sort of bargaining chip or commodity that has a value attached to it, that is always bad for them. The price is paid by the child.'[18] That price is frighteningly high in countries where rapists may bargain to marry their under-age victims in order to avoid prosecution. I shall be looking at this later.

Sometimes, of course, child marriage is not contracted between families at all, but is the result of kidnapping, trafficking, abduction or legal compromise. The 276 Nigerian girls taken from their homes in Chibok in 2014 by the Taliban were clearly taken, not only against their own will, but against the will of their parents and the whole community. The story made international headlines for two weeks. Who can forget the huge demonstrations, the banners held by mothers, with world leaders joining the condemnation, insisting that the girls be returned? Yet, when nothing happened, it then slipped quietly out of public consciousness. A few years earlier, award-winning journalist Kathy Cook exposed the appalling plight faced by girls who had been abducted in Uganda and exploited as child wives in her book *Stolen Angels*. Concy's story makes us shudder with horror at what little girls undergo:

> When I was 10 years old, I was married against my will to a Brigade Commander. The first time he forced me to have sex, I bled and cried a lot. I was in great pain, but my 'husband' had a gun next to him and I had seen him use it before so I tried to stop crying. Every day he called me and demanded sex. Whenever I tried to resist, he beat me to the point of paralysis. Sometimes I felt so weak because we had no food or water, but I had to go to him anyway. The Brigade Commander had a total of 20 'wives' – some were very young, but

most were between 12 and 18 years old. If the rebels raided a village and abducted a beautiful girl, she would be forced to marry the Brigade Commander. Since I was also a soldier who fought, I was more respected than some of the other girls who were only 'wives.' When my 'husband' would go away, I would stay with his other 'wives' and keep them in line. I knew that if any of them ever escaped, I would be killed.[19]

Concy endured years of ill-treatment at the hands of different men, and the trauma continued when she returned to her village. It was help from a children's charity which eventually brought change in her life, and a new beginning. She became one of the fortunate ones. Sadly, too many others have no means of escape.

Wrangling over legislation – some striking examples

In countries sluggish to embrace women's rights, the battle to reform laws on child marriage is inevitably fraught with conflict. Lawmakers have to be persuaded, often against their own traditions.

Pakistan

In Pakistan, when Marvi Memon brought a bill before the National Assembly, she found fierce opposition from conservative religious parties, including her own. Seven per cent of Pakistani girls are unlawfully married before they are 15, according to a 2014 UNICEF report,[20] and Memon wanted to increase the fine for involvement in under-age wedlock from $10 to $1,000 with the option of a substantial jail sentence. It was a radical reforming vision, and children's rights campaigners strongly backed her efforts. Yet opponents fiercely resisted. Many clerics wanted the penalties scrapped altogether; the influential chair of the Council of Islamic Ideology (CII) argued that even the current laws forbidding child marriage contradict the Qur'an. The social media made the contest of views very public. It became hailed as 'Marvi vs Mullahs', with #mullahsvsmarvi even trending on Twitter. Memon stayed persistent: 'These girls are being treated as cattle ... They are dying. We cannot have little girls being married off at 15 and 16 and being forced to produce kids. It doesn't make sense medically, and it doesn't make sense economically.'[21] At the time of writing, the issue is still unresolved. The tragedy is that since Pakistan's government does not track the issue or keep statistics on child marriage and few cases are ever reported to police, the dogged laissez-faire attitude remains hard to shift.

The Middle East and North Africa

Early and enforced marriage across the Middle East and North Africa has put marriage laws under the spotlight in several countries. In **Saudi Arabia**, back in 2008, a case brought before Judge Habib al-Habib in the Saudi city of Onaiza brought the power of tribal and religious forces into sharp relief. The judge refused to annul a marriage contract of an eight-year-old girl who had been married to a man of 47. He did, however, offer a 'concession' to the child victim, and ruled that once the girl reached puberty, she could petition for divorce![22] The judgment was met with incredulity by human rights activists. Saudi's record on its treatment of girls and women faced exposure at the highest level in 2014, when four daughters of King Abdullah used Skype to outline the abuse they had suffered for 13 years, since their mother fled from the kingdom. Their disclosure that women were illegally detained and placed in psychiatric wards to keep them docile had, they claimed, led to the sisters themselves being drugged, abused and kept isolated. In October 2014, their mother appealed for intervention from President Obama, on a visit to Saudi Arabia. But, while the ex-wife claimed her daughters were being starved, Saudi's powerful king continued with trade and arms alliances with the West, right up to his death in 2015. Even in his obituaries, the plight of the four women had faded from public view.

The law and judiciary have also faced the spotlight in **Morocco**. Even though the rights of the child were ratified in Morocco in 1993, judges had been accused of authorizing the marriages of girl minors in an automatic way – around 30,000 child marriages are authorized every year. Article 475 of the penal code, proposed by the Islamist-led government in 2011, generated great controversy. Initially heralded as enlightened, it provided for a prison term of one to five years for anyone who 'abducts or deceives' a minor 'without violence, threat or fraud, or attempts to do so'. Yet the second clause of the article was anything but enlightened; it decreed that if a rape victim under 18 married the perpetrator, 'he can no longer be prosecuted except by persons empowered to demand the annulment of the marriage and then only after the annulment has been proclaimed'. This effectively prevented prosecutors from independently pursuing rape charges, and allowed child abusers and rapists to escape prosecution.

In March 2012 a horrible incident highlighted the issue. Amina Filali, aged 16, had been raped by a man ten years her senior. When she disclosed her terrifying ordeal, she never imagined that she would be forced to marry him. But she was, and his constant brutality towards her drove her, seven months later, to swallow rat poison and kill herself. Her husband's viciousness went on public show, as he grabbed her dying body by her hair, and dragged her down the street.[23]

What followed was an unprecedented public outcry against Article 475, which led to the Moroccan parliament voting unanimously to amend it in January 2014. The campaign of activists had made it clear that *the law effectively protected rapists of girls and punished child rape survivors*. The action of the parliamentarians now confirmed that consent to marriage is a legal requirement, which cannot be given by minors. All this was too late to help Amina, but it was one more vital step away from early, enforced marriage and towards greater justice for future rape victims.

In **Algeria** and **Tunisia** legal reforms have been much slower. By the second half of 2014, both countries still allowed rapists to avoid prosecution by marrying their teenage victims (Article 326 of the Algerian Penal Code and Article 227 of the Tunisian Penal Code). In **Iraq**, legal proposals are becoming regressive rather than liberating. The Personal Status Law – a new Jaafari marriage law proposed in 2014 by a former justice minister and accepted by the Cabinet, would make it easier for men to take multiple wives and allow girls to be married from the age of nine.[24] Although given the volatile situation in Iraq, it may never come before parliament; radio show host Ahlam al-Obeidi was scathing in her condemnation: 'This is not marriage, but rather the selling and buying of young women.'[25]

All these penal codes betray a shocking absence of respect for the girl child, and utter disregard for the suffering of child victims. They also present marriage as a legal loophole for violent men, rather than a relationship of mutual love based on consent and commitment. The situation in many North African countries leaves girl children constantly at risk. With laws like these, violators and perpetrators of child rape continue to walk free.

The future?

There has to be a future for girls without the threat of child marriage. A groundswell of concern across the world now recognizes this. Many initiatives have been set up, statements issued, reports published. The president of the Christian Association of Nigeria called for Christians to stage massive street protests against an amendment to Nigeria law which would allow child marriage. The Elders, an influential group of global leaders founded in 2007 by former South African President Nelson Mandela, gathered dozens of organizations for a two-day meeting in Ethiopia and launched Girls Not Brides, a global partnership committed to ending child marriage. By the autumn of 2014 the partnership operated in 64 countries with almost 360 civil society organizations.

European countries operate their own ban on forced child marriage. Frequently, girls are taken 'home' from Europe to the country of parental origin to be married during the summer months. This is illegal in the UK, but the Forced Marriage Unit handles some 1,500 cases a year, half of them relating to visits to Pakistan. The UK charity Karma Nirvana, which acts as a lifeline to girls at risk of forced marriage, suggests they put a spoon in their underwear if they are suspicious that the trip abroad may be for their wedding, not a vacation! Setting off the airport security alarms by means of metal hidden in an intimate body area gives the girl the opportunity to be searched privately, and disclose her fears.[26]

The first ever global resolution on early and forced marriage of children was led by the UN in 2013. It was supported by a cross-regional group of over 107 countries – almost all countries where child marriage was prevalent, including Ethiopia, Yemen,

South Sudan, Sierra Leone, Chad, Guatemala and Honduras. The outcome was promising, though not without its disappointments. India, with around 40 per cent of the world's 60 million child marriages, and the highest absolute number of child brides (about 24 million), refused to sign.

Other global initiatives have followed suit. The Girl Summit, held in London in July 2014, brought young survivors together with campaigning organizations and faith groups to highlight child marriage and FGM, and get support from governments. It followed the twenty-sixth session of the UN Human Rights Council which discussed early and enforced marriage. With the world's media present, these pivotal meetings provided key opportunities for high-profile public exposure of the issues.[27]

That meeting of the UN Human Rights Council drew in leaders and delegates from countries across the world, including those in which early and forced marriage was a substantial problem. Wide agreement that forced marriage violated the right of a woman to choose a lifelong partner and calls for effective legislation were evident. In the light of future predictions, strong consensus on the urgency of the problem spurred the need to approach it from both a human rights and a child-safeguarding issue. Delegates from the Maldives pointed to the weight of cultural reasons behind the practice – economic gain, religious conformity, preservation of family name and honour. Creative examples were offered to show what had worked to reduce the problem. Delegates from countries like Israel reported on recent changes in their laws to establish 18 as the minimum age of marriage. Syrian representatives spoke of seminars held across the country in the presence of judges and lawyers, and claimed that sanctions led to a decrease in families choosing early marriage. Delegates from Asia and Africa spoke of improvements after engagement with male community leaders who then became committed to finding solutions. A speaker from Egypt shared a pilot scheme for creating early-marriage-free zones. In these zones people had taken part in awareness campaigns and carried out door-to-door visits to educate the public, resulting in a sharp reduction in child marriage.

The commitment was to keep the issue firmly on the agenda way beyond 2015, the year of the realization of the millennium goals. Suggested provisions were crucial: financial remedies, clear legislation, education, more effective legal mechanisms and obligations to implementation. The goal was sound: to eradicate early and enforced child marriage within a generation. The strategy was laudable: to gather ever greater international support until a tipping point is reached. No words sum up the task ahead better than those of Ban Ki-moon, UN Secretary-General in 2013: 'I urge governments, community and religious leaders, civil society, the private sector, and families – especially men and boys – to do their part to let girls be girls, not brides.'[28]

But action on the ground is also where it counts. Advocacy and protection organizations like Karma Nirvana and the YWCA, local initiatives like Care Ethiopia[29] or EKATA in the Bogra district of Bangladesh,[30] work tirelessly to raise awareness and change attitudes. No one is in any doubt that deep attitudinal changes are desperately needed within cultures reluctant to relinquish patriarchal traditions. Without these changes, the rights of the girl child might be spoken about, protocols signed and laws passed, but serious implementation of her fundamental human rights will remain a long way off. With them, millions of young girls could enjoy childhood and face an entirely different future.

5

Whose 'honour'? Killings and femicide as reprisals for shame

He told me that in his society, a man is like a piece of gold, a woman is like a piece of silk. If you drop gold in the mud, you can clean it. But a piece of silk is ruined.[1]

Killing in the name of preserving honour only brings dishonour to the family and largely, the country.   Kamna Arora, India

Shock and shame gripped communities in the UK when the fate of 17-year-old Shafilea Ahmed was fully revealed. The eldest daughter of five children born to parents from Pakistan, she was murdered in front of her siblings at their home in the north of England. The parents objected to her white, non-Muslim friends and her lifestyle, and were furious at her reluctance to accept their control over her life. After months of family rows, they stuffed a plastic bag into her mouth and closed her airways with their hands until she suffocated. Having disposed of her body, they then reported her as missing. Her decomposed corpse was found the following year, but it was to be nine years of painstaking police inquiry before the offenders were brought to trial. There, they were forced to listen to the testimony, finally brought against them by Alesha, their younger daughter, who told the court of their repeated attacks and abuse of Shafilea; how they had threatened her with a knife and gun, had drugged her, and locked her in a room for days without food. She said that her sister had been 'torn between the allure of a Western lifestyle and their demands she wear traditional clothes and agree to an arranged marriage'. On the night Shafilea died, her sister spoke of her gasping for air as her parents suffocated her. As the other children ran upstairs in shock, she saw her father carry a wrapped blanket to the car, which she believed contained her sister's body. The couple were found guilty of murder and sentenced to life imprisonment.

> On sentencing, Mr Justice Evans told the couple, 'Your concern about being shamed in your community was greater than the love of your child . . . A desire that she understood and appreciated the cultural heritage from which she came is perfectly understandable, but an expectation that she live in a sealed cultural environment separate from the culture of the country in which she lived was unrealistic, destructive and cruel.' He added: 'You killed one daughter, but you have blighted the lives of your remaining children.'[2]

The media widely described this as an honour killing – carried out to protect the values which some families feel they are required to uphold. Yet 'honour' is a strange word to use with reference to such cruel and barbaric treatment of children who do not fall in line with the wishes of their parents. What family could possibly be honoured by the murder and mutilation of its daughters?[3] For the detective superintendent in charge of this case, there was nothing honourable about it at all. He said quite simply that the savagery meted out to Shafilea was a 'vile and disgraceful act' and a 'clear case of murder'.[4]

Opening closed doors to see beyond

Phyllis Chesler, professor of psychology and women's studies at Richmond College, City University New York, conducted a ground-breaking study of 'honour killings' worldwide between 1989 and 2009. Carefully analysing the killings of 230 victims in 29 countries (including Canada, UK, USA, Afghanistan, India, Pakistan and Germany) she found that they were overwhelmingly against women (93 per cent), there was intense family collaboration (42 per cent of the murders were carried out by multiple perpetrators), victims were young (average age worldwide was 23) and that, outside Asia, a high proportion of the girls were murdered for being 'too Western' (91 per cent in North America, 71 per cent in Europe). More than half the victims were brutally tortured before they died, enduring multiple stabbing, bludgeoning, burning, throat-cutting or beheading. She also concluded that although 'honour' killing was carried out occasionally among Sikhs and Hindus, the majority were Muslim-on-Muslim crimes – in her study, 91 per cent of perpetrators were Muslims.[5]

Chesler's study showed an escalation in known 'honour' deaths over the 20-year period, though it was not clear whether this reflected an increase in killings, or better reporting. It is evident from her findings, and from studies since then, that the task of producing accurate figures of the actual extent of this crime is fraught with difficulties. When so much of it occurs in countries where brutal practices exist in the dark shadows of kinship cultures, hidden in family structures away from the public gaze, these killings are insidiously absorbed within the society and slow to hit the global headlines. Yet, behind closed doors, horrifying 'punishments' have, for many years, been meted out on girls who fall foul of family traditions, or want to live like their peers. In more rare cases it has been enacted against sons also. The records that do exist give us a glimpse of the scale, but the figures are erratic. In Pakistan, for example, honour killing (often referred to as *karo-kari*) is suspected to be the cause of death for up to 10,000 women each year, but official records account for less than a tenth of these figures. As long ago as 1997, the independent Pakistan Human Rights Commission reported that in Sindh province some 300 women were victims of 'honour killings'.[6] A human rights watch report published in 1999 claimed that in 1998, 888 women were killed in the single province of Punjab.[7] But the official average figure offered for the whole country has been consistently between 900 and 1,000 a year.[8] When most cases go unreported (and almost all go unpunished), it is extremely difficult to find out how many women recorded as having died in accidents, or through sudden illness or suicide, were actually murdered in 'honour' attacks. And what about all those who simply 'disappeared'?

Pakistan: 'honour' absolves murder?

Pakistan is one of the countries most noted for this practice, and the cultural attitudes which fuel the slaughter become transparent in the tragic stories of its victims. The case of Samia Imran back in 1999 illustrates the worst of them. A young married woman, seeking a divorce from a violent husband, Samia went against the wishes of her family by engaging Jilani and Jahangir, a law firm of two sisters, known for their concern for women's rights. She had sought safety in Shirkatgah, the only women's refuge in Lahore, as she pursued her case. However, her visit to the lawyers' office in Lahore ended abruptly. Her mother entered with a male associate who shot her dead. The aftermath was also shocking; none of Pakistan's political leaders condemned the attack and members of Pakistan's upper house demanded punishment for the two women lawyers. The Muslim clergy in Peshawar also joined the outcry against the lawyers, asking for them to be put to death for trying to help Samia Imran!

Writer Suzanne Goldenberg takes up the story:

> Three days after Samia's death, the Peshawar Daily Mashriq ran an advertisement announcing the dates for a demonstration against 'a dirty conspiracy against Islam, Pakistan, family life as we know it'. The targets were Jilani, Jahangir and the women's shelter, and so violent were the threats against the lawyers that they moved the courts to prosecute for incitement. The courts did not respond.[9]

Bringing a case to court is difficult enough. A UN Commission on Human Rights report noted that the 'great majority' of the honour crimes it examined in Pakistan went 'unpunished either because no complaint was ever filed by relatives of the victims, or because the police refused to file a complaint'. Even in cases where 'murderers reportedly surrendered themselves to police with the murder weapon . . . no action was ever taken against them'. Suzanne Goldenberg concurs: 'Those who kill for honour [in Pakistan] are almost never punished. In the rare instances [that] cases reach the courts, the killers are sentenced to just two or three years.' She pointed out that Hana Jilani, the lawyer who witnessed Samia Imran's murder, had collected 150 case studies and in only eight cases did the judges reject the argument that the women were killed for 'honour'. Yet '[a]ll the others [perpetrators] were let off, or given reduced sentences'.[10]

Amnesty International also recognizes that perpetrators receive far greater protection than the victims: 'the judiciary ensure that they usually receive a light sentence, reinforcing the view that men can kill their female relatives with virtual impunity.'[11] The police invariably take the man's side, producing what Nighat Taufeeq calls 'an unholy alliance that works against women'. She goes on: 'The killers take pride in what they have done, the tribal leaders condone the act and protect the killers and the police connive the cover-up.'[12]

All this was vividly brought home in a murder in May 2014. Farzana Parveen, a 25-year-old pregnant woman, was beaten to death in front of the high court building in Lahore by family members enraged that she had married against their wishes. Her family had brought a case of kidnapping against her husband and she was due to testify against them, but it was never to be. The large crowd of witnesses became mere onlookers as one of her brothers and male family members attacked her with blunt objects and stoned her till she died. Despite her screams for help, no one went to her assistance and some reports said even policemen watched the incident.[13] Although her father was arrested, all the attackers managed to escape.

This time, at least, there was public condemnation. Abid Saqi, a former head of the Lahore high court bar association, felt that this public 'mutilation to bits' of a young woman 'right in front of the doors of justice' showed a 'complete breakdown of law and order'. Others, like human rights activist Tahira Abdullah, felt it showed the consequences of a deep-seated cultural and religious control of women. Under the criminal laws of Pakistan the killers could be prosecuted for double murder, because both the woman and her unborn child were killed. But under the Islamic-tinged legal system, killers were effectively allowed to walk free, as close relatives of murder victims were given the right to forgive the perpetrators. In her view it was vital for the country to follow the civil code rather than sharia law.[14]

Anyone party to an alleged 'dishonour' can be targeted for honour killings. An extraordinary case in the Kohistan area in 2012 illustrates this. When a mobile phone video showed footage of women and men dancing and clapping at a wedding, men from the women's families decided they had been shamed. Reportedly, they killed eight people: the four women shown in the video, a fifth girl acting as a messenger and three brothers from the men's family. What followed was a dispute which, because of the local complications, could not be settled even by the Supreme Court. Bizarrely, the legal wrangle seemed not about the right of these men to kill the five women and two of the men. It was simply about whether they also had the right to kill the third brother who had not been in the video. In justification, the women's family are said to have argued that since the perpetrators had killed five of their women, the custom also allowed them to kill five men![15]

The mindset which defines family 'rights', as in many stories like the one above, indicates why laws are slow to be introduced and even slower to be implemented. Yasmeen Hassan, author of *The Haven Becomes Hell: A Study of Domestic Violence in Pakistan*, argues that the concepts of women as property and honour are 'so deeply entrenched in the social, political and economic fabric of Pakistan that the government, for the most part, ignores the daily occurrences of women being killed and maimed by their families'.[16] There was little effective legal redress until an Honour Killings Bill was passed in 2005, raising the bar for punishments of such crimes. However, this bill failed to amend the *Qiyas* and *Diyat* ordinances, which allow guilty perpetrators of 'honour' crimes to avoid criminal prosecution if they were forgiven by the victim or her family. Because, as in Farzana Parveen's case, the victim's family is often also the perpetrator, victims could still be violated with impunity.

Further laws passed in Pakistan in 2012 offer greater protection to women, but the gap between the dignity and rights of women and men remains huge. Dr Tahira Shahid Khan, who works in a women's resource centre, argues that it hinges on the assumption of ownership – just as any owner can decide the fate of his property, men can decide the fate of women. 'Women are considered the property of the males in their family, irrespective of their class, ethnic or religious group . . . The concept of ownership has turned women into a commodity which can be exchanged, bought and sold.'[17] That's why activist Sana Saleem feels that attitudes stuck in the past, along with the right of relatives to pardon killers, remain a major impediment to proper legal implementation. For her, legal changes must be reflected in cultural transformation: 'It's great that we have new legislation but without the police and the courts reforming, changing their attitude to women, then nothing can change.'[18]

Such changes of attitude must also address the issue of protection and reparation for victims of violence. For women subjected to honour attacks do not always die. And there is little comfort for those left alive. Women can be cut, maimed, blinded or disfigured for life and left dependent on their attacker without any other form of livelihood. In graphic and shocking detail, we read how this affects one victim:

> Zahida Perveen's head is shrouded in a white cotton veil, which she self-consciously tightens every few moments. But when she reaches down to her baby daughter, the veil falls away to reveal the face of one of Pakistan's most horrific social ills, broadly known as 'honour' crimes. Perveen's eyes are empty sockets of unseeing flesh, her earlobes have been sliced off, and her nose is a gaping, reddened stump of bone. Sixteen months ago, her husband, in a fit of rage over her alleged affair with a brother-in-law, bound her hands and feet and slashed her with a razor and knife. She was three months pregnant at the time. 'He came home from the mosque and accused me of having a bad character,' the tiny, 32-year-old woman murmured as she awaited a court hearing . . . 'I told him it was not true, but he didn't believe me. He caught me and tied me up, and then he started cutting my face. He never said a word except, "This is your last night."'[19]

The allegations here about Zahida's 'bad character' are a familiar echo. Any contact, even conversation, between a man and a woman outside wedlock can be seen as evidence of illicit sex and breach the honour of the woman's family. Such allegations against women by husbands or relatives do not have to be substantiated. The mere expression of suspicion by the woman's family is evidence enough; the community demands no further proof! As one human rights activist (in Baluchistan) points out, the distinction between a woman being guilty of sexual impropriety and a woman being alleged to be guilty is irrelevant. 'What impacts on the man's honour is the public perception, the belief of her infidelity. It is this which blackens honour and for which she is killed.'[20]

So, despite laws, an unwritten, unlawful but widely accepted code means that the 'ownership' of women continues to confer 'rights to vengeance' on would-be assassins in Pakistan. And in these patriarchal communities women are left persistently vulnerable to injustice, brutality and death. It is hardly surprising, therefore, that many women live in isolation and fear, with threats of violent reprisal discouraging any plan to flee from family control. In any case, where would they go? There are few women's shelters or places of safety. Transport is not easy. Women seen travelling alone receive abuse from strangers or police, and male relatives can easily be alerted to their whereabouts. We can begin to see why, for those women whose lives have become intolerable, suicide appears the only means of escape. Writing in the summer of 2014, Tahira Abdullah pointed out that Pakistan is 'now at a crossroads where we have to decide whether we continue going down the Talibanisation route or whether we go down the rule-of-law route'.[21] Without this redirection, women will continue to be at risk. Real justice for women still seems beyond the distant horizon.

Honour killings in the Middle East

My focus has been on Pakistan, but there is no shortage of examples of honour killings right across South Asia, the Middle East and elsewhere. In south-eastern Turkey, 16-year-old Medine Memi was murdered by relatives for talking to boys. Her body was found in a hole 2 metres deep under a chicken pen, with tied hands, and lungs and stomach filled with soil. She had clearly been buried alive.[22] In Egypt, Karima Metawe, 20, was rumoured to have left her home in Alexandria, Egypt, without permission. To 'restore family honour' she was strangled to death in front of her baby by her two brothers and an uncle.[23] In Bangladesh, Hena Begum, 14, was beaten by family members and died after being publicly flogged by order of the village council, whose members sentenced her to 100 lashes. Her 'crime' was that she had been raped by her 40-year-old married cousin.[24] In Yemen in 2013, a girl was burnt to death by her father for talking to her fiancé before the wedding.[25] In Jordan, one woman was knifed to death because she wanted to

66

continue her education and refused to marry the man chosen for her by her family. Another woman was shot five times because she ran away from her husband who continually beat and raped her. Yet another had her throat slit because of suspected adultery – her husband saw her speaking with a man from their village.[26]

In South Lebanon (al-Wazzani) in 2013, the body of a teenage girl was found with stab wounds in her head and sides. Seven months pregnant, she had been killed by her 21-year-old brother for bringing shame on the family. An investigation later revealed that the brother had raped her, and the child she was carrying was his. His murderous attack was nothing to do with her so-called immorality; it followed her refusal to undergo a late abortion.[27]

In each of these dreadful cases, as in so many others, guilt is falsely imputed to the girl who then bears the full weight of punishment. The perpetrators might call this 'honour', but its proper names are sadism, hypocrisy and injustice.

Murders of women in Turkey rose by 1,400 per cent between 2002 and 2009, and women's rights activists believe most of the increase was in honour killings.[28] In countries such as Jordan, Morocco, Lebanon and Syria, 'honour crimes' were, until recently, legally sanctioned; and defence of the family honour was considered a mitigating factor in acts of violence. Legislation often awards lesser punishment wherever the victim is considered to have 'provoked' the crime by violating cultural norms. For example, Article 548 of the Penal Code in Syria, and Article 340 of the Penal Code of Jordan, provided for an exemption from penalty if a man kills his wife or female relative after finding her 'committing adultery with another'. In Syria, a reduction in penalty is provided for a man who kills or injures his female relative after catching her in a 'suspicious state with another'. In Jordan, Article 98 provided for a reduced sentence if the crime was committed in extreme 'rage'. A Jordanian parliament member who opposed the reforming of the penal code betrayed appalling, but widespread, gender prejudice: 'Women adulterers cause a great threat to our society because they are the main reasons that such acts take place . . . If men do not find women with whom to commit adultery, then they will become good on their own.'[29] Nevertheless, 5,000 protesters, including members of the Jordanian royal family, took to the streets of Amman in 2000 demanding the repeal of the penal code condoning 'honour' killings.[30]

The Lebanese parliament agreed in 2011 to abolish Article 562 of their code which, for years, had effectively protected honour killers. And despite conservative resistance in the Middle East, most of these penal code articles are being repealed. Yet reform remains sluggish. We might have assumed that younger generations would be more opposed to such violent actions against women and girls. A study in 2013 carried out by a researcher at Cambridge University found otherwise. In surveying over 850 teenagers in Jordan's capital city, Amman, it found that one third of all teenagers involved in the research actually advocated honour killing. Almost half of the boys and one in five of the girls believed that killing a daughter, sister or wife who has 'dishonoured' or shamed the family was a justifiable punishment. So, well into the twenty-first century, the 'risk factors' for attitudes in support of vigilante murders of women were depressingly evident.[31]

By 2015, the rise of the so-called Islamic State in Iraq and Syria (ISIS) had taken atrocities against women to a new, barbaric level. In October 2014, Islamic State militants kidnapped and tortured Samira Saleh al-Naimi, a lawyer and human rights activist, who had bravely criticized them for destroying places of worship. Now reconstructed as 'apostate', she was killed for the 'honour' of Islam. A few weeks later they publicly stoned to death a young woman allegedly taken in adultery, whose father refused to forgive her.

The global spread of atrocity

Over the past few decades, with increasing migration, the practice of 'honour' killing has spread from those countries where women are known to be at risk to countries with stronger legal protection for women. As it has become more exposed in 'open' societies, the real danger to young women in 'restrictive' societies has become frighteningly obvious. Negative attitudes towards women along with control have been put under the spotlight to reveal how brutality and murder have been masked under norms of discipline or submission. The challenge to countries in Europe and North America is to face up to the responsibility of protecting their own citizens. But it is also to find the will and resources to stand with those committed to combating the problem globally.

Honour killings in the UK: a shocking scenario

In the UK, it used to be assumed that daughter-violence occurred in isolated pockets, carried out by particularly repressive and autocratic parents. But increased reporting over the past two decades has disclosed a different image. Within many of our urban areas, girls from families originating in countries with a tradition of honour killing are being subject to control and violence at home in quite deliberate defiance of all child-safeguarding laws. Where the legal framework of their new country restricts their right to assume command over their daughter's choices and future, such parents apparently see themselves as above the law. In a media-dominant society, these issues are given more public exposure, which in turn makes it easier for neighbours to tip off the police about what they hear and see, providing their own anonymity can be preserved.

Yet, despite increased awareness of the abuses, the government has been ready to admit that it does not know the true scale of the problem. A survey of police statistics in 2012 shows that 2,823 so-called 'honour' crimes were reported in the UK in 2010 – shocking figures in themselves, but gleaned from only 75 per cent of police forces. A quarter of forces could not provide any statistics; their classifications contained no separate category for identifying this form of cruelty or attack. Inevitably, therefore, it is still possible for families to cloak violence and draw a veil of silence across their atrocities, continuing to believe that control is their entitlement. People outside the minority ethnic community are often very reluctant to 'interfere' – including, sometimes, even the local authorities. It requires a brave intervention of friends or teachers to alert the social services or police to the issue – brave because they themselves can become the focus of reprisal. But it is also cowardly and negligent for authorities to ignore these violations of the human rights of vulnerable minorities. The effect of all this is that those who face family abuse often do so in intense isolation.

However, more cases are reported in the UK than in countries like Pakistan, even though the numbers of incidents are almost certainly lower. One British writer gives a brief 'roll-call' of some of them, noting the length of time it often took for justice to be done:

> It took ten years for Mehmet Goren to be jailed, in 2009, for murdering his daughter Tulay, because she fell in love with an older man of a different Muslim sect. Last year, Gurmeet Singh Ubhi was found guilty of murdering his 24 year old daughter Amrit because the Sikh girl was dating a white man. There are others too – Heshu Yones, Banaz Mahmod, Nuziat Khan – the list of women murdered in the UK over their 'honour' is depressingly long.[32]

To this list might be added the names of Samaira Nazir, who died with 18 stab wounds and three separate cuts to her throat because, though from a Pakistani background, she wanted to marry her Afghan boyfriend,[33] and Laura Wilson, an English girl from Yorkshire, repeatedly stabbed in the head, then drowned by her Asian boyfriend, Ashtiaq Ashgar, for bringing shame on his family.[34]

The outcome of such murders in the UK is more likely to be careful investigation and due process of law. Most of those responsible are now in prison, some serving life sentences. But according to campaigner Jasvinder Sanghera, other 'honour crimes' still go unheeded, even by civic leaders: 'I've yet to see community leaders, religious leaders, politicians, Asian councillors give real leadership on this.' For her, their reluctance is 'extremely irresponsible', 'morally wrong' and 'morally blind'.[35]

There is inevitably pain for those caught up in the crossfire. Sometimes, it is a mother who is the victim, leaving behind unsolved problems for her children. The daughter of Surjit Athwal, a woman forced into marriage at the age of 16, spent years wondering what had happened to her mother when she failed to return home from a trip to India. She was told that she had gone off with another man. Almost a decade later she would learn the truth:

> I was seven when I last saw my mum. She was off to India with my grandma for a family wedding. I wanted to go too but they wouldn't let me. My last memory is watching her walk out of the house. She would never come back and it would be nine years before I

understood the real reason why: my grandma and dad had arranged to have her murdered out there.

My mum was killed because she wanted to leave her unhappy marriage. She was expected to act like a 'traditional' wife, waiting on everyone hand and foot. But she wanted her independence, to wear western clothes and have a job. She was killed for wanting her freedom.

I think about my mum every single day.

Surjit's husband and mother-in-law were given life sentences in the UK for her murder. Yet, ten years after the death, those paid to carry out the killing were still free in India. Her daughter campaigned in 2014 for full justice for her mother, utilizing the social media. She highlighted the plight of all British women and girls who have no say in how they lead their lives but are 'intimidated, attacked, forced into marriages against their will and in the worst cases, like my mother, killed'. Her petition closed with almost 95,000 signatures.[36]

. . . and across Europe

Honour crime exists throughout Europe, although the level of reporting is generally lower than in the UK. Scandinavian countries, for example, are noted for their child-respect policies which build child protection into mainstream social consciousness, so have sometimes been slower to identify abusers who have very different attitudes towards women and children. In Finland, police fear that fewer than 5 per cent of cases come to light. One senior officer in that country believes that the seriousness of the situation is not understood, even by the officials who deal with it. He urges officials to develop more familiarity with other cultures so that when women and family members from such cultures come to report threats of violence, they might be 'met with a different attitude'.[37] The problem is not peculiar to Finland. Allegations of indifference from European nationals have been made in many European countries. But such 'indifference' can be more an uncertainty about how to react to culturally separate groups. There is always concern about how to reinforce legal safeguards without being accused of racism or undermining ethnic culture. Whatever the reasons for indecision, there is little doubt that the tally of abuse, assault and murder of girls by certain family members is much higher in every country than the cases recorded in police statistics.[38]

Again, we could give a roll-call of killings across the European continent. In Italy, Hina Saleen had her throat cut by her father because she refused an arranged marriage and wanted to integrate into Italian society. In Sweden, Fadime Sahindal was killed by her abusive father for going public about her love for a Swedish boy.[39] In Denmark, 18-year-old Ghazala Khan was shot dead two days after her wedding, because her Pakistani family were opposed to her choice of husband.[40] In Germany, five women were murdered in quick succession, including Hatin Surucu: gunned down by her Turkish brother for adopting Western ways.[41] In Switzerland, 16-year-old Swera was axed to death by her Muslim father for dating a Christian boy, and trying to escape from home.[42] I could go on. Such deaths occur in societies which already have protective laws against gender-based violence. Defiance of the law by repressive, dominant communities cannot be overestimated.

North America

Reports from Canada and the USA uncover a similarly depressing scenario. A case which captured worldwide attention in 2009 brought honour killings to the forefront in Canada. Afghanistan-born Mohammad Shafia, 58, his wife and son were all found guilty, after a ten-week trial, of the first-degree murder of Shafia's first wife and his three young teenage daughters. The gap between cultural attitudes was spelled out in the judge's comments to the convicted trio:

> The apparent reason behind these cold-blooded shameful murders was that the four completely innocent victims offended your twisted notion of honour that is founded upon the domination and control of women; a sick notion of honour that has absolutely no place in any civilized society.

Sometimes, pleas of innocence are easy to dismiss. In the USA, Tina Isa, a bright American high-school student in St Louis, Missouri, longing to study aeronautics, was held down by her mother while her Palestinian-born father, Zein Isa, plunged a butcher's knife into her chest six times, telling her to die quickly. She had been described as a 'tramp' and a 'whore' by her parents for wanting to play sports, go on school trips, and take a job in a fast-food restaurant. They called 911, reporting they had killed their daughter in self-defence. But their case fell apart since Zein Isa had been under surveillance as a member of a Midwest-based terrorist cell linked to a jihadist group. FBI agents heard, on tape, every second of the seven-minute family argument and subsequent terror and screams from the dying girl. The parents were convicted of first-degree murder.[43]

Understanding the sociology of honour crime

Honour crime makes no sense unless one recognizes the cultural pressures that give rise to it, and recognize the common characteristics of such crime, committed even in countries with more rigorous protective laws. The sense of entitlement in parents to enforce what they want for their sons and daughters overrides all else. The despising of the mores of the host culture fuels a powerful bid to cut their children off from its influence. Tradition is highly valued, while 'liberty' is not; death is seen as preferable to dishonour. Consequently, there is a low regard for the law of the land they live in, especially when this law restrains the power of the family to control the lives of its members.

In his book *The Honour Code*, Kwame Anthony Appiah emphasizes the acceptance of honour codes – shared norms that determine entitlement to respect. These codes bind people together in the same 'honour world' which provides some bulwark against the different perceptions of a host country. 'Honour codes' have implications for how the right to respect is protected and what is seen as a violation. There are also chilling implications as to how members of the 'honour world' support those who take action against those who bring 'shame'.

Usually, as in the country of origin, several members of the family may collude in the violence, murder plan or subsequent cover-up. Murder victims 'disappear' and authorities may be told that they have returned to the country of origin. Because that is easy to check, more often they are reported as missing persons. If a body is found, and death was clearly the result of a violent attack, the plea is usually that there was no unlawful killing, but parents acted in self-defence, or that the victim died of self-inflicted injury. In cases which are brought to court and result in conviction, violent parents usually show no remorse. Sometimes, they believe their actions to be a gesture of defiance against the 'moral laxity' of the host society. Convictions do not seem to deter others from similar actions against their children. As Diana Nammi of the Iranian and Kurdish Women's Rights Organisation (IKWRO) explained: '[t]he perpetrator will be even considered as a hero within the community because he is the one defending the family and community's honour and reputation.'[44] So they continue to maintain that what they did was right, even though the rest of society now classifies them as murderers.

International law recognizes honour killing for what it is: a barbaric, brutal and entirely unjustified form of violence, mostly against women, which ruins lives and destroys relationships. It acts as a terrifying deterrent to women who dare to exercise choice over crucial areas of their own lives and futures. If women stand against the practice and all the assumptions about them that it embodies, they risk even further violation and can become perpetual targets. All who care about justice should acknowledge the persistence of those women's rights activists who have opposed these practices for so many years – women from Pakistan, Iran, Iraq, Turkey, Syria, Morocco, Egypt, Lebanon, Jordan . . . the list is long. Their challenge is that we should now mobilize action where it is needed. For it will take the combined effort of governments, religious leaders, law-enforcement agencies and campaigners to implement laws and change the endemic mindset of 'ownership'. As we honour the many women victims who bravely continue to resist the power wielded against them and become beacons of hope to others who have little chance of justice or reparation, it is surely time to celebrate their courage, and rally together to their support.[45]

6

Nowhere to run, nowhere to hide: violence in the home

———◆◆◆———

We were always told that they'd put us in foster homes where people would rape us if we ever said anything. So we explained away the bruises and my mom wore big sunglasses whenever she left the house. And we invented car accidents if the bruising was too bad to cover with make-up.

Emily Andrews, *The Finer Points of Becoming Machine*

In an article for the US magazine *Glamour*, editor-at-large Liz Brody tells a story familiar to people who work alongside survivors of domestic abuse. For readers who have been victims, the details may be sickeningly reminiscent.

> Not long before sunrise on a Midwestern Friday, college student and part-time waitress Alexandra Briggs sat in her one-bedroom apartment, meticulously applying thick makeup all over her face, neck and arms. It took two coats to cover her boyfriend's teeth marks and the cigarette burns he'd inflicted, along with her newly purpling bruises; her pants hid the spot on her thigh where he'd stabbed her with a fork. When she finished, he drove her to the Original Pancake House for her 7:00 a.m. shift. 'I'm sick,' she told her boss as she clocked in and headed to the restroom.[1]

Alexandra Briggs was one of the fortunate ones. She had a sympathetic boss who had long suspected, and now recognized beyond doubt, that the student was the victim of intimate-partner violence. Her boyfriend would later admit in court that he had hit her repeatedly with a small bat that morning, and strangled her until she slumped, unconscious. A ruptured eardrum and broken nose were just two of the injuries she had suffered. This was no isolated attack but a form of relentless aggression which left deep scars on her body, mind and spirit. Because of her boss's intervention, this student escaped further brutality, and her abuser received a ten-year jail sentence. Others have become part of US homicide figures.

Half a world away, a woman in Bangladesh is struggling with the long-term impact of an acid attack. Sarah Turley describes in *The Guardian* how, two years after the incident, its effect is still all too evident:

> Nurbanu, a softly spoken woman of 35, is sitting under the shade of her corrugated iron kitchen roof in Shatkhira, south west Bangladesh. The acid has left the skin on her face thin and creased like tissue paper, and she is holding her daughter Mallika's hand – something she has become accustomed to because the acid left her blind, and she needs Mallika's guidance around her home.[2]

Nurbanu's 'offence' had been to divorce her husband, after years of his brutality and infidelity. For that she was subject to his 'punishment' – a vicious acid attack on her body, which distorted her features and ended her sight. It meant she had to return, with her three children, to her husband's house, for her blindness and disability gave her no other option. Domestic violence was not criminalized in Bangladesh until 2010, so with no recourse to law, unable to work to support her children, and with no welfare system, she had to take the only course open to her.

Alexandra's and Nurbanu's stories are not isolated ones, either in the USA or in Bangladesh. In the United States, according to the US National Center for Injury Prevention and Control, women experience about 4.8 million intimate partner-related physical assaults and rapes every year,[3] with, in 2007, an estimated 1,640 ending in death.[4] In Bangladesh, the World Health Organization suggests more than 50 per cent of women experience some form of domestic violence, with around 3,000 acid attacks reported in one decade. In both countries the reported level is known to be much lower than the actual incidence. In Bangladesh, even if women do report the crime, they have no guarantee of redress. Out of 121 attacks reported in 2010, there were only seven convictions.[5] In the USA the stigma of domestic assault remains high:

typically, fewer than 20 per cent of battered women even seek medical treatment following an injury.[6] What is very clear is that in countries as distinct as the United States and Bangladesh, women are suffering both the physical impact of intimate-partner violence, along with dreadful emotional and economic consequences.

Some consequences are impossible to exaggerate. Acid attacks occur every other day, archetypically on women who have resisted sexual advances, or upset their husbands in some way. Apart from the shocking bodily and visual impact, women who have survived acid attacks have difficulty finding work, and if unmarried, finding a husband. We can understand how the very threat of such attacks can produce compliance in a woman who is powerless against her assailant.

How big is the global problem? Trying to collect the data

According to Michelle Bachelet, former UN Women Executive Director, up to seven in ten women continue to be targeted for physical and/or sexual violence in their lifetime. This is not helped by the fact that 603 million women live in countries where domestic violence is still not a crime.[7] Although it is not always so visible or overtly brutal as that suffered by Nurbanu, intimate-partner violence is the most prevalent form of gender violence and does affect women of all cultures. The UN reports that 48 per cent or more of women in Zambia, Ethiopia and Peru suffer violence at the hands of a current or former intimate partner.[8] The World Health Organization's study of ten countries found, despite considerable variation between countries, cities and rural areas, that domestic violence was widespread in each of them.[9] Ten separate domestic violence prevalence studies carried out by the Council of Europe found consistently that one in four women – a quarter of the female population – suffered domestic violence over their lifetime.[10]

Accurate data of numbers and incidents are very hard to come by, so figures from these studies are crucial in trying to establish the scale of the problem. Occasionally, estimates are challenged by people who claim that the level of domestic violence to women is wildly exaggerated. In fact, the opposite is more likely to be true. In countries where no careful research has been carried out, little reliable data exists at all, and figures recorded by official institutions, law-enforcement agents or NGOs can be woefully inadequate. As always, a considerable gap exists between the number of incidents reported to the police or authorities and those unearthed by researchers. Take Turkey, for example. A study by the Hacettepe University Institute of Population Studies interviewed 12,000 women in 2009 and discovered that 42 per cent of women aged 15–60 across Turkey, and 47 per cent of women in rural areas, had experienced physical or sexual violence perpetrated by their husbands or partners. Yet only 8 per cent of the victims went to the police or sought help. Without this study and the 2011 report we would have scant evidence of the scale of the problem.[11]

The 2011 Human Rights Watch report on family violence in Turkey[12] shows clearly why so few women seek help from the authorities. They are not encouraged to. The report documented appalling experiences of domestic violence against women of all ages. In Istanbul, Ankara, Izmir, Van, Trabzon and Diyarbakir, women and girls as young as 14 told of being raped, stabbed, kicked in the stomach when pregnant, and beaten with hammers, sticks, branches and hoses, to the point of having broken bones and fractured skulls. The catalogue of horrors included being locked up with dogs or other animals, starved, shot with a stun gun, injected with poison, pushed off a rooftop, and subjected to severe psychological violence. Yet, far from victims receiving help from the state authorities, the report found that an appeal to such agencies often compounded the distress. Women who informed the police were often chided, shamed, treated with impatience and told to come back another day. Not infrequently, they were sent back to a violent partner after the man had assured his interrogators that there was no problem. Unsurprisingly, levels of violence against women in Turkey are seen as the worst in Europe, with these types of abuse more prevalent only in sub-Saharan Africa, East Asia and the Pacific. And even though outcry from parliamentarians and pressure groups did result in a new law in March

2012, introducing tough measures against abusers, and boosting state assistance and protection for victims,[13] most people recognize that it would take changes in cultural outlook to solve the problem effectively.[14]

It is rare, then, for the size of the problem to be detected by police authorities. In all societies, individual incidents of domestic violence often only come to light when women present themselves for treatment to health professionals, or are investigated for other symptoms. Even then, despite the suspicions of those who are making a diagnosis, the cause of injury can be masked by the victim as 'accidental' or disguised by other signs as a 'mental health issue'. It may take a whole cluster of symptoms to alert medical authorities to the real source of the problem. Since victims of domestic violence are also prone to post-traumatic stress disorder, psychosis, depression, anxiety, panic attacks and attempted suicide, unravelling the complexity can be daunting.

Sometimes, indeed, the violence is detected only when the victim dies. Partner abuse is the gateway for yet more serious crimes as very many women don't survive their ordeal. Several international surveys suggest that over half of all women who die from homicide are killed within the family, the majority by current or former partners.[15] Key studies have reported that in Australia, Canada and Israel this accounts for 40 to 70 per cent of female murder victims; in India, 22 women were killed each day in dowry-related murders; in South Africa, a woman was killed every six hours, and in Guatemala two women were murdered, on average, each day – all by partners.[16] In Europe, too, seven women are said to die every day from domestic violence perpetrated by men.[17]

What exactly is domestic violence?

There is no subtlety about an acid attack, a fractured skull or a murder, yet for many women the experience of domestic abuse is much more complicated than horror impacts. It might occur without physical violence, but involve psychological abuse, or emotional trauma. Manipulation, mind-games, undermining, financial or even spiritual violation are not infrequent. In some cultures, it is usual to find a whole cluster of these different aspects interwoven in the experience of a single victim. What they all have in common is that they form a pattern of coercive and controlling behaviour, which takes away freedom and destroys a sense of self-worth.[18]

In some cultures, because 'wife chastisement' is seen as a justifiable part of marriage, some women expect to be subject to physical 'discipline' and see this as problematic only when it becomes prolonged or extreme. In other cultures, where there are no such norms, it is difficult to identify any single context for domestic abuse. Abuse can begin at the start of a relationship, but it can also suddenly erupt after years spent together. It can occur in 'forced' marriages, where the woman has few legal rights or protection, or it can occur in relationships where the woman has chosen her partner and is 'protected' by the law. It can follow a generational pattern, where the abuser has grown up in a dysfunctional family or with a violent parent, but it can also begin without any previous family patterns of abuse. It can be affected by poverty and scarce resources, but also found in highly affluent contexts. It can be part of overall violence in society – war or tribal fighting – or it can occur in situations of peace and calm. It can be related to trigger points – unemployment, financial loss, depression – or it can come without warning. It can be accompanied by irritability and anger, or it can be a calculated and deliberate way of inflicting pain on another. It can be associated with alcohol or drug abuse, but be inflicted too by those who are stone cold sober. In short, domestic abuse covers so many multiple forms that even those who are enveloped within it do not always recognize it for what it is. At its core, it happens because an abusive person *chooses* to behave in a way that gives maximum power over the other. The abuser deliberately acts to dominate and control.

Male victims

This book is about violence against women, but it is only fair to note that abuse is also suffered by men in relationships, and in same-sex partnerships. In fact, in the UK, the incidence of abuse against men is rising; and those on the receiving end face very specific dilemmas. The indications are that men who are abused by their partners in countries like the UK and USA are even more reluctant to seek help than women. Not only is an abused man likely to feel embarrassed and humiliated at having to make such a disclosure, but he is liable to face other problems. He might encounter a shortage of resources, scepticism from police, and major legal obstacles, especially if he is trying to gain custody of his children from an abusive mother. Counsellors report different gender responses in that an abused man might justify his partner's behaviour, or feel he needs to protect her from public exposure. Sometimes he believes he might change her. He knows, too, that if he retaliates, the situation can become much worse; men are strongly cautioned against responding physically to bodily attacks. If the police are called, it is far more likely that he will be seen as the one perpetuating violence. Most men do not try to find 'safe houses', and in any case there are very few men's refuges, partly because abused men are less likely to be pursued or hounded by partners. Very often abused men stay with their partners because they fear for their children and do not want to lose them, but they become nervous and constantly anxious within the relationship.

In real situations, wherever abuse occurs, and whoever the injured party, the experience is deeply damaging and destructive. And in recognizing that men too can be victims, we cannot minimize the harm that their partners can inflict on them. Helplines like the Men's Advice Line run by Respect are a sobering testimony to the number of men who face violence and cruelty at home. There are also many appalling stories of isolated men who suffer in silence and endure abuse for decades without ever seeking help.

We do need to acknowledge, however, that despite horrifying incidents of male-partner victimization, overwhelmingly it is women who suffer from domestic violence. We see this reflected even in the ratio of male to female deaths through domestic attack. They comprise 40 to 70 per cent of female murder victims[19] but just 4 to 8 per cent of male victims. Closer scrutiny of individual cases also reveals that there are often different circumstances behind these fatal attacks. Although violent women certainly do exist, and can act with appalling viciousness, they rarely murder their victims.

Studies done on women who do kill their partners indicate that most of these women are, paradoxically, not normally prone to violence, but often have endured beatings for years and their retaliation is a last desperate attempt to be free.[20] Karen Ingala Smith's penetrating analysis of UK homicide figures shows that men are more likely to be killed by someone they were abusing; women are more likely to be killed by someone they were being abused by.[21]

What are the signs?

We can see from the complexity of domestic abuse that it is difficult to construct a definitive list of signs that someone is a victim, whether that person is male or female. Because individuals may not identify their experiences at the hands of their partners as domestic violence, they may neither seek help nor realize help is available. Sometimes, an abusive person's personal characteristics are exactly the same qualities that first attracted the partner. For example, a woman might initially regard a man who always wants to know where she has been as intensely romantic and loving. Only later, when she finds she cannot act or move without his supervision, does she realize she has become imprisoned by a controlling tyrant. There can also be a collusion of silence between both the violator and the victim, where the perpetrator lies to deny what is happening, and the victim hides the truth because of fear or shame. As Amy Buckley points out, the victim may defend the abuser, due to 'fear, coercion, threats, denial, shame, [or] blame economic necessity and events relating to the cycle of abuse'.[22] Sometimes, couples have become so skilled at playing 'happy families' that even close friends or relatives may not detect the real truth about the relationship.

Yet in relation to women's experience of domestic abuse, there are patterns which constantly recur. An abuse victim often becomes isolated from family and friends. She may be jumpy or anxious in her partner's company, or be reluctant, unable even, to speak for herself. She may have regular unexplained absences from work, have little access to money, and be cautious about having visitors at home. She might show little interest in her appearance, paying no attention to clothes or hair. Those around her may notice that her partner is constantly checking up on her – texting, phoning, interrogating – requiring her to answer his questions or meet his requirements. And, even though the abuser is careful to inflict wounds which cannot easily be detected, she may, of course, present inexplicable injuries, where explanations do not match the evidence.

If we try to draw up an accurate profile of a typical abuser we are beset with the same problems. For example, some violators do lose control very easily, and become caught up in demonstrations of anger which get completely out of hand. Often, a man will blame his partner for making him angry and out of control, and thereby bringing the problem on herself. He will deny that he is violent, or punitive, and assert that he is simply reacting to the situation his wife leaves him with. Yet although domestic violence often does build up in a crescendo, it has very little relation to the woman's behaviour, for she is in a 'no-win' situation. The majority of perpetrators are not, in fact, men out of control, but are very much in control. They know exactly how to hurt their victim, how to inflict the maximum pain without detection. Women have come to clinics with their bodies covered with burns, yet largely hidden by clothing. Women have described how their throats have been squeezed almost to the point of asphyxiation, and then, as they were losing consciousness, released. Violent and brutal tactics employed by abusive men will be used regardless of whether they feel anger or not. Only rarely is domestic abuse simply an angry outburst; it is far more frequently a very deliberate choice to hurt, damage and control the other.

Unequal women

In many cultures the scale of domestic violence is intrinsically linked to women's unequal status. This is the case in those countries which provided our earlier examples. In his study of intimate-partner violence in Bangladesh, Syed Masud Ahmed points to the gender inequalities deeply embedded in that culture, where 'extreme poverty, patriarchy, systematic discrimination from birth, illiteracy, early marriage, and unequal power relations make women vulnerable to gender-based violence, especially domestic violence'. He goes on to point out that the 'patrilocal marriage system, where the young bride moves to the in-law's (*sic*) household away from her natal home, makes the situation worse'.[23] Inequality, patriarchy and isolation all compound the problem.

Turkey also has manifestly unequal gender relations. In 2015, women gained 17 per cent of seats in the national parliament, although locally there are only 37 female mayors out of a total of almost 3,000. Women represent merely 29 per cent of the paid workforce,[24] and have little disposable income of their own. Figures on illiteracy released by the government in 2010 showed great disparities between men and women: 3.8 million of the 4.7 million people without literacy in Turkey are women.[25] In 2014, Turkey ranked 69 on the United Nations Development Programme's global Gender Inequality Index, with the World Economic Forum ranking it 125th out of 142 in its Global Gender Gap Index in the same year. [26] Yet even university education is no guarantor of freedom from domestic violence in countries where it is sanctioned traditionally. An official study involving Qatar University female students disclosed that 63 per cent of them had been beaten, usually by male relatives.[27]

Where gender inequality is rarely challenged, it can be part of the cultural norm for women to be chastised in the home: commended even, as a way of maintaining orderly family life, and work discipline. A man interviewed in Lebanon assumed this to be a matter of fact:

> My first wife didn't obey me so I had to hit her repeatedly. I disfigured her; I broke her nose and cut off all her hair. Then I repudiated her. My second wife, she was also rebellious and disobedient so I broke her leg. She made me so angry, I wanted to kill her. But I married again on Saturday, my third wife, and I believe this time I made the right choice . . . It is my right to beat my wife if she doesn't carry out all her duties towards me and my family.[28]

Statements like this do more than send shivers down the spine, and make us fearful for the new wife. They also disclose the size of the problem to be overcome if women are to know freedom from violence.

In the Rakai District of Uganda, a survey of 5,109 women of reproductive age found that 30 per cent of women had experienced physical threats or physical abuse from their current partner – 20 per cent during the year before the survey. Three fifths of women who reported recent physical threats or abuse recounted three or more acts of violence during the preceding year. Just under half reported injuries. Yet most of those who responded – around 80 per cent of both men and women – regarded it as justifiable for wives or female partners to be beaten by the man in certain circumstances.[29] Ten years after this study, I found a similar response when I visited rural communities in north-east Uganda. A questionnaire was given to community members at the beginning of a self-evaluation community project. To the question, 'When would it be appropriate to beat your wife?' possible answers included 'when she burnt the meal' or 'when she went out without telling me'. Although 'never' was also a possible answer, very few men chose that option. In fact 86 per cent of the respondents thought they would be justified in beating their wives if they went out without permission.

The HIV & AIDS pandemic has also brought more risk to women. They can be blamed and 'punished' for infecting their husbands. In one of many cases, when a man hacked his wife to death with a machete in Rukungiri, Uganda, after learning he was infected with HIV, it was more than a case of ignorance.[30] It also exposed deep-seated acceptance of male promiscuity and a belief that women must be responsible for every ill.

In cultures where women have greater autonomy and higher educational attainment we might expect to find a different response. And indeed we do. A consistent finding of studies carried out on gender relations is that where women have more control over resources – through education or income – they are more protected from domestic violence.[31] These factors provide some balance to the distinct gender hierarchy which gives men the right to exercise patriarchal authority. The hope is that measures which empower women, economically and politically, will bring positive changes in family attitudes and behaviour. This hope was borne out for me in conversations with women both in Uganda and in rural communities in the north of Ethiopia. Having been encouraged to form local 'self-help' projects, the Ethiopian women met each week and 'banked' their weekly savings together. It was not long before these mutual savings had grown large enough to make loans to group members to begin small business enterprises. After four years, most of these women had become successful small entrepreneurs, educating their children, beginning literacy classes themselves, and reaping benefits in health and sanitation. When I asked if it might also have changed their relationships with their menfolk, they looked self-consciously at each other and laughed. Slowly, one of the braver ones spoke up: 'Yes, now that I have a business my husband no longer beats me; he respects me as his equal.' The Ugandan participatory project showed similar encouraging results.

Empowerment for women inevitably challenges patriarchal cultures, encourages education, spearheads legal change and brings readjustment in gender relations. Yet we need to recognize that none of these signs of progress can *guarantee* safety for women. The context is also very important. In fact, studies show that, in particularly conservative settings, women who achieve high autonomy may actually face an increased risk of violence.[32] Traditional male leaders in kinship networks or communities can resent the perceived challenge to their own authority. So violence can be used as a way of bringing women back into line and reasserting where the 'power' really lies. Sometimes, domestic change is simply slow to fall into step with legal and educational changes.

'Equal' women

This factor becomes more evident when we look at societies where women do occupy key positions in business, politics and the professions. For even in these cultures, domestic violence afflicts the lives of millions of them, often co-existing paradoxically alongside skilled professional competence and high educational achievement. Stories describe women who are strong and capable in the boardroom, yet suffer abuse and violation in the bedroom. In fact, in many ways, intimate-partner violence is harder to defeat when it exists despite laws and public disapproval. Those who endure such abuse become more isolated, their pain hidden behind a wall of shame and confusion, their experiences challenging the concepts of success and achievement which are so treasured in affluent societies.

Evidence in many countries confirms this. In the UK, domestic violence accounts for 18 per cent of all recorded violent crime,[33] with the police receiving reports of incidents every minute, or 1,300 calls a day.[34] The Freephone 24-hour National Domestic Violence Helpline, set up by two key organizations – Refuge and Women's Aid – received over a quarter of a million calls in its first 12 months. Yet we know only a relatively small proportion of victims call the helpline or police. Analysis of crime figures over a number of years by Sylvia Walby and Jonathan Allen revealed that every year there were 13 million separate incidents of physical violence or threats of violence against women from partners or former partners.[35] Of all crime, it also has the highest rate of repeat victimization: the British Crime Survey indicated that each victim experiences an average of 20 incidents of domestic violence in a year, often increasing in severity each time. The cost to the National Health Service is substantial. The bill for treating just mental health problems arising from domestic violence rose from an estimated £176 million in 2004[36] to £3.6 billion in 2014.[37]

Victims are not always adults. In a ground-breaking study in the UK on violence in teenage relationships, researchers found many examples of 'coercive control' by adolescent boys towards their girlfriends, some of whom were as young as 12. From extensive interviews they found clear evidence that 'some teenage girls, especially those with a history of family violence or with an older or much older boyfriend, are at serious risk of harm due to their partner's violence'. Nearly 11.2 per cent of the girls in their sample described the violence from their boyfriends as 'severe'[38] and most of the girls who experienced physical violence confessed to feeling extremely scared during the attack. It was dangerous to retaliate, and many tried to protect themselves against injury through non-violent protective defence of their bodies. Yet it was not clear that these teenagers understood how pathological such treatment was; the researchers noted that violence had almost become normalized in their experience, seen as part of intimacy. They expressed their own concern at the vulnerability they found among girls, especially where there was an age differential.

> Victimisation rates for girls with a much older partner are extremely concerning. Over four-fifths of girls with an older partner experienced emotional violence, three-quarters experienced physical violence and as many as three-quarters also experienced sexual violence. It is clear from these figures that many of these girls experienced multiple forms of violence from an older partner.[39]

This and other studies make it clear that intimate-partner violence is an urgent problem not only in overt patriarchal societies, but also in countries that pride themselves on being gender-egalitarian. As even young relationships become sexualized, and subject to associated pressures, the experience of violence at the hands of a partner becomes harder to address. The same reluctance to seek help from external sources found in adult victims is found even more conclusively in the study of teenagers discussed above. It is often only with intervention from a close friend or peer that the real situation becomes evident.

There's the door – why stay?

The question asked regularly is why do women stay in abusive relationships? Yet, however easy it looks from the outside, breaking away from partner violence is far from straightforward. Nurbanu, in Bangladesh, had little choice. She had no other means of livelihood; her blindness and profound disability increased her dependency on her abusive husband. Other women stay because of financial hardship, even more so when they have been denied access to their own earnings for most of the relationship. If there are children, mothers may stay in the violent relationships for their sake, believing that as long as a partner does not abuse them, they need a father. And by the time they have been constantly undermined and put down by abusive partners, few women have the self-confidence needed to take the initiative to leave. Any woman can easily believe she cannot cope elsewhere. In any case, where would a victim go? Without family to take her in, or friends or shelter, she could quickly become destitute and more vulnerable. As the years go on, and the violence becomes a familiar part of everyday existence, it can be difficult for a woman to envisage any other kind of life.

Even when the woman is young and strong she might find it difficult to leave. The teenagers in the UK study frequently found it hard to extricate themselves from relationships, sometimes because the experience of having a boyfriend had given them a status they were reluctant to lose, sometimes because of fear of reprisal – threats of bad-mouthing or recrimination proliferated if they did go. In the USA, one 24-year-old student tried to explain to *Glamour* magazine why she had stayed for two and a half years with a boyfriend who hit her, threatened her and used violent, abusive language towards her. She had been in denial about the reality of what was really happening.

> We've grown up in a different generation, where women are leaders, we have careers, children – we break glass ceilings . . . We expect to be strong and independent. When the abuse began, I thought, I can handle this on my own.

By the time she realized she could not, she found she was trapped in a cycle of violence. Another victim, a PhD student in clinical psychology, testified to the way humiliation ate away at her self-esteem.

> People think, You don't have kids, you're a beautiful girl – what's keeping you with him? . . . Well, I started out a confident, strong girl. Five years of someone telling me, 'If you just shut up, I wouldn't have to hit you,' and I started thinking, 'maybe I should shut up.'[40]

Ending a violent relationship does not automatically bring freedom. The researchers in the UK study on violence in teenage relationships pointed out that '[f]or those with very violent partners, ending a relationship did not, regrettably, mean that the control or violence stopped; in a minority of cases the violence actually intensified'.[41] In any sadistic relationships, those who attempt to get away can find themselves at even greater risk. Statistically, the time a woman is in most danger of being killed is when she is trying to leave an abusive partner, or in the aftermath of leaving – as we saw in the opening article by Liz Brody.

Take the experience of April Singiser, 22, a San Diego nursing student. Over the course of three years her boyfriend threw food at her and held her hostage in his apartment when she wanted to leave. She hid her embarrassment and shame, confiding in no one, still believing she was strong and could cope. But after she tried to break up with him, he grabbed a switchblade, forced her into her Honda Civic at knifepoint, and made her drive. 'He was telling me, "You shouldn't have left me; I'm going to take you to an Indian reservation where I can kill you and no one will find you," and holding the knife to my throat.' It was only when she drove off the freeway and hit a red light that April managed to leap out of the car and run for her life to the car behind, screaming that he was going to kill her. 'It was literally the first time she'd ever asked for help.'[42]

When Quasona Cobb asked her violent boyfriend to move out of her apartment he pulled out chunks of her hair, dragged her down the hall, put his foot on her stomach and with his lighter in his hand began dousing her body. Recognizing the acute peril she was in, and terrified he would set fire to her, she agreed to stay with him. The danger is real, not only to the woman herself, but to anyone she loves or who intervenes on her behalf. Arlene Gordon, a 42-year-old assistant analyst, went to her daughter's apartment to ask the abuser to leave, but did not return. The police found her unconscious, face down on the bed and set alight. Her head had been crushed with a heavy object, and the heat from the burning had melted a plastic bag over her head into her hair. Months later, she was still fighting for her life in hospital.[43]

There seem to be no boundaries around acts of retaliation towards some women who have managed to break free. Jean Say emigrated from the Ivory Coast to the UK, with a long history of violence. For many years he inflicted abuse upon his wife, tormenting her with jealousy and subjecting her to aggressive, possessive behaviour. His wife went to the police with allegations of rape, but they did not investigate them. Increasingly afraid, she eventually left her brutal husband, taking her two children. His revenge came during a custody visit from his children six months later. With no sense of compassion or humanity, he waited until they had finished playing computer games, then slit their throats and phoned his former wife to ask her to collect their bodies. Sitting calmly by their corpses when the police arrived, he was willing to face conviction and jail in order to inflict the maximum pain on their mother. He succeeded. She was heartbroken and expressed her sheer devastation in court, describing them as 'the most beautiful, thoughtful and fun-loving children who brought so much joy into my life'. Their father's cruel and wicked act had left a huge void in her life. 'Not one moment goes by that they are not in my thoughts.' It was a searing, tragic loss of precious, innocent life. But he had made exactly the impact he intended.[44]

Legal protection and the courts

To curtail acts of violation, and ensure justice for victims, properly framed laws are needed, along with strict law-enforcers, careful lawyers, understanding courts and impartial judges. And herein lies another problem. Laws take place within prior cultural frameworks. The difference between nations that endorse male-dominant frameworks and those that endorse gender equality is reflected in the way laws are shaped, framed and understood. In many countries, state laws exist alongside religious laws and religious courts which might be operating with a different goal or focus. Very often we fail to recognize that the law itself is a 'site of struggle' and cultural frameworks can restrain fair and just outcomes. For legal scholar Archana Parashar, domestic violence needs different legal responses for women in northern and southern nations.[45]

We can take two examples. In India, the Domestic Violence (Prevention) Act (DVA) of 2005 was passed in a context of women as 'economic dependants' and where a variety of religious personal laws restrain equality for women. Its breakthrough is that it names violence to women as a subject of civil law. But because its concern is with the 'right' of the violated woman to stay in the matrimonial home, its remit is narrow. The courts are empowered to allow a woman, subjected to violence, to occupy the home to the exclusion of the violent husband. But, as Archana Parashar points out, although the law gives women time to get out of a violent marriage, the wider social, economic and cultural conditions block her exit. Women 'cannot realistically expect either maintenance or a share of property on divorce. The right of residency in the matrimonial home (legally the husband's house) is therefore an empty achievement.'[46] She believes a thorough revision of legislation is needed which recognizes the layers of inequality underpinning domestic violence, and reaches a more integrated response.

For our second example we could go to Lebanon or another Middle Eastern country where women usually resort to religious courts to address their complaints against an aggressive or brutal spouse. Such courts are set up to deal with domestic conflict, but within the context of ensuring the security and stability of the family. Consequently, the courts' focus is more on the preservation of family life than on securing protection for women. So they typically solve personal status matters such as divorce, custody and inheritance through commending counselling or guidance measures. A case for divorce could be supported and granted to a woman after proven evidence of violence against her. But the courts are not mandated by law to protect women from violence, or to prosecute and punish abusers.[47]

Sentencing and the judiciary

These issues are less relevant in countries where courts have a broader remit, and where the laws against domestic violence stipulate punishment for offenders. A much stronger likelihood is that men will be given custodial sentences or restraining orders, and that proper, protective measures will be granted to their victims. In some cases the woman can be further safeguarded by being removed to an undisclosed safe place and given a new identity. But it has taken many years to reach this level of awareness. A largely male judiciary has, in the past, made extraordinary comments about women 'exaggerating' about their experiences, or of 'not suffering much' in relation to domestic violence. They have also focused on a woman's own 'nagging' or 'unreasonable' behaviour towards her partner as providing mitigating circumstances. Even today, many anomalies and old stereotypes still need to be overcome. That is one of the reasons why many women remain reluctant to bring their abusive partners to court. Not only are they likely to find reliving the violence disturbing and traumatic, but they might themselves feel under attack and consider the sentences very disappointing.

In a newspaper article in 2005, Katharine Viner deplored the attitude of the judiciary in many cases of intimate-partner murder. In the light of what she found, she argued that 'Britain is not getting any safer for women, however many get to be CEOs.'

> But perhaps the most shocking thing is the sentencing. Time and again, men who kill their wives get short sentences because courts believe a woman's infidelity, or even her 'nagging', is bound to provoke a husband to commit murder. A recently reported example is Paul Dalton's killing of his wife, Tae Hui. Dalton punched her, she died, then he cut up her body with an electric saw, and stored the pieces in a freezer. He was cleared of murder on the grounds of provocation; the judge said that he had suffered 'no little taunting on her [his wife's] part'. Dalton received just two years in jail for her manslaughter, but got three years for what many might consider the lesser crime of preventing a burial. He is appealing against the sentence.[48]

Viner has a strong point. When Dalton had been having an affair with his receptionist, blaming the dead woman for 'provocation', even though she was unable to give her version of events, seems extraordinary. The cultural baggage may not be as deep and traditional, or so strongly economically underpinned, as that in India or Lebanon, but it has been a struggle to part from the assumption that the man's point of view is given high priority.[49]

Sometimes this takes absurd forms as in a case reported in the USA in December 2012. Judge Johnson took ten years off the sentence of a man who had beaten his terrified ex-partner with a metal baton, and threatened to mutilate her face and genitals with a heated screwdriver, before committing rape. The judge's reason? His explanation drew a sharp intake of breath from all his listeners. He argued: 'I'm not a gynaecologist, but I can tell you something, if someone doesn't want to have sexual intercourse, the body shuts down. The body will not permit that to happen unless a lot of damage is inflicted, and we heard nothing about that in this case. That tells me that the victim in this case, although she wasn't necessarily willing, she didn't put up a fight.' Thankfully, the outrage which followed this judgment brought a public admonishment from the Commission on Juridical Performance and a rebuke that 'the judge's remarks reflected outdated, biased, and insensitive views about sexual assault victims who do not put up a fight'.[50] Odd judges may still give odd judgments, but, thankfully, public opinion is catching up with reality.

The same reality was reflected in the outcome of the awful Jean Say case mentioned above. He was given a custodial sentence of 30 years, and is likely to end his life behind bars. Welcome evidence exists that courts are taking more seriously the fact that violent killings are murder, not justifiable retaliation, and that justice requires appropriate punishment.

Conclusion

The widespread experience of intimate-partner violence illustrates the complexity and breadth of violence against women. Though we find it in every country across the world, its specific shape still often relates to cultural conditions in those countries. It is compounded by traditional practices where girls are denied education and pushed into early and forced marriages. It is bolstered by attitudes that husbands have the right to 'punish' their wives for failing in their duties. It is underpinned by dowry requirements and preference for sons. It is buttressed in affluent societies by stigma, fear of humiliation and disengagement, and masked by distorted views of women's sexuality. It is shielded by legal indifference whereby many cultures ignore the pleas of women trapped in violent relationships, even when they are subject to physical, psychological or sexual assault. And even in those countries where domestic abuse is acknowledged as a criminal offence, it can remain difficult for a woman to find protection from a vicious partner.

The Council of Europe's 'Istanbul Convention' remains one key expression of the urgency of the problem of intimate-partner aggression, and our need to safeguard women. The UK government owes it to its citizens to ratify this urgently. It rightly maintains that 'violence against women seriously violates, impairs or nullifies the enjoyment by women of their human rights, in particular their fundamental rights to life, security, freedom, dignity and physical and emotional integrity'. How very true. Women will not be safe anywhere, until they are safe at home.

7

Money, sex and violence: trafficking and prostitution

———◆•◆•◆———

Sexual exploitation eroticizes women's inequality and is a vehicle for racism and 'first world' domination, disproportionately victimizing minority and 'third world' women.　　Women's support project[1]

We, the survivors of prostitution and trafficking gathered at this press conference today, declare that prostitution is violence against women.
Manifesto, joint press conference for Coalition Against
Trafficking in Women and the European Women's
Lobby (CATW–EWL), 2005

In northern Vietnam, trafficking has become so acute that communities say they are living in fear. 'I worry so much about it, as do all the mothers in the villages, but it has happened to a lot of girls already,' said Phan Pa May, a community elder from the Red Dao ethnic minority group. '. . . I'm worried about my granddaughter. We always ask where she is going, and tell her not to talk on the phone or trust anyone.' Activists working to combat trafficking in Vietnam said police and authorities take the problem 'very seriously'.

The shelter in Lao Cai opened in 2010 and has helped scores of female victims. [One of them,] May Na, from the Hmong ethnic minority, was 13 when her uncle took her across the border and forced her to marry a Chinese man. 'I could not accept it. They left me at home alone and I climbed over the wall and ran away. I was wandering for more than a day, lost, sleeping in the streets, crying,' she said. Eventually, Na ended up at a police station, but because she spoke neither Chinese nor Vietnamese – only her native Hmong – it took police a month to figure out what had happened and return her to Vietnam.[2]

Human trafficking was once called slavery. Abolitionists exposed the sheer injustice and atrocity of taking people from their own communities by coercion and force, and transporting them to distant places to work without freedom, for the benefit of others. The conditions of slavery were appalling; the ill-treatment, brutality, deprivations and harsh punishments were dehumanizing.

Today, 200 years after slavery was abolished, human trafficking is again part of the global landscape. The action, the means and the purpose of trafficking are almost the same as they were all those centuries ago. In 2000, the UN officially defined the 'act' as 'the recruitment, transportation, harbouring or receipt of persons'. The 'means' are the 'use of force, deception, coercion or abuse of power' to lure victims. The 'purpose' is the exploitation – sexual, forced labour, domestic servitude, begging – to which traffickers subject their victims.[3] These definitions might sound detached, yet they convey, incontrovertibly, the wrongness of subjugating people into slave labour for the profit of others. They also convey something of the vulnerability, defencelessness and experience of violation. Modern slavery involves 'millions of people who cannot walk away, who are trapped and denied freedom and lives of dignity, and bound only to serve and profit the criminals that control them'.[4]

New evidence that women were being trafficked across national boundaries began to emerge in the early 1980s. Initially, women trafficked to Western Europe had come from Thailand and the Philippines, but now they were being brought from Latin America, West Africa and the Caribbean. Following the end of communism there, traffickers became active also in Eastern and Central Europe. As a global crime, trafficking now affects nearly every country in the world; the 2014 UN *Global Report on Trafficking in Persons* found people from at least 152 different nationalities trafficked and detected in 124 different countries,[5] and around 47,000 victims were known to have been trafficked. Yet, like every other form of violation we have looked at, accurate numbers of victims are very hard to come by. Detection rates are low, secrecy and cover-up are high, and victim-control makes it hard for investigative agencies to penetrate the systems. In many countries, people can disappear without trace; records of missing children or migration of 'workers' are rarely documented with any precision. From their broad research, the International Labour Organization (ILO) estimated in 2012 that 20.9 million people globally are victims of forced labour,[6] while the Global Slavery Index 2013 suggested the total of trafficked victims is approaching 30 million.[7]

Who are the victims of trafficking?

Although the approach to trafficking often presents it as gender-neutral, inevitably it is women and girls, the most vulnerable members of a community, who are at greatest risk from trafficking. Trafficking is gender-biased in most regions of the world, especially affecting women caught up in poverty and already marginalized. Of global victims detected in 2009, 59 per cent were women, 17 per cent girls, 14 per cent men and 10 per cent boys. Shifts in percentage over the years rarely alter the gender ratio but do reflect the fact that women victims are getting younger. In some countries this is pronounced. In European and Central Asian countries, only around 16 per cent of detected victims are youngsters, but in Africa and the Middle East children comprise around 68 per cent of victims. In Haiti, the second country listed by the Global Slavery Index, children are the most at risk from trafficking; abuse can even penetrate the generous system where poor rural children (*restaveks*) get food, shelter and education from urban families in exchange for doing light work. Runaway restaveks sometimes end up in the streets, in forced begging and commercial sexual exploitation.[8]

Women and girls are victimized in every region of the world, as Louise Shelley points out in her excellent study, *Human Trafficking: A Global Perspective*. In countries where particularly low social status denies them access to education, property, economic rights and participation in the political system, girls have little protection. They can be seen as commodities to use rather than persons to value, and sold off to 'repay a family's debt, provide cash for a medical emergency or compensate for an absence of revenue when crops have failed.'[9]

In some countries, the consequences of other forms of discrimination play into the trafficking of women. In Ethiopia, women and young girls migrate from rural areas in order to escape early marriage, poverty, violence at home, abusive relationships, exploitative labour, limited education and drought, only to become victims of commercial sexual exploitation in urban centres like Addis Ababa.[10] In the Syrian refugee crisis, human trafficking is linked with problems of abuse, rape and exploitation, and one activist notes an increase since 2012.[11] In Nepal, as many as 20,000 young girls from the poorest areas are trafficked into brothels or domestic servitude as far away as the Middle East. In China, in the aftermath of selective abortion, girls and women are trafficked for marriage.

Three decades after China's controversial one-child policy, millions of men of marrying age cannot find spouses, so some desperate families look to human traffickers to find their sons a bride. The Chinese Academy of Social Sciences estimated that, by 2020, there could be 24 million more men than women of marriageable age.[12] Myanmar's north-eastern border region with China has become notorious for the transport of girls, and more than half the human trafficking cases in one province involved young brides for sale in China.[13] Human rights workers across South East Asia say they are witnessing 'systematic' trafficking of girls into China for forced marriage or sex: from Mongolia, North Korea, Russia, Burma, Laos and Vietnam.[14]

Vietnamese girls are sold for up to $5,000 as brides or to brothels. Michael Brosowski, the founder of a rescue programme (the Blue Dragon Children's Foundation) which brings back trafficked girls from China, describes the process of entrapment:

> The girls are tricked by people posing as boyfriends, or offering jobs. Those people do this very deliberately, and for nothing other than greed and a lack of human empathy . . . It is likely that many of the girls end up working in brothels, but due to the stigma of being a sex worker they will usually report they were forced into marriage.[15]

(This is not unusual. In Turkey, the myth of 'temporary marriage' to Syrian refugee women puts a 'veneer of respectability' on sexual abuse and exploitation. The trafficking–prostitution link is in evidence across Europe and the Americas.) Being returned to Vietnam is not, unfortunately, the end of the story. It is usually the beginning of therapy. Psychologist Chau knows the score:

The girls have been in a living nightmare, sometimes for years. Separated from their families, imprisoned, repeatedly raped and beaten, and threatened with worse if they don't comply. Tricked and let down by friends, boyfriends and neighbours; people they thought they could trust. It takes a lot of courage and determination for girls to escape from their captors, face them in court, return home and start again.[16]

China is both a country of origin and a destination for trafficking. Chinese women are trafficked from poor, rural provinces to wealthy urban and coastal provinces for sexual exploitation. Both girls and boys are trafficked for illegal adoption, involuntary labour, and begging. People from south-west China have been trafficked through Myanmar into countries like Thailand and Malaysia. China's Ministry of Public Security reports that many women fall into the hands of criminal gangs and the number of Chinese women forced into overseas prostitution is rising.[17]

Global trafficking flows

Huge numbers of people involved in the criminal trade resource well-developed trafficking flows, which link the origin and destination of victims. Almost half detected victims are trafficked within the same region, for example from Vietnam to China, Albania to Kosovo, Haiti to Jamaica. When the destination is South East Asia, Africa and the Pacific, victims will have come almost exclusively from within the region. More than a quarter of all trafficking takes place domestically, within the country of origin. There are obvious reasons for this: it is cheaper, more convenient, and easier to manage. Shorter distances for travel minimize the risks for the traffickers, and victims are more likely to trust people who speak their language and are not going to transport them thousands of miles away. Trafficking flows do span greater distances to America and Western and Central Europe, bringing victims from a great variety of origins (112 nationalities were identified in these regions in the UN Report). Yet the majority of the victims there, also, come not far from the destination country. Managing trafficking flows across vast distances requires enormous planning and execution, and a high level of criminal organization. Regions of Africa, the Middle East, Europe, South and East Asia, Eastern Europe, America, Central Asia and the Pacific are crossed by about 460 distinct trafficking flows.

Most women are trafficked from poorer to more affluent areas, though poverty and affluence occur in the same society, and many countries function both as origin and destination. The upsurge in trafficking is a downside of globalization: the international mobility of people, trade and communication and fewer border controls make it easier. Over the past decade sex trafficking has followed a spiral of demand: increase in availability increases sex services, which further increase demand, so local resources are not enough and more women are brought in to fill the ranks.[18] In countries with legalized prostitution, trafficking flows seem higher than in countries where prostitution is prohibited. The criminalization of prostitution in Sweden seems to have had the effect of shrinking the market for street prostitution and resulted in a decline in women trafficked to Sweden.[19]

Who are the traffickers?

Trafficking networks consist of economically and politically motivated criminals who intersect with local traffickers and the larger world of transnational crime. They employ criminal specialists to forge false documents, hire thugs to intimidate victims, and use money-laundering channels to move their proceeds.[20] Predictably, most of them are men; in more than 50 countries, men comprised two thirds of those prosecuted or convicted for trafficking over a three-year period.[21] Yet women are involved; their participation in trafficking is far higher than in other crimes. In most countries, offences by women are below 15 per cent of the crime total (the average is 12 per cent), but 30 per cent of trafficking offences are by women. In Eastern Europe and Central Asia, women form a staggering three quarters of convicted traffickers, most typically involved in the trafficking of girls. Louise Shelley describes their roles:

> Women exploit other women in domestic servitude. Women in couples often facilitate the trafficking activities of their husbands

and lovers. Yet women can also act independently. In many regions of the world, women who have aged as prostitutes recruit the next generation of trafficked women . . . Women often train the trafficking victims, run the brothels and maintain control of their victims through violent means. The largest smugglers and traffickers can sometimes profit substantially from this trade, as has been seen in China where women have headed large smuggling operations.[22]

In other regions women are more likely to be carrying out duties more exposed to the risk of detection and prosecution than those of male traffickers, and are normally found in lower-ranking positions of the trafficking networks.[23] The relative ease with which their activities are detected suggests that even within this industry women can act as a buffer for rich male traffickers who have developed careful ways of staying hidden. Yet, as Shelley points out, their active participation should not be underestimated. 'Human trafficking is the only form of transnational human crime in which women are significantly represented both as victims and perpetrators.'[24]

Most traffickers come from the country they operate in, but a quarter of those convicted for trafficking are foreign nationals. The ratio is higher than for other crimes, especially in destination countries in Europe and the Middle East. They often come to those countries deliberately to develop a trade in trafficking, bringing compatriots over who learn the system and know how to find 'trade'. Perpetrators become skilled at procuring victims. If they had to rely on kidnapping or hostage-taking, the incidence would be far lower than it is. The approach is far more sophisticated, especially in Europe and North America. At a European gathering to combat trafficking, an Albanian survivor told me how local traffickers befriend vulnerable girls struggling with loneliness, poverty or abuse, gaining their confidence, then betraying them. Trisha, a Canadian victim, describes her own difficulty in understanding what it was all about:

We didn't have the language of trafficking or an understanding of exploitation. There weren't brothel owners, there were men or women who ran hotel rooms or apartments. There weren't pimps, there were 'boyfriends' or brothers – seemingly someone who cared about you.

So many people today have this image of a trafficking victim tied up in a room or black and blue with bruises – they don't understand that many of the girls and women being trafficked are in love with their traffickers or pimps, and that these exploiters use subtle coercion, not just outright violence. The relationships are multi layered, complex; remember most exploiters have been at this for years and they know the best way to control a prostituted woman is through mental and emotional manipulation. The upside for them is this doesn't leave bruises. I knew a pimp who actually went to community college to take psychology to control his girls; he just saw it as an investment of his time.[25]

Detection and reporting of forms of trafficking

People are trafficked for many purposes. Forced labour accounted for more than a third of trafficking from 2007 to 2010 and could be greater as detection rates vary. (European countries and the Americas have higher levels of victim detection and report low levels of forced labour. Africa, the Middle East, South East Asia and the Pacific have lower rates of detection, and report higher levels of forced labour.) People are also trafficked for begging, illegal adoption, participation in armed combat, rituals and crime (usually petty street crime), but these accounted for only 6 per cent of the detected cases in 2010 and the latter examples were largely in Africa.[26] Victims trafficked for the removal of organs comprised a small 0.2 per cent of detected cases, yet were spread through 16 countries across continents.[27] The 2014 *Global Report* leaves us in little doubt that trafficking for sexual exploitation is still by far the biggest form detected worldwide.

The commodification of women is very evident in the 'try before you buy' policy reported by the Lithuanian charity Caritas Lithuania. Women in London were said to be bartered over by pimps who were invited to take and rape the women, and then come back to the trafficker with a price.[28] Yet, despite this kind of piecemeal evidence, detection rates are low everywhere because trafficked victims rarely report their plight. Women often fear reprisals from their keepers or retribution from authorities. They may face detention, prosecution and deportation for illegal entry or unlicensed prostitution. Those deported are in danger of being trafficked again. In recent Greek cases, trafficked women found little protection from the law and were often charged with other offences. Gangs exercise great power and control, and the covert nature of trafficking means that it remains one of the most hidden of all crimes. It is also the most damaging for its victims. They are extremely vulnerable to human rights abuses and deprivation of liberty; the isolation, sexual violation and physical torture compound the suffering. Tragically, trafficked women become part of the homicide figures. Those who survive have to overcome years of psychological damage and fear, and learn to trust again. Healing and finding new self-worth can take a long time.[29]

International response

On Christmas Day 2003, a significant day of hope and new beginnings, a UN protocol came into force that marked the reality of trafficking as a serious international problem, and supplemented the United Nations Convention against Transnational Organized Crime.[30] By August 2012, when 152 countries had ratified the Protocol,[31] trafficking had become defined and recognized by the international community. In 2014, over 250 Nigerian teenagers trafficked for prostitution in Ghana and Europe were reported to have been rescued and reunited with their families. The Nigerian High Commissioner to Ghana linked cross-border human trafficking with the smuggling of arms.[32] In the UK, growing concern for trafficking led to the Modern Slavery Act, 31 July 2015, which gave victims extra protection and increased the custodial sentence for convicted traffickers to life.

In some countries, however, there remains a massive gap between Protocol and implementation, and, in spite of legislation, the problem grows. Uganda, for example, has a terrible trafficking problem but few convictions. Uganda's honorary consul in Malaysia said more than 600 Ugandan jobseekers were trafficked into the sex trade in Malaysia. Uganda's director of Interpol reported that Ugandan women were also being trafficked to India, Thailand, China, Egypt, Iraq, Afghanistan, Indonesia, India and the United Arab Emirates.[33]

Corruption charges against key officials, and slowness to prosecute, leaves victims at risk.

Nevertheless campaigns are growing across the world, led by both humanitarian and faith-based coalitions, like the Coalition Against Trafficking in Women, Abolition Scotland, Stop the Traffik, the Global Freedom Network and the International Justice Mission (IJM). Some organizations operate both advocacy campaigns and rescue missions, as in the well-planned 'sting' operation in the Dominican Republic in April 2015. A sex party had been arranged (costing $500 for each person) where the well-heeled 'guests' were actually Dominican state prosecutors, US law-enforcers, and NGO leaders. When the girls were brought in, the party ended abruptly and seven suspected traffickers were arrested. Twenty-nine girls, 14 of them under the age of 17, were freed into the care of IJM and the National Council for Children. With the traffickers denied bail, and the girls in a safe shelter, IJM's aftercare programme helped them through anxiety and trauma, and started them on the long road to restoration.

The eradication of trafficking needs commitment and strategy from law-enforcers, at least equal to that of organized criminals, and here the criminals got it. Trafficking succeeds because of the vulnerability of victims, and sex trafficking is one more aspect of the global problem of violence against women. But it can be eliminated. With an international will for change, we can all support a movement which protects the vulnerable, petitions parliaments, supports NGOs, holds law-enforcers to account, and fights corrupt economics. It is time to end this twenty-first-century slavery, and release the captives.

Prostitution

Beyond the Streets, an organization that works with women in prostitution, believes that there are fundamental overlaps between trafficking and prostitution. The social and economic inequality between the exploited and exploiters means that the sex industry itself is a 'theatre for gender power dynamics to take the stage'.[34]

It is important to make that link evident, because some current observers with liberal views, especially in Western democracies, want to put the two into very separate categories. They argue that, yes, trafficking is wrong, but prostitution is a career option adopted by adult women, who have a moral right to do what they wish with their own bodies and should have freedom of choice. Governments have no mandate to produce restrictive legislation. These critics insist that once prostitution is sanitized of its 'dirty sex' stigma, and regulated and licensed, it can take its place officially in the economy as a job alongside any other.

Unsurprisingly, we often find that underneath this view lies a gender-neutral, laissez-faire concept of economics, in which 'similarly situated individuals' make complementary choices: one to buy sex and the other to sell it. The process in which one individual merely purchases sex from another is a simple economic transaction exchanging sexual pleasure for money; the product of free, unfettered market choices, unconstrained by social forces. The view is summed up in an interview, in the *Guardian* newspaper, with a man who had just visited a brothel in Amsterdam: 'Prostitution is not bad . . . women do it for money, €50 for each client. They look happy. I don't believe they are trafficked or forced to do it.'[35]

Legal responses of governments – Germany

Politicians have not been slow to adopt this outlook and it is reflected in well-intended legislation in both Holland and Germany. In Germany, a law of 2002 had attempted to de-stigmatize prostitution by removing prohibitions and allowing prostitutes to apply for regular work contracts. The vision was to transform stigmatized back-street prostitutes into autonomous businesswomen, who had 'chosen their profession freely and to whom Germany now wishes to offer good working conditions in the sex sector of the service industry'.[36] A five-part series in *Spiegel* in 2013 commented:

> That's the 'respectable whore' image politicians seem in thrall of: free to do as they like, covered under the social insurance system, doing work they enjoy and holding an account at the local savings bank. Social scientists have a name for them: 'migrant sex workers,' ambitious service providers who are taking advantage of opportunities they now enjoy in an increasingly unified Europe.[37]

The German law was opposed from the start by many activists, including women like Alice Schwarzer, influential founder and editor of the feminist journal *EMMA*.[38] Later, many others were to argue that the law had not changed the situation for women in prostitution. The idea that it would increase the bargaining power of sex workers with their brothel employers, based on contracts, better work conditions and taxation was probably unrealistic.

In the meantime, with increased demand for women, there had been a surge in human trafficking to Germany; in 2004 a Turkish gang leader had been sentenced to nine years in prison for pimping, human trafficking, assault, extortion, weapons violations and racketeering. His gang controlled the night clubs in Cologne's entertainment area, grooming girls for work in the brothels. The tide of trafficked women into Germany swelled over the next years (quite consistent with research charting the correlation between the legal status of prostitution and inward trafficking[39]). By 2011 it was suggested that 68 per cent of women working in the German sex industry came from abroad (still lower, however, than the staggering Dutch figure of over 80 per cent).[40] Although trafficked women may well have been cajoled or duped rather than kidnapped, they were still caught up in work conditions which they had not chosen and subject to treatment which they hated.

An increase in trafficked victims seemed to be just one of many downsides to the legalization of prostitution in Germany. The Family Ministry of the German government reviewed the law's impact in January 2007, and found that only 1 per cent of the sex workers surveyed had signed any employment contract. They also saw little evidence of better working conditions, and concluded that deregulation had 'not brought about any measurable actual improvement in the social coverage of prostitutes'. The ability to exit the profession had not increased, either, and there was 'no solid proof to date' that the law had reduced crime.[41] In its 2013 series, *Spiegel* suggested that police officers, women's organizations and politicians familiar with prostitution were convinced that the well-meaning law was little more than a subsidy programme for pimps, and made the market more attractive to human traffickers.[42]

Why the theory doesn't work

Critics of the thinking behind the liberalizing of prostitution are not hard to find. Law professor Dorchen Leidholt, who has spent years engaging with issues of human rights and legislation, questions the whole basis on which the laws in Germany and Holland operate. She argues that the model of prostitution entertained by most individual-rights-oriented libertarians as a neutral economic transaction between equal individuals is naïve and culturally ill-informed. Prostitution is not about women making money in a free-market economy; it is about pimps, brothel owners, pornographers, travel agencies, club owners and governments making money off women's bodies. She argues, from her years of experience in the court context, that there is no symmetry between sex workers and their clients, or pimps. When the uninformed 'symmetrical economic transaction' model is applied to prostitution, it merely reinforces the status quo of women's powerlessness and turns a blind eye to fundamental issues of injustice and violation. Her critique is sharp:

> Far from being about similarly situated individuals, prostitution is a paradigm of sexual and racial inequality. In fact, prostitution doesn't have much to do with individuals. Individuality is the very attribute that prostituted women are denied – along with that related characteristic, humanity. In prostitution, a woman's history is erased. Her name is changed. The act of prostitution means projecting back *his* fantasy. To the pimp or brothel owner she's a commodity. To society, she's a whore or nonentity.[43]

For Leidholt, far from being an activity entered into by equal individuals, prostitution embodies a 'system of male power over and against women', in which women's human rights are constantly violated. Her rebuttal of the idea that prostitution is a 'chosen career' is well made, for concepts like 'choice' have to be understood within the social and economic context of real women's lives. 'Choice' is a fiction unless it is taken by someone who has the cultural, personal and economic capacity to *choose*. In real life, rather than in theoretical constructs, it simply is not the case that the majority of women in prostitution have had the luxury to reflect on career options. The idea that they have been able carefully to weigh up the economic advantages of selling their bodies, over entering a career in human resources, catering or social work, is farcical. As Leidholt's work makes clear, the reality is that many women's entry into the sex industry is underpinned by long histories of violence, neglect and abuse; drug dependency and absence of choice often keep them there. Before we can talk meaningfully about women in sex work rationally considering their options, we have to acknowledge the layers of disadvantage most of them have already experienced.

A submission made in 2014 in the UK, by the End Violence Against Women Coalition (EVAW) to Amnesty International, puts this succinctly:

> [S]o-called 'free' choices – 'consensual' choices – in prostitution are actually decisions made in conditions of already existing inequality and discrimination. Women's choices should not be measured simply by where they end up (in prostitution), but by the circumstances in which these choices must be made. Choices made in conditions of being unequal cannot be considered 'free'.[44]

This was an echo of the statement of prostitutes themselves to the Joint Project of the Coalition Against Trafficking in Women and the European Women's Lobby (CATW and EWL) in 2006:

> Women in prostitution do not wake up one day and 'choose' to be prostitutes. It is chosen for us by poverty, past sexual abuse, the pimps who take advantage of our vulnerabilities, and the men who buy us for the sex of prostitution.[45]

The Nordic solution

Sweden came to a very different conclusion with regard to prostitution from that of Germany or Holland. Gunilla Ekberg, a lawyer working for the Swedish Ministry of Industry, Employment and Communications, commented wryly on the Dutch situation:

> [N]ot every country in the world is equally enthusiastic about the idea that prostitution should be seen as a form of work, or that

> sexual exploitation of women by men should be commercialized
> and legalized . . . In Sweden, it is understood that any society that
> claims to defend principles of legal, political, economic and social
> equality for women and girls must reject the idea that women and
> children, mostly girls, are commodities that can be bought, sold,
> and sexually exploited by men.[46]

Officially recognizing that 'prostitution is male sexual violence against women and children' and that 'prostitution and trafficking . . . should not be separated',[47] the 1999 law prohibited prostitution, not by criminalizing the prostitutes but by producing strong sanctions against brothel owners, pimps and customers. The law was further strengthened, in 2005, to make punishable all attempts to buy sexual services, whether purchased on the street, in brothels, massage parlours, escort services or anywhere else.

In 2008, the Supreme Court Justice (later Justice Chancellor) Anna Skarhed was appointed by the Swedish government to lead an official inquiry into the effects that the law had had on prostitution and human trafficking in Sweden. The report, submitted in 2010, was confident that the law had achieved its objective both in reducing street prostitution and acting as a barrier to human traffickers.[48] The results in Sweden have encouraged parliamentarians and legal researchers from other countries to consider similar legislation. In June 2015, Northern Ireland followed Sweden, Norway, Iceland and Canada in making the buying of sex a criminal offence.

The diversity of political responses to prostitution highlights the problem of addressing the issues involved with any sort of global integration. Although many legislators are looking to pass laws so that the lives of vulnerable women might be improved, the theoretical underpinnings of their legal decision may leave them open to making situations worse. Those who are strongly wedded to myths of consensuality in the prostitute–client or prostitute–pimp relation can push a view of women's freedom in prostitution which bears little resemblance to lived experience. For every ten so-called 'career prostitutes' there will be 10,000 who have been forced into this form of work through poverty, rape or male domination. Outside countries of Africa, Asia and Latin

America, it is all too easy to forge a climate where people with vested interests collude with libertarian politicians to hurl allegations of paternalism or moralism at those who want stronger legislation. From the (now defunct) Californian COYOTE organization (Call Off Your Old Tired Ethics) to the French 'Hands Off My Tart' petition in 2013,[49] there has been no shortage of invective against opponents, designed to put those who see the problem in terms of justice and violence on the defensive. The End Violence Against Women Coalition simply dismissed the tirades, and rejects the labelling of their ideas and activities.

> Our critique of prostitution is not moralistic, nor do we condemn or infantilise women who are involved within it, rather we argue this is a patriarchal institution through which women are exploited, marginalised, abused and stereotyped. Prostitution, and other structures in which women are objectified, reinforce and perpetuate stereotypes of women, especially where this intersects other aspects of social identity such as race/ethnicity, age and class.[50]

These intersections can also become intergenerational, especially in the poorest countries of the world. Louise Shelley points to a further blurring of trafficking and prostitution, common in India where trafficked women succumb to AIDS, leaving daughters who are orphaned and without any contact with family. 'Often the brothel keepers maintain the girls, and then prostitute them even younger than the age of ten. The sexual slavery of the mother therefore continues on into the succeeding generations.'[51] The well-being of future generations must surely also be addressed by the legislators.

Sex work and sexual violence

When commercial sexual exploitation of girls and women is accepted as part of the public life of societies, the full story rarely is told. Many girls and women find themselves trapped in a life of physical, sexual and psychological abuse which is public yet hidden from view. In situations of both trafficking and prostitution, women are extremely vulnerable to violence and human rights violations. In extreme cases it can result in homicide, which can occur irrespective of the legal provisions of a country. This became evident in the UK both in 2009 after the murder of five women in Ipswich, Suffolk, and again in 2010 when three sex workers in Bradford, Yorkshire, were brutally killed. A detective chief superintendent who had investigated other such murders admitted to being 'staggered by the level of excessive brutality inflicted'. One woman working as a prostitute had survived 47 knife wounds. What she was able to tell the police of the hateful language and savagery she had been exposed to confirmed the sadism and loathing of the men who inflict this barbarity.[52]

None of this would surprise clinical psychologist Melissa Farley. In her authoritative article in *Psychiatric Times*, she refers to prostitution as 'paid rape' and sees violence as the norm for women in prostitution. Incest, sexual harassment, verbal abuse, stalking, rape, battering and torture are all points on a continuum of violence which occur regularly.

> Prostituted women are unrecognized victims of intimate partner violence by pimps and customers ... Pimps and customers use methods of coercion and control like those of other batterers: minimization and denial of physical violence, economic exploitation, social isolation, verbal abuse, threats and intimidation, physical violence, sexual assault, and captivity ... The systematic violence emphasizes the victim's worthlessness except in her role as prostitute.[53]

Farley describes the experiences of a woman who prostituted primarily in strip clubs, but also in massage, escort and street prostitution:

> In strip club prostitution, she was sexually harassed and assaulted. Stripping required her to smilingly accommodate customers' verbal abuse. Customers grabbed and pinched her legs, arms, breasts, buttocks and crotch, sometimes resulting in bruises and scratches. Customers squeezed her breasts until she was in severe pain, and they humiliated her by ejaculating on her face. Customers and pimps physically brutalized her. She was severely bruised from beatings and frequently had black eyes. Pimps pulled her hair as

a means of control and torture. She was repeatedly beaten on the head with closed fists, sometimes resulting in unconsciousness. From these beatings, her eardrum was damaged, and her jaw was dislocated and remains so many years later. She was cut with knives. She was burned with cigarettes by customers who smoked while raping her. She was gang-raped and she was also raped individually by at least 20 men at different times in her life. These rapes by johns and pimps sometimes resulted in internal bleeding.[54]

Worse than this physical violence, however, was how the woman described her psychological damage: 'you become in your own mind what these people do and say with you.'[55]

There is very little difference between her experiences and that of Ayesha, a woman trafficked from a village in Bangladesh to Kolkata by someone she trusted. The picture of systematic, sadistic 'grooming' for compliance is one which has been painted thousands of times across the world. It also lays bare the myths of choice and career.

To 'break me in,' I was raped several times a night for nearly a month before the madam started selling me to men for money. It was typical for me to have ten to twelve buyers every night. They were usually abusive, treating me as if they owned my body. I have a deep scar on my neck from a knife blade, which I got trying to save a young girl in my house from being gang raped. It almost killed me.

Later I would learn that my story was not unique. There were hundreds of us – young girls from Bangladesh, Nepal and other parts of India, sold into brothels. To keep us isolated the brothel owners forbid us to speak to girls in other houses . . . I tried to leave that dungeon many times. Memories still flash in my mind of my hair being pulled, of being dragged through the dirt streets by the brothel owner after a failed escape. Even though I cried, screamed for someone to help me, people just stood by watching, without even a look of sympathy.

When people tell me that women choose this life, I can't help but laugh. Do they know how many women like me have tried to escape, but have been beaten black and blue when they are caught? To the men who buy us, we are like meat. To everybody else in society, we simply do not exist.[56]

Thankfully, Ayesha was ultimately able to leave this life behind, and not follow so many women into an early death through AIDS, infections or sheer brutality. Through Apne Aap, an organization combating trafficking of women, she was able to protect her daughters and to move on. Stories like hers must be celebrated, and organizations like those supported – Samaritana (Philippines), Rehab (Mali), The Garden of Hope (China). But our task is also to identify the false assumptions that surround the understanding of sex work and acknowledge how deep are the problems facing women caught up in these forms of oppression across the globe. We need to hear Leidholt's point that the sex worker has the function for many misogynists of representing generic woman. She is 'de-individualized and de-humanized', bought and sold for all the distinctively female parts of her body. She stands in for all of us, and she takes the abuse that we are beginning to resist.

Most women's support groups agree that advocacy for the vulnerable, and work towards the elimination of male violence against women, is undermined so long as the abuse of women and girls through commercial sexual exploitation goes unchallenged. Demarcation between trafficking and prostitution is blurred and confusing; attempts to draw strong legal boundaries problematic. So long as prostitution is seen merely as a myriad of individual acts of transactional sex, rather than a highly organized industry of paid rape, closely allied to trafficking, its harms are made invisible. Try telling the 20-year-old girls dying of AIDS in a Bangkok brothel that they must be free to enjoy this career they've chosen. Whether in strip clubs or local brothels in capitals like Amsterdam or cities like Cologne, the sex industry is one in which women are both prostituted and trafficked. Domestic sex workers will operate alongside trafficked women and share the same vulnerability. The very least the international community can do is produce clear, protective legislation.

8

Rape

―――◆◆◆◆―――

We are told to forgive and forget . . . But I couldn't forgive and I couldn't forget . . . Then I realized . . . I have a right to remember and I leave the forgiving to a higher being.   Rape survivor

Selective abortion, FGM and honour killing are types of violence against women prevalent in particular cultures and traditions. Rape is different. There is no society on earth where rape is absent. It is there in affluent, educated countries and in cultures which struggle with poverty and illiteracy; it exists in dark urban alleys and bright sunlit beaches. It can happen in our capital cities and rural communities, be found in families, schools, professional work environments, sports complexes and religious institutions. Even in areas known for their peace and security, rape cannot be completely eliminated. We would struggle to identify any place, in any context, anywhere, where all women are safe from its intrusion. An article in *The Independent* reinforces that with regard to the UK:

Rape and sexual violence against women are endemic everywhere . . . Those punches, slaps, kicks and bile-filled screams are happening all around us – yes, undoubtedly on our own streets. A quarter of women will face this abuse at some point in their life and – horrifyingly – two women will be murdered by their current or former male partner each week.

It's not just the overt aggression. It's the sexual harassment and objectification of women by men that provide fertile ground for this violence. In a poll by End Violence Against Women this year, 41 per cent of women aged between 18 and 34 had experienced unwanted sexual attention in London. Some men may regard a few 'jokes' about rape as a bit of harmless banter, but it all helps normalise violence against women.

As a country, we still don't take rape survivors seriously.[1]

How societies differ is not dependent on the presence of rape, but on the level of tolerance they give to it and what legal and protective provisions they offer women. And progress here is an uphill struggle. It is true that in societies formerly marked by official indifference towards rape, attitudes do change, but how often are those changes sustained? A beautiful young university student, Jyoti Singh Pandey, was viciously gang raped on a New Delhi bus in December 2012, and died from her injuries. Cries of outrage and huge demonstrations followed across India, and the outcry was effective. Laws against rape were tightened, a host of stringent new punishments were introduced, and, for repeat offences, even the death penalty was brought in. With better protection against other forms of violence, including acid attacks, it seemed at last that there were laws strong enough to address these crimes. Yet eight months later in August 2013, another brutal gang-attack in Mumbai left a young woman critically ill and scarred for life. Reporters, once again, had rape as their headline:

> A 22-year-old photojournalist was gang raped while her male colleague was tied up and beaten in an isolated, overgrown corner of India's business hub of Mumbai, police said on Friday . . .
>
> The assault comes amid heightened concerns about sexual violence in India. The gang rape and death of the 23-year-old student on a moving bus in New Delhi in December had shaken a country long inured to violence against women and sparked protests demanding better protection for women . . . About 1,000 people, including members of several local journalists' associations, gathered Friday evening in south Mumbai to stage a silent protest. Some wore black armbands, while others carried placards reading 'Stop rape' and 'City of shame.'[2]

To those who protested, these were shameful acts of brutality and hatred. To those who committed the acts they probably seemed perfectly appropriate expressions of their feelings about women. It is clear that high-profile public condemnation did not prevent this rape and will not itself eradicate rape in the future, for most rapists seem impervious to public opinion and appear to see such treatment of women as their entitlement. They also believe they will go unpunished.

Let's talk numbers – how big is the problem?

In the USA the fight against rape has a great ally in President Obama. He used the Grammy Awards in 2015 to announce the need for Americans to change the culture on violence against women. His statement that nearly one in five women in the USA had been a victim of rape or attempted rape sent commentators off to investigate crime figures. Numbers of rape cases reported to the police in the last annual official publication were around 80,000. Yet the US Justice Department estimates that 300,000 American women are raped every year, and the National Center for Injury Prevention and Control puts the number much higher at 1.3 million. Obama's figure would apply to nearly 20 per cent of the female population which translates to 22 million women. The number comes, in fact, from a survey released in September 2014 by the Federal Centers for Disease Control and Prevention, and is regarded as broadly accurate.[3]

Similar statistical discrepancies exist in most record-keeping countries. In the UK between 2009 and 2012, figures showed an increase of 26 per cent in total rape cases recorded by the police. In one year, 2011, rape cases against women had shown an increase

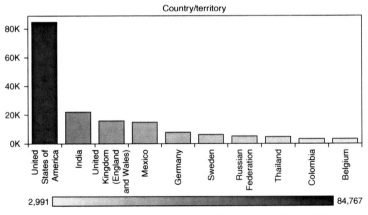

Top 10 countries with highest reported rape incidents (2004 to 2010)

of 5 per cent, bringing the number of attacks to 14,624.[4] Yet even with these higher levels of reporting, the figures fall far short of the 85,000 women who are estimated to be victims of rape in an average year.[5]

Reliable international comparisons are even more difficult. According to the UN table, the United States produced the highest figure for police-reported rape, and if total numbers are tallied, then Europe and the Americas do consistently top the charts. But if we look at reported rape cases per head of population, a quite different picture emerges: Australia, Botswana and Lesotho rank highest.

These kinds of comparisons offer us little. In so many countries rape is barely reported at all, so police records grossly underestimate the proportion or suggest there is no real problem. Yet, in those same countries, organizations like the Mothers' Union are busy mobilizing communities on campaigns against rape, and going out together to protect schoolgirls! In other countries, draconian laws deter women even from taking action to protect themselves. In October 2007 a woman in Iran was arrested after killing an official in the Ministry of Intelligence, who, she said, had been trying to rape her. She was tried and spent five years in prison. Despite public criticism of the trial and an international campaign calling for her reprieve, she was executed in 2014.[6]

Rape reporting and convictions

Underneath these difficulties of collecting data lies the problem faced by victims. What will happen if they do report their experiences of rape to the police or authorities? Many of them already know. Fear of reprisal, stigma and rejection, or not being believed, can be crippling to those who are struggling to come to terms with what has happened. In many cultures, even in those where the law is clear, victims also feel that there is little chance that their reporting will make any difference or bring any benefit. The sense of defeat is perfectly understandable. With little hope of justice, why would women initiate a process which could engulf them in yet further suffering?

In 2014 in the UK, the Commissioner of the Metropolitan Police suggested that more than 80 per cent of rape and sexual violence victims did not trust the system enough to come forward after being attacked.[7] Even when women did report the incident, they faced the unlikelihood that their rapist would come to court. A report disclosed that only around 15 per cent of rapes recorded in 2012–13 as crimes by the police resulted in rape charges being brought against a suspect. This was in spite of the fact that the identity of the suspect was often known.[8] Thirty-six per cent of alleged victims dropped their cases.

A decrease in the proportion of reportings which result in conviction could suggest a 'justice gap' for victims. Professor Betsy Stanko, now working for the Metropolitan Police, pointed out in 2014 that the profile of alleged victims in London had not changed significantly in eight years, and most reports of rape – 87 per cent – came from women whose characteristics made them vulnerable. Around a third were under 18, most were known to the perpetrators, between a quarter and a fifth had been in an intimate relationship with their assailant, a disproportionate number suffered from mental illness, and a large minority consumed alcohol or drugs. Women and girls with learning difficulties were found to be particularly at risk of facing obstacles to justice; they were 67 per cent less likely than those without to have their case referred by police for prosecution. Mental illness reduced the chances by 40 per cent. Stanko was critical of the predominant focus of detectives on proving 'lack of consent' rather than addressing exploitation or vulnerability. Surely, a woman who could not easily understand the arguments surrounding 'consent' was at a great disadvantage? Stanko's stark observation was that for such women and girls, rape had been effectively decriminalized.[9]

There is a long way to go, even in a country where rape is a highly punishable offence, before rape is taken as seriously as it should be and potential victims are protected. Underlying negative attitudes to women can still cloud responses from authorities. This became alarming clear in the UK in 2014, when a 19-year-old woman made an official complaint for gross misconduct against the West Midlands Police to the Independent Police Complaints

Commission. She had reported a sexual assault, and the police phoned her mobile in response, but were unaware that their conversation with each other was being recorded. On her voicemail, the officers can be heard discussing the statement they needed to draft, and which she should sign, referring to her as a 'slag' and a 'bitch'. They were suspended, pending a full inquiry.[10]

Thankfully, cases like these are becoming rarer, and in the UK at least, the better news is that policing rape is changing. More informed personnel are being called upon to advise the police, and police do undergo more rigorous training in handling rape reporting. The result is that a more sensitive approach is taken to victims and far fewer cases are likely to be categorized as 'no-crimes' than before. This confidence now has to seep through to those who survive these ordeals and need justice.

Changes are taking place in many countries, but are often long in coming. A 22-year-old journalist, raped in Nepal in 2008, found that her assailant was given a light sentence by a district court and quickly released. Supported by the Federation of Nepalese Journalists she took her case to the Supreme Court. Seven years later, in December 2014, the man received a five-year prison sentence. The victim said at the end of the trial: 'In these seven years, I had to quit my profession. I was threatened several times. I was forced to leave the country for almost 15 months. I went through mental trauma. However, I never gave [up] the hope for justice.'[11]

The cost of rape

Rape continues to be a massive problem in terms of social resources. Its economic price-tag is enormous. The World Health Organization, the World Bank and Chambers of Commerce have all commissioned studies which look at the financial costs to societies. In the aftermath of the gang-rape case in New Delhi for example, a survey of 2,500 women by the India Associated Chamber of Commerce and Industry disclosed that this attack had affected productivity in several major cities. Nearly 82 per cent of those surveyed said they started to leave work early, and very few worked beyond their normal end of day, which impacted productivity in

IT and the outsourcing sector by 40 per cent.[12] In England and Wales, rape is estimated to cost almost £27 billion annually;[13] and $4.2 billion each year in Canada. These costs are increased if domestic violence is included. It has been estimated that US victims lose nearly eight million days of paid work each year, the equivalent of more than 32,000 full-time jobs.[14] The total annual financial cost of violence against women and girls in the UK is estimated at £40 billion.[15]

Costs are often related to loss of wages, productivity and taxes, and to the demands made of the criminal justice systems. But expenditure on health care and social services must also be factored in. During a two-year period in the USA an estimated 105,187 females were treated in a medical emergency department as a result of non-fatal injuries sustained from sexual attack.[16] Surgery, including fistula operations, is costly. If the attack is violent there can be broken bones, internal bruising, scarring and repeated bleeding, which may need long-term medical attention. Victims have to be screened for sexually transmitted infections; help has to be offered for painful future intercourse. Mental health units, counselling services and victim support groups all need to be provided. It is probably not surprising that, by the time all these have been included in the figures, the cost, in the UK alone, of each single rape has been estimated to be a staggering £120,000.[17]

Health consequences are significant not simply for economic reasons. For the women who suffer, they can be severe and long term. Not only are there possibilities of pregnancy, and of becoming exposed to infections, but other health hazards multiply. Links have been found between non-consensual sex and irritable bowel syndrome, high cholesterol, cardiovascular problems, stroke and heart disease.[18] Rape can also increase women's risk of developing chronic physical diseases later in life, including diabetes. It is quite simply beyond doubt that sexualized violence – everything from forced penetration to long-term sexual slavery – has chronic, wide-ranging mental and physical health consequences. Long after the headlines have passed and surgery has been completed, these continue to be endured across the world by rape victims and their children.

Mental disorders following trauma

Post-traumatic stress disorder (PTSD) is, as the name suggests, a mental health problem which results from traumatic experience. It can follow any kind of shock – a road accident, being in a burning building, or sudden bereavement. It is also the most common and most well-studied mental disorder following sexualized violence. The findings are sobering. Population-based studies published in the *Archives of General Psychiatry* and the *American Journal of Psychiatry* have repeatedly shown that people who report sexualized violence are at higher risk of PTSD than those who have endured extreme traumas like sudden bereavement and exposure to combat or disasters. Studies on survivors of sexualized violence document this high prevalence of PTSD globally. Nearly three in ten women in the USA have reported some form of fear or trauma following rape or physical violence by an intimate partner.[19] In countries like Liberia, Rwanda, Bosnia and Croatia, Bangladesh and the Democratic Republic of Congo the experiences are compounded.[20] And the problems do not stay with PTSD. Other resulting mental health problems often manifest themselves in depression, anxiety and suicidal behaviour.

Karestan Koenen describes the after-effects she suffered, following a brutal rape she had endured 20 years earlier as a Peace Corps volunteer in Niger, West Africa:

> As a result of my rape, I developed full-blown post-traumatic stress disorder (PTSD). I was plagued with unwanted memories, I felt numb, could not eat or sleep, and was constantly on guard. I was hopeless about the future and often wished he had killed me because living with the shame of the rape seemed unbearable. I also found out my attacker was likely HIV positive and, due to the lack of prophylactic medication for HIV in 1991 and inconclusive testing, feared for months that I had also contracted the disease.[21]

For those who endure rape, a great price is paid which lasts for years. Along with the identifiable consequences of sexual violence come a large number of problems associated with trauma, not least fear and low self-confidence, which can emerge at any time in panic attacks and high anxiety levels. In cultures with high levels of rape which go largely unpunished, I have often been told by women that the possibility of a violent attack is never far from their minds. It acts as a reminder of their powerlessness when confronted with brutal assault. Not surprisingly, across the world, women and girls limit their behaviour in a way that men and boys do not. Rape focuses the mind. Marshall University Women's Centre in West Virginia is right to suggest that 'rape functions as a powerful means by which the whole female population is held in a subordinate position to the whole male population, even though many men don't rape, and many women are never victims of rape'.[22]

The experience of rape can change a woman's personality and temperament. She can almost become someone else, devoid of confidence and living with loss. The inroads the ordeal can make on her disposition are exposed in an article, 'Rape Victim Cries Every Day and Sleeps in Clothes':

> Alice woke one night to find a half-naked intruder kissing her. She had no idea who he was, although he was telling her that she knew him. When she resisted, he put a 10 inch pair of scissors to her neck and raped her. Alice was only rescued when her flatmate came home and interrupted an attempt to rape her again.
>
> Afterwards she was traumatised. This was exacerbated by the fear that she had contracted HIV or had become pregnant. The 38-year-old social worker now felt her life had completely changed. Where before she had been independent, she was now afraid to be alone in strange places. She felt nervous on crowded public transport. Alice had to move house, because she couldn't bear to sleep in the same room, but even in her new house, she repeatedly checked that all the windows and doors were locked. Despite the fact that she felt she was using all her strength to stay strong, she still cried every day. She found it hard to sleep because of nightmares.
>
> Fortunately for Alice, there was a lot of evidence against her attacker, and so he was convicted and given a life sentence. On sentencing Alice said: 'He didn't just rape me – he has stolen my independence, my confidence, my freedom and my happiness.'[23]

The price paid in terms of a survivor's mental and emotional health, and the crisis of identity are tragically all too common.

Harvard psychiatrist, and specialist in trauma study, Judith Herman warns about the deep-seatedness of the effects: 'Traumatized people suffer damage to the basic structures of the self. They lose trust in themselves, in other people, in God . . . The identity they have formed prior to the trauma is irrevocably destroyed.'[24] This is an observation made also in Jodi Picoult's novel *The Tenth Circle*: when Trixie's parents are struggling even to talk about their young daughter's sexual violation:

> It was a catch-22. If you didn't put the trauma behind you, you couldn't move on. But if you did put the trauma behind you, you willingly gave up your claim to the person you were before it happened. It was why, even when they weren't actively discussing it, the word *rape* hung like smoke over all their heads.[25]

Many common reactions which rape survivors experience combine to build up the damage identified by Herman. Powerlessness and loss of control are high on the list – the sense of helplessness, and fear of never being in control again. Emotional numbness, inability to cry and periods of prolonged shock go along with these. Disturbed sleep, flashbacks, a sense of unreality, mood changes, loss of confidence, isolation can become woven into a survivor's psychology. Emotions can also seem confusing and paradoxical – anger and hatred for the perpetrator can blend with personal guilt and shame and become focused in self-loathing and disgust. Fear and anxiety can be expressed as hostility; grief can freeze into depression. Some victims even wonder if they were to blame; or if, in their judgements, they are now being unreasonable: they worry that their action might cause pain to other people.

> In the beginning I even felt sorry for the guy, which later seemed completely out of place . . . I was not sure if he really knew what he had done. And I thought about his son, who I knew of, right away. I was thinking that it was not the child's fault, that he had a dad like that. I felt even bad, considering that he might go to jail and the son would not have his father around . . .
>
> I imagined how police would go to the guy's house and how he would react. When I found out that the guy was married I asked myself: how must his wife feel? I seemed to be concerned about

everybody else but myself in the beginning. I constantly tried to recall what happened and if I had sent out some wrong signals! I kept questioning myself and doubting myself. I blamed myself and felt ashamed.[26]

Such confusion of emotions is quite common, but can hold up recovery. So can denial. It is commonplace for the perpetrator to deny that what he has done amounted to rape, but it is not unusual for the victim to be confused about it too. In an attempt to regain the stability she enjoyed before the attack, she might begin to suppress the memory of what has happened, to ignore or reconstruct the situation. This is all the easier when the attacker is known to her and respected by others, and goes on with his life as though nothing has happened. For who is going to believe her when she tells a very different story? Can she even believe it herself? Caring therapy from skilled counsellors is crucially needed to refocus emotions and come to terms with the damage that has been done.

Many women in such situations can therefore be reluctant to classify their experience as rape. In a landmark study of the intimate relationships of adolescents in the UK, one third of the girls in the study were found to have endured some form of sexual violence. Yet the authors reported that none of the girls who had been clearly physically coerced into sexual intercourse defined what they went through as 'rape'. Many of these girls were used to levels of intimidation and force in other aspects of their relationship, and had even come to see violence as an endemic part of intimacy. Some had been subject to high levels of control throughout the whole of the relationship, and seemed to feel it was a requirement on them to accept unwanted sex. It is interesting that in reflecting later on the trauma they had undergone, the abiding emotion expressed by many of the girls was guilt at their weakness in having given in to sexual pressure. They often blamed themselves, even though they had found it difficult to refuse, and had communicated reluctance to their boyfriend. When Tasminder, a girl in the study, was asked by the interviewer how she had dealt with her reluctance to comply when her boyfriend was trying to force her to have sex, her response was: 'I didn't, I just went with the flow really. I was just crying, I was just crying and crying and crying.' Her reply strongly countered the frequent suggestion from boys in the survey that it was easy for them to misunderstand the 'signs' of non-consent. The authors comment:

> In Tasminder's account, the sexual violence continued even though the victim was clearly distressed throughout her ordeal. Thus, in this situation, as in many others, it was not that the 'signs' of non-consent had been misinterpreted. Her partner was clearly aware that he was forcing his girlfriend into sexual intercourse.[27]

Coercion and power

In the above study the girls found to be most at risk from sexual violation were those in relationships with older men, and who had experienced forms of violence at home. Power inequalities, in these cases in terms of age, strength and money, often go along with incidences of rape. These factors can be even more noticeable when the rapist is well known, and when the surrounding community allows a veil of silence to cover his behaviour. The horrific sex-exploitation scandals of Rolf Harris and Jimmy Savile in the UK illustrate how dangerous to children this can be.

Manuela Picq identified the same problem in Ecuador, with the story of a 77-year-old Ecuadorian man, Jorge Heriberto Glas Viejó, who for a year had sexually abused, and then made pregnant, a 12-year-old girl whose mother was his employee. He sponsored the girl at a school, which he directed, but was reported to have taken her out of school on bogus doctors' visits and driven her to a motel. As with the Harris and Savile abuses, Picq sees this as indicative of the way rape and inequality often go together.

> As rapes often are, this case is embedded in power inequalities, socio-economic as well as political. First, Viejó raped the child of his subaltern, a low-income single-mother living in rudimental conditions. He abused a girl of lower social class whose education he sponsored in an institution he directed. Second, the accused benefits from political authority as the father of the minister coordinating non-renewable resources and strategic sector, aggravating gender and class inequalities in access to justice.

Threats and economic pressure almost had the mother abandon the case. Fired from her job, with her two children expelled from school and a newborn to care for, the mother started peeling garlic to afford the $30 monthly rent.

The case would have gone unnoticed was it not for coverage by El Universo, the pariah newspaper of Ecuador, stirring up feminist networks and the pro-bono support from the Bar Association of Guayas.[28]

As with Savile, in Viejó's case no questions were ever raised and no teacher ever objected. The abuse continued until the girl passed out in school exams and medical exams revealed she was pregnant. Then, after a year-long criminal investigation, Viejó was released for 'lack of flagrancy' and disappeared.

Rape travels alongside trafficking and prostitution as the exercise of power over vulnerability. And that power is often layered and multi-faceted, pitting the economic, political or social status of the perpetrator against the insignificance of the victim. When the unbalance is made even more uneven by the lack of safeguarding measures, or indifference from authorities, trying to bring redress can simply feel like a task too overwhelming, and impossible to achieve.

Rape culture

In many societies, the passive silence about sex abuse can be compounded by the presence of an active rape culture which normalizes and excuses it. Rape culture is perpetuated through the use of misogynistic language, the objectification of women's bodies, the glamorization of sexual violence and the entitlement given to men. Gender definitions themselves play a part in it. When 'manhood' is defined in terms of dominance and sexual aggression, then it is hardly a man's fault if he expresses this aggression towards a woman. The high level of rape carried out by soldiers in conditions of conflict is regularly justified this way. Defining 'womanhood' produces more ambiguous results. Women can be perceived as submissive, innocent and sexually passive, or as whores just waiting to be raped ('she was asking for it'). Either way, they are at risk.

Other facets of rape culture are easily recognized: trivializing sexual assault, showing tolerance towards sexual harassment, inflating false rape report statistics, publicly scrutinizing a victim's dress, mental state, motives and history. One of the more alarming recent developments in many Western societies is the proliferation of 'jokes' about sexual violence. The growth of social media and the internet has brought a proliferation of sites specializing in sick rape jokes which go unmonitored and unregulated. 'Jokes' like 'I had sex with a girl in public the other day, and I was amazing! So amazing in fact that she was screaming before we even started' can clock up hundreds of endorsing comments within minutes of posting. Beyond the internet, the appalling rape-entertainment culture among the worst of the stand-up comedians has proved hard to combat. One brave woman in the audience of a Daniel Tosh comedy gig heckled 'Rape jokes are never funny' after he had told several in a row. His response was to insult her by suggesting it would be funny if she had been raped by five guys. He later had to apologize, but has continued his banal and empty patter, enjoying the support of those who will always laugh.[29]

Rape culture has been exposed, not simply by sociologists studying social mores, but by organizations committed to bringing change. The Rape Is No Joke (RINJ) campaign, a Canadian anti-sexual assault organization founded in 2011 in response to 'rape joke' and pro-rape content on Facebook, has pressured media and law-enforcement agencies. A Socialist Students initiative in the UK of the same name has also been active. It refuses to accept that attempts at humour are innocuous and in a different league from any actual violence. Its stance is that:

> this 'comedy' is lazy and un-intelligent. But it also, combined with prolific violent pornography on the internet, 'lads mags' in every corner shop and aggressive sexual imagery in advertising, adds to a culture that accepts, and even glorifies rape and sexual assault.[30]

Rape culture has also been challenged by other more controversial approaches. On 24 January 2011, a Toronto police constable, Michael Sanguinetti, made a monumental error during a session on crime prevention at Osgoode Law School, York University. Addressing the issue of rape, he interrupted a senior officer to declare: 'I've been told I'm not supposed to say this – however, women should avoid dressing like sluts in order not to be victimized.' Although he later apologized for the remark, it was seen as reflecting the way rape culture blames the survivor of a sexual assault while taking the onus away from the perpetrator. Inevitably, it triggered a storm of protests. When, just a month later, a judge in Manitoba gave a suspended sentence to a convicted rapist, the 'SlutWalk' movement was launched in Canada. (The judge also later apologized and the rapist was re-tried and given a prison sentence.)

SlutWalk rallies have now spread across the world – taken up by women as far apart as Latin America (*La Marcha de las Putas*) and India (*SlutWalk arthaat Besharmi Morcha*). Contrary to how they are often presented by the media, the majority of women on these marches are not typically semi-naked, or mimicking prostitutes, but simply claim the right to wear whatever they wish. The rallies are not about the rights of women to walk down the road in sexually seductive and titillating clothes, but are about the rights of women to walk down the road. The London group expressed the point of the movement:

> All over the world, women are constantly made to feel like victims, told they should not look a certain way, should not go out at night, should not go into certain areas, should not get drunk, should not wear high heels or make-up, should not be alone with someone they don't know. Not only does this divert attention away from the real cause of the crime – the perpetrator – but it creates a culture where rape is OK, where it's allowed to happen.[31]

Although many women have found SlutWalk empowering, and endorse the point it makes against rape culture, the marches have also attracted criticism from women campaigning against rape in other ways. The main reproaches to SlutWalk have been that it is culturally insensitive and lionizes promiscuity. It is accused of giving out ambiguous messages about sex, which led one writer to label it a 'self-contradictory trainwreck'.[32] The attempt to hijack a term – 'slut' – backfires for some, since its connotations are simply too powerful. Feminists Gail Dines and Wendy J. Murphy have suggested that the word 'slut' is 'beyond redemption', inextricable from its long-loaded context in the opposition between woman as Madonna and woman as whore. 'Women need to find ways to create their own authentic sexuality, outside of male-defined terms like slut.'[33] Probably the most critical response comes in the Open Letter from women of African descent – anti-violence advocates, activists, scholars, organizational and spiritual leaders. They pointed out: 'As black women we do not have the privilege or the space to call ourselves "slut" without validating the already historically entrenched ideology and recurring messages about what and who the black woman is.'[34] The most powerful combating of this ideology comes from African American writers themselves, especially Maya Angelou, Toni Morrison and Alice Walker.[35] Their poetic and literary brilliance in depicting the history of black American women and the realities of abuse have been publicly acclaimed, with Morrison awarded both the Pulitzer and Nobel prizes. Their writings offer far greater depth and challenge than any march could. So, whatever the future for SlutWalk, other ways of challenging anti-rape culture and campaigning against violence against women are likely to be more inclusive and effective.

Recovery and moving on

What anti-rape movements have in common is the call for public recognition that rape is endemic in culture, that it is profoundly wrong, and that it needs to be countered legally, socially and in terms of attitudes about gender. That includes marital rape. An outcry in Lebanon in 2015 called for the elimination of an amendment to a law drafted five years ago, effectively protecting rapist husbands.[36] Public acknowledgement that rape should never take place in any context, at any time, is vital for the healing of those who have suffered. Restorative justice also requires that provision for reparation be built into the legal response.

Evidence of the damage that rapists have caused can be seen in the public arena as well as in counselling centres and in the silent trauma of women's personal lives. The need, therefore, is for rape to be combated on all fronts. School curricula, police training programmes, public awareness literature, legislation, poetry, art, counselling and sentencing all contribute to changing the culture and to the healing of those who suffer.

Whenever it is possible for perpetrators to hide, to avoid exposure and continue to damage others, those who are vulnerable continue to be at risk. It compounds the sense that justice for victims remains a long way off. Yet the complacency of the perpetrators may be ripe for a fall. A report from Merseyside in the UK is reassuring to all those who are still in limbo after their ordeal:

> Hundreds of evidence bags containing the DNA evidence of rapists lie in two tall freezers deep in the heart of a hidden location where women and men seek help after becoming sex attack victims.
>
> They are all from people who did not feel strong enough to go to the police but consented to medical evidence being taken to be used at a time when they may be ready for their case to be shared.
>
> For row upon row there are swabs taken from victims each coded by a number to protect the anonymity of the person brave enough to have asked for help.[37]

In other countries where rape is not a capital crime and rape victims are often prosecuted for adultery, signs of hope are also beginning to emerge. In Afghanistan in October 2014, the human rights group Women for Afghan Women successfully sheltered a girl raped by a mullah in a mosque, and the man was brought to trial. Against all odds he received a 20-year prison sentence. Other women may now be encouraged to break silence and seek justice.

For those still struggling with fear and defeat from sexual violation, words of survivors and activists bring support. I leave some of them with you now, in the hope that they might reassure those in pain that rape does not have the last word in their lives.

> I survived this torture which left me paralysed for years. That's what that night was all about, mutilation, more than violence through sex. I really do feel as though I was psychologically mutilated that night and now I'm trying to put the pieces back together again. Through love, not hatred. And through my music. My strength has been to open again, to life, and my victory is the fact that, despite it all, I kept alive my vulnerability. Tori Amos

Rape

And I have seen the ugly face of hatred
As it ripped my flesh and seared my soul
Mocking my refusal with malicious, brutal force.
But I am learning to erase that gaze
And seek instead the gentle face of love
Which stoops to soothe my fear with tender touch
And travels patiently in step with me
On the long journey towards peace.

Prophetic visions (Isaiah 61)

They speak of binding for the broken-hearted
Freedom for captives
Release for prisoners in darkness and confusion.
A crown of beauty instead of ashes
Oil of gladness instead of mourning
A garment of praise instead of a spirit of despair.
I believe all this is true.
And I wait in trusting hope, ready to receive.

Survivors' workshop

9

War and sexual violence

The greatest pleasure in life is to defeat your enemies, to chase them before you, to rob them of their wealth, to see those dear to them bathed in tears, to ride their horses, and to ravage their wives and daughters.
                                                                Genghis Khan

War is bad enough on its own and has brought untold misery to millions of people since history began. But there is an accompanying aspect of war which makes it even worse.

> It was dusk when armed Seleka rebels dragged the teenager from the road leading north towards Kobe. They pulled her into the jungle and raped her for several hours. She was abandoned near Route Nationale 10 and, after stumbling into the town of Kaga-Bandoro, was taken to hospital. 'There were five of them raping her until they tore her vagina. Her family paid the [hospital] expenses until she got well,' said her friend, Lisa Moussa, 17.
>
> Moussa was more fortunate. As soon as she saw the rebels, she began running. They tried to kill her, shooting until she stumbled and fell. The gang caught her and frogmarched her to a police station and threatened to rape her until her father paid 6,000 Central African francs (£7.90) for her release.[1]

Tragic stories like those of Moussa and her friend have been repeated across the world, often with the accompanying narrative of police impotence or collusion. A paradox lies here. War is traditionally fought by male military combatants, yet from every international or non-international war zone we hear reports of brutal violence against women. In our contemporary world, according to Amnesty International, 90 per cent of casualties in modern warfare are civilian and of these 75 per cent are women and children. The implications seem clear:

> Women and girls are uniquely and disproportionately affected by armed conflict. Women bear the brunt of war and are the vast majority of casualties resulting from war. Women are 80% of all refugees and displaced persons. Rape and sexual violence targeting women and girls are routinely used not only to terrorize women, but as strategic tools of war and instruments of genocide.[2]

The general breakdown of moral and social order which accompanies war and conflict has been seen to unleash high levels of abuse, exploitation, rape and trafficking. Increased tensions and the higher availability of weapons all leave women particularly vulnerable. Trust can fly out of the window as the threat of gender-based violence spreads like gangrene. It is perpetrated by neighbours, family members, strangers and even humanitarian workers. But the most reported incidents are committed by 'men in uniform'.

Judith Herman believes there is a significant link between combat and rape as the public and private forms of organized social violence. They both occur predominantly in adolescence and early adult life. In many countries boys are conscripted for military service in their early teens; the United States Army enlists young men at 17, and in many other countries it is younger. The period of highest risk for rape is in late adolescence – half of all victims are under 20. Herman concludes:

> The period of greatest psychological vulnerability is also in reality the period of greatest traumatic exposure, for both young men and young women. Rape and combat might thus be considered complementary social rites of initiation into the coercive violence at the foundation of adult society. They are the paradigmatic forms of trauma for women and men respectively.[3]

We can see this even more forcefully where the breakdown of social order has become widespread, even normalized. Daily life becomes hazardous, and dangers lurk in the wake of every task. For women whose trauma includes experience of assault, the effects are unforgettable, and the scars slow to heal.

The number of women involved in coercive violence is staggering. In the 100 days of genocide that ravaged the small African nation of Rwanda, an estimated 250,000 to 500,000 women and girls were raped.[4] In Sierra Leone, between 1991 and 2000, about 64,000 internally displaced women endured sexual assault. In the Balkans tensions of the 1990s, thousands of women in Bosnia-Herzegovina and Kosovo experienced terrible violations involving mass rape: 20,000 to 50,000 women were violated in the Bosnian conflict over three years. During the Liberian civil war, from 1999 to 2003, about 49 per cent of women aged 15 to 70 experienced sexual violence from soldiers or armed militia. In the early 2000s Janjaweed paramilitary and Sudanese government troops raped and murdered tens of thousands of non-Arab women in Darfur. In the Democratic Republic of the Congo, an estimated 200,000 surviving rape victims are alive today, although the figure for those who were killed will probably never be known. In 2013 rampant violence against women was reported in the civil war in Somalia, and reports from Syria said that 90,000 women and children had fled rape and sexual persecution.[5] Yet fleeing guarantees no safety, for reports of gender-based violence towards women refugees – from Iraq, Somalia, Chad, Syria – flood out from the internally displaced person (IDP) camps that take them in.[6] As recently as 2014, chronic instability and lawlessness in the Central African Republic opened up another wave of violence against women, and the brutal barbarity of Islamic State fighters continues the vicious process. Yet none of this awful scenario is new. Sexual violence was prevalent in Europe as far back as the 1914–18 War; it was in Asia during the Asia–Pacific Wars, and across more than one continent in the Second World War. One hundred years after the outbreak of the First World War, the *National Catholic Reporter* called for us to properly recognize gender-based violence in war for what it surely is:

> Beheadings and bombings are seen as terrorist acts, but the systematic rape, abduction, and trafficking of women as a war tactic is still viewed only as a women's or humanitarian issue. Until we recognize these acts of sexual violence as acts of terrorism and not simply as a humanitarian concern it will be difficult to combat these ongoing, catastrophic attacks on women.[7]

War atrocities against women take multiple forms. Slaughter, maiming, burning, kidnapping, gang rape, sex slavery and every imaginable form of torture have all been documented, sometimes in sobering detail. There is no age-determinant for victims. Women as old as 80 and girls as young as four have routinely suffered sexual abuse at the hands of rebel forces, and even their own; they can also be at risk of sexual exploitation from the very military groups commissioned to protect them. When millions of women and girls are so vulnerable in conflict zones it can seem that no woman is safe. For not only is the violence and suffering which many women experience in everyday life more heightened and widespread in war; it is also the case that the violation of women becomes a deliberate and conscious strategy.

Stories from the past – Korean 'Comfort Women'

One strategy has been to exploit women's sexuality as a commodity for the use of military troops. The women who are used in this way have to live the rest of their lives coping with the physical and mental pain of repeated sexual violation and torture. The story of the 'Comfort Women' of Korea highlights the point chillingly. Korea had been annexed by the Japanese in 1910, who exercised harsh control over the lives of the people. In the 1930s Japan turned much of its aggression on China and fought in a number of local-ized skirmishes or 'incidents'. In one of these, the Shanghai Incident in 1932, rape by Japanese soldiers became extreme, leading both to venereal infections and deep anti-Japanese resentment. The Japanese wanted a fighting force which could focus fully on warfare and death. So the question was how to prevent rape and disease while ensuring that the soldiers would be pliable to the demands of battle. The answer was to establish a regime of 'comfort stations' in the military bases, and bring girls over from Japan's colonized and occupied regions. Young girls were brought from Korea as well as from Taiwan, the Philippines, Malaysia, East Timor and China, sometimes lured through the promise of training and pleasant work, at other times simply abducted. The lives of the girls or the concerns of their families were irrelevant. The key requirement was that the aggression and morale of the soldiers would be maintained, and their sexual demands met by a ready supply of women. The women themselves could be regularly 'cleaned out' for public use.

From the early 1930s, through to Japan's surrender at the end of the Second World War in 1945, girls like 13-year-old Geum Joo-Hwang and 14-year-old Lee Ok-Seon were forced to provide sex for Japanese soldiers in the military bases. All these girls, many barely reaching puberty, were expected to 'service' up to 40 soldiers a day, and would be beaten and chastised for any reluctance to serve. Frequent pregnancies were resolved by violent abortions; bodily injuries were ignored unless they prevented them from carrying out their roles. Looking back at the 'comfort station' regime 70 years later, Lee Ok-Seon said simply, 'It was not a place for human beings. It was a slaughter house.'[8] Unable to endure the horrors of this lifestyle, many girls killed themselves, throwing themselves off cliffs, or hanging themselves by any means available. No one knows for certain how many girls of Korea suffered and died at the hands of the Japanese; it is estimated that more than 200,000 were taken, but the majority of those transported to Thailand, Japan, Cambodia, the Philippines and Australia never returned.

It was not until the 1990s that one of the survivors finally broke her silence, and told about her treatment as a sex slave. Her witness was soon followed by around 250 others, emboldened to speak out also. Since then, their case has been taken up by the United Nations and many member countries, who have called this 'one of the largest cases of human trafficking in the twentieth century'. They have also named the treatment the women received as 'gang rape, forced abortions, humiliation, sexual violence, resulting in mutilation, death or eventual suicide'.[9] Japan has given some acknowledgement of what the women have suffered, but for those in Korea their statements lack clarity and accuracy. Demonstrations outside the Japanese embassy in Seoul have continued every Wednesday for the past two decades, and, as the women themselves have succumbed to frailty and death, their supporters have multiplied in number, protesting in capitals across the world.

At the end of 2013 I visited South Korea and met some of the surviving 'Comfort Women' – *Halmonis* ('Grandmothers') as they are now known. They were elderly women in their eighties, each of them still struggling with the physical ravages from their prolonged violation, and talking of how difficult it had been to pick up the threads of life. They still bore the visible scars on their bodies, indelible marks of the brutality of male aggression. Many survivors had been isolated for years – from their homeland, their families, their language. None of the ones who returned had ever been able to have children. One of the young women with me in our visit was from Japan. She listened in shocked silence as the elderly Koreans shared their ordeals, then confessed to me quietly. 'I never knew; at home they have never told us.' It was distressing for each of us to listen to the experiences of the *Halmonis*. Their desire now was that their stories should be told, that pressure might be put on the Japanese to admit and compensate for the complete collusion of their government with the policy of kidnapping and sexual slavery. They have yet to receive what they demand.

The creation of fear and disruption

The *Halmonis'* story is an appalling example of sexual slavery in warfare. But the widespread rape of women has not only been used to encourage soldiers to fight. It has also been used to terrify the 'enemy'. The gender-specific roles played by women puts them at particular risk of violence and terror, especially in societies crippled by armed conflict. In countries in Africa and the Middle East they are often hemmed in with fear. An Amnesty International report indicated that women in Darfur were more vulnerable to attack because they were responsible for children and family dependants so became primary targets for brutality. As care-givers, they would usually be together in the village, which would leave them more accessible to aggressors, whereas the men would be away, tending cattle. Women would also be beaten for information, or to disclose where the men might be hiding. When terror did strike, the women could not easily flee, as they would first look to the safety of their dependants. One 40-year-old described the process:

When the Janjawid came, they put fire on our huts and they beat the children and the women. I have seven children and six are here with me now, I put one on my back and one in front and the others were holding my hands and we ran. Also my grandmother was with me. On the way there were many Janjawid and they were beating people and we saw them raping women and young girls.[10]

It takes little imagination to sense the anxiety and panic that all this causes among these women. Attackers might strike them at any time. They cannot maintain the life of the community because it becomes dangerous to travel out to get wood or water. They have huge responsibilities towards others more vulnerable than they. And they can always be used by enemy militia to undermine the very structures their lives were built upon. A 28-year-old mother in West Darfur, pregnant with her next child, tells a story that reflects so many others:

I was collecting water in the river bed, just outside town when I met a group of men in military uniform who asked me to bring them some water. I brought them some but the men threw the water in my face. I went home carrying my buckets of water and those men followed me. When we were close to the village, they told me to come to their camp. I refused but they pulled me. My mother was around and asked them to stop. The men started to beat both of us. My mother fell down on the ground. One of the men took me aside and raped me.[11]

Amnesty records how African women in Darfur were also systematically tortured and raped in front of their families not only to frighten other women and degrade them, but also to humiliate their menfolk. The men were forced to look on, unable to defend their wives, mothers, sisters or daughters from armed attack.[12] It is a pattern reproduced wherever fighters disrupt local relations; a report from the Women's League of Burma documented an incident when eight troops from the SPDC Light Infantry Battalion 515 raped five women in front of their tied-up husbands.[13] As Desiree Lwambo points out, in her study of men and masculinities in Eastern Congo, when men were left unable to protect their females it undermined their physical strength and challenged very effectively their general dominance. It reduced them, too, to being victims of violence.[14]

Much of the vengeance from opposing fighting groups was in fact directed towards the men, and their demoralization. Women barely mattered in this process. Yet an even greater humiliation was inevitably experienced by the woman. Not only did she no longer feel safe in her own body, or free to go about her normal daily routine, but as a report from Physicians for Human Rights records, she faced future destitution. Even if she had attempted to fight off her attacker before she was ravaged, a raped woman was likely to be rejected by her family and divorced by her husband.[15] This could have a disastrous, traumatic and isolating result, and rob any young woman of a life without hardship.

> I am 16 years old. On[e] day, in March 2004, I was collecting fire-wood for my family when three armed men on camels came and surrounded me. They held me down, tied my hands and raped me one after the other. When I arrived home, I told my family what happened. They threw me out of home and I had to build my own hut away from them. I was engaged to a man and I was so much looking forward to getting married. After I got raped, he did not want to marry me and broke off the engagement because he said that I was now disgraced and spoilt. It is the wors[t] thing for me.[16]

This young woman's tragic story gets worse. Made pregnant by the assault, she was attacked and beaten by the police in her eighth month for conceiving out of wedlock, and imprisoned along with a score of other pregnant rape victims. These girls were then forced to fetch water and clean and cook for their captors for hours every day and eventually compelled to pay a fine. In situations where women are blamed for being victims, the line between army violation and police 'protection' is indeed a very thin one.

Why has sexual violence become a weapon of war?

It is not only in its power to humiliate or produce fear that sexualized violence has become a potent weapon of war. As women are key in holding the honour of an ethnic or religious group intact, their violation can be used to tear down and destroy the society of the 'enemy', as a form of ethnic cleansing. Gita Sahgal, human rights and women's activist, believes that because women are seen as the reproducers and carers of the community, rape is often used in ethnic conflicts as a way for attackers to impose social dominance and redraw ethnic boundaries.[17] For, even though women are not treated on parity with men in many cultures, their sexuality and procreativity ensures generational continuity, as long as it remains under the control of their own menfolk. So the rape of women by hostile groups can be aimed at the destruction of the progeny of the family; reinforced by the brutal abortion of the foetus of the victim, and subsequent traumatic genital injury which impairs the women's future ability to produce offspring. For many women the shame of rape is now compounded with infertility. If rape results in pregnancy there is a different kind of shame, for a child born of rape is likely to be rejected by the community along with its mother. In warring societies such as the Democratic Republic of the Congo, where much of a woman's value is placed on having children, this leaves her in an extremely weak situation. Systematic rape can thus annihilate an ethnic community, and the perpetrators can force their victims to give birth to their own lineage.

> Chibalonza Pascaline refuses to tell her 4-year-old who her biological father was. 'How can I tell the child her father is someone who did this to me?' she asks . . . as she slowly rolls a sock down her left leg, revealing mangled scars and burns just below her knee.
>
> Pascaline was held for eight months by the Interahamwe, a Hutu militia also known as the Democratic Liberation Forces of Rwanda (FDLR), which has waged a brutal war throughout Congo's eastern corner since fleeing across the border after Rwanda's 1994 genocide. She was beaten and raped daily. She tried to escape once but her captors caught her. They contemplated killing her, but instead tortured her. She was four months pregnant at the time. Four years and one surgery later, Pascaline feels sad and angry, even with her daughter. Yet she knows Rolande is not to blame.

At the time of interview, Pascaline lived with 42 others in a safe house set up for victims of war violence by Heal Africa. Through counselling and support they were being helped to bond with the children they had never wanted to bear. In Pascaline's case, there was huge progress:

'The child comforts me, especially when I see her playing with other children but also playing with me and laughing and smiling,' she says. 'I hug my child with a lot of happiness and I really forget some of my problems.'[18]

Gender-based violence is carried out for other reasons also. Enemy militia might rape women to increase the food insecurity of those they are warring against, and procure a community's resources for themselves. Because the tasks of searching for firewood and cultivating crops fall to women, militia groups in DRC have been found to target these women strategically so they can gain supplies and build up reserves while starving the enemy. Wherever women carry out similarly gendered tasks – for example in camps for IDPs – they can become targets for violent assault.

Lisa Jackson's 2008 documentary *The Greatest Silence*, filmed in the Congo, offers rather more indirect reasons for rape. In cultures where superstition is widespread, bizarre notions about women and sex can become woven into ideas of masculinity and power. This was evident in comments from Mai Mai fighters, interviewed in the film, who believed that rape released their 'magic potion' and so fortified them for battle. Without rape, this 'magic' was unavailable to them and military success could not be ensured. One of them explained 'We had to rape women in order to make it work, and beat the enemy.'[19] Others were more prosaic, insisting that rape was ordered by their superiors, and even if they did not want to rape the women involved they were afraid of the consequences of disobedience.

Sometimes the violation is so horribly destructive that even these explanations seem superficial. The only conclusion can be that corrosive motives lie deep within.

Beyond . . . usual kinds of abuse, there were other cases where the rapists inflicted severe injury on their victims by penetrating their vaginas with sticks or other objects, or by mutilating their sexual organs with such weapons as knives or razor blades. A gynaecologist said that in his many years of work he had never seen atrocities like those committed against women who had been raped whom he has treated recently. Among the cases are women whose clitoris and vagina lips had been cut off with razor blades. He said that one of his patients explained this by saying, 'It is just hatred.'

The father of four daughters, the doctor commented, 'I have the feeling that if you are born a woman in this country, you are condemned to death at birth . . . Why are we silent about this?'[20]

However, the 'men in uniform' who are usually reported as perpetrators are not always enemy troops. Often a country's own soldiers carry out violence, without provocation, against their women. Swedish researchers interviewed soldiers in the Forces Armées de la République Démocratique du Congo (FARDC) to find out why. The men pointed to the gruelling demands they faced, claiming it was a response to their frustrations over hunger, poverty, or being too long in the bush without women. One soldier spoke of how anger over the lack of resources in his life took on the form of rape, murder and looting. 'You feel you have to do something bad . . . You mix it all: sabotage, women, stealing, rip the clothes off, killing.'[21] If women are available, they simply take it out on them. The result is that in these situations women remain at high risk. They become targets for the ruthlessness of the enemy and scapegoats for the dissatisfactions of their own side.

Sexual violence in conflict is usually indiscriminate – except when the wives or daughters of opposing leaders are assaulted. Any woman in the path of perpetrators can become a victim. In the 2002 Human Rights Watch report on sexual violence in the eastern DRC, *The War within the War*, many women were keen to explain that they were not personally targeted, but were just in the place where warring soldiers were looking for people to violate. Often they were relieved that the rape was over quickly, and they were then allowed to go, rather than be abducted and kept for weeks as the sexual property of their captors. But for most victims there is little consolation.

I was at the Heal Africa hospital in Goma, a wonderful healing centre founded more than 20 years ago by a Christian Congolese surgeon, Kasereka (Jo) Lusi, and his wife Lyn. Their vision for serving the people of Eastern Congo with holistic care in a time of constant conflict involved them in training medical interns, repairing limbs and organs, along with caring for victims of sexual violence and performing fistula operations. In one year alone (2013) more than 5,000 cases of sexual violence were identified and treated. The hospital was a landmark, both medical and spiritual, in a very dangerous place. When I arrived, a beautiful 17-year-old girl had been carried into the compound and carefully handed over by a group of women. They had found her lying in blood, after being gang raped. On her face, physical trauma, sexual violation and emotional agony fused into near-total despair as she wept and rocked backwards and forwards in the arms of a nurse. As the nurse held her close, gently cradling her face, and praying compassionately over her, the girl simply repeated one word over and over again, '*Pourquoi? Pourquoi?*'[22]

Listening to stories in the Democratic Republic of Congo, I found it all too easy to understand why gender-based violence is so powerful. It is a weapon every bit as formidable as guns or grenades. It is also easy to understand what makes rape so effective. It is inexpensive, easy to use, available everywhere, and inevitably hits the target. Louise Nzigire, a social worker at Panzi Hospital in Bukavu, says rape is a 'cheap, simple weapon for all parties in the war, more easily obtainable than bullets or bombs'. With all her experience of helping survivors, she has no doubt of its intent. 'This violence was designed to exterminate the population.'[23]

Increasing potency of the weapon

Over the past 30 years, the potency of sexual violence in warfare has increased, especially in Africa. The pandemic of HIV & AIDS has doubled the impact. A significant difference between the use of rape in conflicts before 1990 and since then has been the ability to transmit HIV to the victims, compounding both the fear and the consequences of violence. In her report on the Rwandan genocide, Françoise Nduwimana gives voice to one of the many rape victims.

For 60 days, my body was used as a thoroughfare for all the hood-lums, militia men and soldiers in the district. A man named Mugenzi gave the orders . . . Those men completely destroyed me; they caused me so much pain. They raped me in front of my six children. My genitals were completely mutilated[.] They came, they raped me like animals. None of them used protection . . . Three years ago, I discovered I had HIV/AIDS. There is no doubt in my mind that I was infected during these rapes.[24]

Mutilation of victims was a deliberate policy during the Rwandan genocide, as a ploy to destroy ethnic characteristics as well as sexual organs. It was encouraged by media propaganda and stereo-types, not least of Tutsi women who were regularly portrayed as 'evil seductresses, transformed into pistols to conquer Rwanda'. Unless checked, they would be the weapons used to destroy the Hutu men. In her book on the Rwandan conflict, Llezlie Green maintains that the existence of hate propaganda, targeting Tutsi women, strongly implied that sexual violence was not a mere side-effect of the conflict but rather an integral part of the genocidal campaign.[25] With the enlarged awareness of HIV & AIDS, warring groups were quick to grasp this as an additional way of inflicting devastation on the 'enemy'. Not only the scars of rape but the ravages of AIDS would leave victims with no hope for the future. Researcher Stefan Elbe reports an account given by a rape victim in Rwanda who claims she was taunted by her attackers with threats of AIDS. 'We are not killing you. We are giving you something worse. You will die a slow death.' There are even claims that women captives in Rwanda were taken to soldiers who were known to be HIV positive, so that they could be raped by them.[26]

Displacement camps and gender-based violence

War produces another humanitarian crisis: homelessness. By the beginning of 2013, the total number of forcibly displaced persons worldwide had reached a record 45.2 million people. More than half of the world's refugees came from five countries affected by war: Afghanistan, Somalia, Iraq, Syria and Sudan. The conflict in Syria, alone, forced 647,000 people to flee, mainly to neighbouring countries.[27] Almost half a million people, predominantly from Somalia, were living in four camps in Kenya.

The biggest camps are like small cities, but with very noticeable differences. The social structure is fundamentally unstable; the economics are fragile; the geography is chaotic. An extended mass of tents, housing people who have no historic connection with each other, sprawls in all directions, absorbing constant new arrivals. In truth, they are not communities at all. Instead, the tentative organization that has been put in place is disturbed by every incoming displaced group.

Displacement has gender-related significance. It has been estimated that of the 120,000 refugees who fled along the Syria–Jordan border during the conflict in Syria, two thirds were women and children. They sought safety in camps like Zaatari in the Jordanian desert. Yet, like those Sudanese women who fled to camp Breidjing in Chad, Afghan women who went to Iran, or Pakistani or Somali women who escaped to Dadaab camp in Kenya, safety often eluded them. 'There is a tendency to think that once [women] have crossed the border, they are safe,' says Melanie Megevand, a specialist in gender-based violence at International Rescue Committee. 'But they just face a different violence once they become refugees.'[28] In fact there is evidence in the hundreds of camps that currently exist that gender-based violence escalates among displaced communities.

For many women at Zaatari in Jordan, the idyll of a secure haven from violent armed conflict was brutally shattered within days of arrival. Human rights violations, public health issues and sexual violence quickly removed any anticipation of freedom and left them trapped within confined spaces. Women at the camp complained that men regularly entered the communal kitchens to harass lone women, so they retreated to cook on portable gas stoves outside their tents. They also expressed fear at using the latrines after dark as sexual assault regularly took place there.[29] Rape, trafficking, forced marriages were perpetuated in the camps; family members joined in the abuse, with many of the sexual violations taking place in public. Records of teenage pregnancies and an average of eleven births a day at Zaatari have underlined the risks faced especially by adolescent girls. Inevitably, those victims who survive abuse and rape are stigmatized and further traumatized by ongoing maltreatment.

So many stories have poured out of IDP camps over two decades. They describe an epidemic of harassment, assault and sexual violence. Between October 2004 and the first half of February 2005, doctors from Médecins Sans Frontières (MSF, Doctors Without Borders) treated almost 500 rape victims in numerous locations in South and West Darfur. In 2011, a women's rights activist from a camp in the Somali capital, Mogadishu, reported that her colleagues had taken 32 rape cases to the hospital in two days alone: 'We have had the problem of rape in the city but what we are witnessing now is on a scale never seen before.'[30]

Refugees are, by circumstance, foreigners among the people whose government gives them refuge. And this heightens the problems already faced. Many women living in the Zaatari camp noted that, in public places, Syrian women were treated differently from Jordanians; they were identified by their accents and singled out for harassment and discrimination. Unlike them, Jordanian women were able to go out and about independently, whereas almost all the Syrian women did not feel safe going to the marketplace alone. Girls at school faced the risk of being bullied, or receiving unwanted sexual attention which put many of them off attending school altogether.[31] There was also perceived anger from the Jordanian women that young Syrian girls were being married off to their men.

The experiences of these women are replicated throughout hundreds of other IDP bases. There is no longer any doubt of the reality of violence against women both in the refugee camps and beyond. Data once left for committed journalists to uncover, through whatever *ad hoc* means they could assemble, is now the subject of painstaking investigation done by research teams, academics and councils. Yet, although governments and agencies are very aware of the dangers for women in these camps, there seem to be few strategies to bring change. Even when resources exist, the restraints on women mean they may not be used. In the study of Syrian refugees in Jordan, a disturbing 83 per cent of women interviewed did not know of any services available for survivors of sexual violence in their community.

Assessing the scale and taking action

Médecins Sans Frontières voiced a serious problem in relation to Darfur. It was almost impossible to calculate accurately those who had been subject to gender-based violence. Given the great sense of shame, humiliation and fear felt by victims, attitudes which discouraged them even from going to a health facility to receive treatment, the number of victims recorded could be only a partial representation of the real number of those violated.[32]

Collecting accurate data about rape in conflict, and bringing justice to victims, does require the involvement of survivors. But as MSF found, whether living at home or in distant displacement camps, most survivors are unwilling to report their experiences. Lauren Wolfe, who has spent some years carefully investigating the atrocities against women in Syria, knows the problems:

> [I]t's difficult to gather all this documentation in the middle of a war, especially one as chaotic as Syria's. Much of the testimony comes piecemeal, as survivors trickle out of the war zone and into refugee areas, where they are living in tents or the crumbling ruins of buildings. Often once they've spoken to an investigator or reporter they move on, more concerned with making a life for themselves and their families than sticking around for the slim chance of a prosecution.[33]

Erin Gallagher, former investigator of sexual and gender-based violence for the UN's Commission of Inquiry on Syria, concurs. Having spent months speaking with Syrian women and men in camps in Jordan and Turkey, she concludes:

> The reality is that they have much to lose and little to gain by doing so at this point in time, for many reasons ... It takes a lot of courage and strength for a victim to speak up and they may be on their own with little support as they do it. In addition to the shame and isolation a victim may feel, they now are in an insecure environment due to the war. They may now be living in a large refugee camp with no privacy, surrounded by people they don't know or trust.[34]

These analyses are borne out by the painstaking UN Women report on gender-based violence among Syrian refugees. Both women and men in the Zaatari camp told interviewers that women were unable to speak openly about sexual assault and said rape survivors were often afraid to discuss what had happened to them. Women said that a woman could face abuse from her brothers or male family members if she did disclose information, because such claims would disgrace the family.[35]

This is not simply a problem for refugees. It faces all victims of gender-based violence in war. There are problems with reporting to police: officers might ask for a bribe, re-rape the informant, or simply laugh. There is insecurity about what happens to the information they divulge. There are problems in eyewitness corroboration and impartial investigation. There are issues with tribunals and witness protection. When we add in fear of family rejection, discouragement from the authorities, poor safeguards from retribution, and limited hope of justice if they do disclose, why indeed would vulnerable women take such enormous risks?

Yet bringing cases to law is vitally needed. Change has to come. Unless it does, it will be hard to avoid the end-of-war forecast made by Ann Jones in her dispatch from the West African front:

> And here's a little-known reality: When any conflict of this sort officially ends, violence against women continues and often actually grows worse. Not surprisingly, murderous aggression cannot be turned off overnight. When men stop attacking one another, women continue to be convenient targets. Here in West Africa, as in so many other places where rape was used as a weapon of war, it has become a habit carried seamlessly into the 'post-conflict' era. Where normal structures of law enforcement and justice have been disabled by war, male soldiers and civilians alike can prey upon women and children with impunity. And they do.[36]

The way forward

Rape, used as a weapon of war, has been recognized as a 'step' towards genocide by the United Nations Security Council. During the United Nations General Assembly in New York, 2013,

149

a Declaration of Commitment to End Sexual Violence in Conflict was launched by UK Foreign Secretary William Hague and UN Special Representative, Zainab Bangura. Endorsed by two thirds of UN member states, it contains practical and political commitments to eliminate the use of rape and sexual violence in war situations, and assures both victims and perpetrators that justice will be pursued. The need now is for the issues to be given such priority that women's stories are taken seriously across the world, and that countries respond with tighter legislation and sentencing. Once new levels of accountability are put in place, it becomes harder for perpetrators to escape conviction.

This has been seen in the Congo. After years of helping victims of rape, and tireless advocacy for legislation by Lyn Lusi, the members of Heal Africa and their friends in Goma were to see laws enacted and rapists sentenced and imprisoned. At one military tribunal in Rutshuru in 2010, ten officers were found guilty of rape and other war crimes. Since then, many warrants have been taken out, extradition requests made to Rwanda, and 175 convictions brought for human rights violations, most of them rape, in the nine months up to June 2014. Sadly, many investigations were stalled, men convicted later released and many acquitted. In the shocking Minova case where it was confirmed that at least 135 victims, including 33 girls, had been raped, the Operational Military Court of North Kivu tried 26 FARDC soldiers, and in May 2014 convicted only two of rape. Their superiors were also exonerated. So we can give only one cheer for justice in DRC. In a report, the UN High Commissioner on Human Rights pointed to the under-resourcing and lack of capacity of military tribunals to investigate and prosecute those responsible for violations. More fundamentally, its concern was with the lack of independence of the military justice system from the military hierarchy.[37] Until power and patriarchy are kept in check by external accountability structures, impunity stays in place. Organizations like Heal Africa must remain a beacon of hope to those waiting for justice.

One vital lesson I have learned from all my conversations with women whose lives are unmitigated by justice is that women and girls are not only victims of war. They are also powerful builders of peace. And even though thousands of them are unrecognized, under-resourced and not integrated into formal peace processes,[38] their efforts in the prevention of conflict and the securing of peace have been crucial. Rosemarie Milazzo's poem, written to Masika, a Congolese woman who suffered brutal assaults at the hands of General Laurent Nkunda's rebel soldiers, is a gentle reminder:

> No, wounded healer,
> no life's in vain!
> Those women you walk with
> find strength in you
> The children you shelter
> find safety too
> Your care and compassion
> heal wounds so deep.

When we, in the comfortable world, reject both indifference and superficial compassion, and face the challenge of raising our voices against war atrocities towards women, things can change. We can allow ourselves to see the scale of the problem, and campaign to bring legislation which secures justice for victims, and punishment for perpetrators. We can also face the deeper issues of the barbarities of war, and oppose the destructive power of trading in arms, where the ruthless win and the vulnerable are always the losers.[39] Only then can we seriously address the possibility of world peace, and change the climate for the future.

10

Why gender-based violence? It's in our genes: exploring our evolutionary heritage

---

Any honest discussion of human aggression must concede that evolution is responsible . . . Did ancestral women recurrently threaten ancestral men's fitness, acting as a selection pressure that generated mechanisms for intimate partner violence?[1]

It could be argued that in order to know how to eliminate gender-based violence, we need to probe its origins. Any remedial measures must respond to the causes of this global problem or they are unlikely to be effective. The problem here is that though the issue has intrigued scholars for decades, there is not one universally agreed 'cause'. Biologists, criminologists, anthropologists, psychologists, political scientists and sociologists have pored over data and offered conclusions, but the disagreements between them can be sharp and pointed. One school of thought sees violence against women predominantly in terms of human procreative history and adaptation. Another sees it as a cultural variant, related in specific ways to social and religious contexts. Some are intrigued by the psychology of the perpetrator, looking for common patterns in the behaviour or cognition of individuals who violate women. Others adopt a systems approach and apply an analysis of relationships in the family. Population studies in conflict zones like the Congo have correlated sexual violence with physical and mental health factors.[2] Conflict theories have focused on structural issues of power, identifying forms of coercion built into hierarchical relationships. Recently, there has even been an appeal to an 'ecological framework' as a way of acknowledging the interplay of personal, situational and sociocultural factors.[3]

In this book I cannot begin to uncover all these approaches. The scope of the next two chapters is simply to look at the debate between the dominant theoretical frameworks which have sought to explain its causes. This in itself is a difficult task, not just because of its breadth, but because theorists use diverse concepts and often talk past each other. Faced with the task of analysing the problem, and drawing conclusions, some focus on data that others find non-significant. Almost all of them bring presuppositions to their work, which predispose them to certain forms of analysis and which are, in turn, challenged by scholars with different starting points. These inbuilt premises often reveal even deeper philosophical assumptions which lie embedded within the research – assumptions about the nature of human persons or human society. None of this should alarm us, however, because scholarship is not, and cannot be, value-free. Beneath careful methodological processes and the testing of hypotheses lie, inevitably, frameworks of meaning. These frameworks decide, often a priori, what is deemed to be of value, how one might study it, and how the findings might be interpreted. Ideas about human development, the meaning of gender differences, and what constitutes social good are folded into the language and structure of the different approaches. It is to these I now want to turn.

Only one place to start?

Some theorists are explicit about their starting point, and dismissive about those adopted by others. They are often quick to claim that theirs is an 'accurate notion of human nature'. But what is it based on? An assertive claim by evolutionary theorist George Gaylord Simpson is still echoed decades after it was made:

> The question 'What is man?' is probably the most profound that can be asked by man. It has always been central to any system of philosophy or of theology. We know that it has been asked by the most learned humans 2000 years ago, and it is just possible that it was being asked by the most brilliant australopithecines 2 million years ago. The point I want to make now is that all attempts to answer that question before 1859 are worthless and that we will be better off if we ignore them completely.[4]

The historical pivot for Simpson is clearly the publication of Darwin's *On the Origin of Species* on 24 November 1859, which he seems to see as the beginning of knowledge. However, scholars from other disciplines would contest that, certainly in the way it is applied by some into the study of human beings. And modern evolutionary psychologists would be less likely than Simpson to describe other explanatory attempts as 'worthless'. They would instead regard many accounts of human social development as 'proximate' against the 'ultimate' nature of evolutionary explanations.[5] It is also true that people who come from an evolutionary perspective often differ among themselves as to how they see the impact of biological history on present-day behaviour. A hunt through the journals for studies on gender-based violence will reveal a variety of explanations. Writers probing male biology and adaptation theories might see violence directed at women as a sub-set of more generalized manifestations of human violence; others looking at the 'survival needs' of the gene could see male violence as a specific aspect of gender relations and gene-promotion. Some scholars might focus more heavily on the ongoing impact of chromosomes, hormones, or gender differences in the brain, others on the processes of adaptation. Some might even absorb anthropological observations of 'coalitional violence' and favour the 'male warrior' hypothesis over those that lean more heavily on details of biology.[6]

Yet, whatever the specific focus, an underlying basic consensus does link the writers; it is the assumption that our biological heritage can, in some way, account for the violence which men inflict upon women. Only through annexing explanations rooted in our evolutionary ancestry can we arrive at truth. As far as some writers are concerned, everything else is 'unscientific' – most especially the claims of social scientists: 'The social science theory of rape is based on empirically erroneous, even mythological, ideas about human development, behaviour and psychology. The literature it has produced is largely political rather than scientific.'[7] Of course, there is not one 'social science theory of rape', and dismissive statements like this betray an ignorance of both the variety of social science disciplines and the different methodologies within them. The result is further dismissal about how the problem might be tackled in society: 'Police officers, lawyers, teachers, parents, counsellors, convicted rapists, potential rapists and children are being taught "rape-prevention" measures that will fail because they are based on fundamentally inaccurate notions of human nature.'[8] Yet all these assertions automatically privilege evolutionary assumptions as the basis from which to criticize others while failing to put those assumptions themselves under any form of scrutiny. Everyone else might have presuppositions, but there is an acute lack of awareness that this is also true of the writer. Nowhere is the dilemma more in evidence than in sociobiology and evolutionary psychology, with their own particular focus on the biological roots of human behaviour. In this chapter, I therefore will take these theories as the main proponent for the evolutionary side, in the task of explaining gender-based violence.

Sociobiology and evolutionary psychology – our evolutionary history

Sociobiological explanations move in and out of fashion. Dating back to E. O. Wilson's book in 1975[9] and Dawkins's selfish gene theory in 1976,[10] the ideas were amended and developed by the evolutionary psychology of Thornhill and Palmer from 2000, and the work of Aaron T. Goetz in 2009/10 onwards. Two key assumptions shaped the original and subsequent ideas. One is that individual organisms – animals, humans, plants, bacteria – are 'survival machines', whose purpose is to give temporary lodgings to our genes or 'selfish replicators'. The second is that all the characteristics we can see currently in nature are most probably 'adaptations' – characteristics which have conferred some kind of survival advantage in the evolutionary history of the particular organism. This includes adaptations related to our minds as well as bodies. Since minds have evolved, along with brains and bodies, then the behaviour produced by minds should also be understood in the light of evolutionary assumptions. Evolution has sculpted our brains with preferences that yield reproductive success. Life for all organisms is about pursuing genetic advantage.

Applied to sex, the central argument is disarmingly simple. Because males produce far more sperm than females produce eggs, different strategies are needed for males and females to maximize their genetic potential. A man can have many children with little inconvenience to himself; a woman can only have a few, and with great effort. In many species, males direct most or all of their energy in trying to copulate, with females providing most of the parental care. A male's success in producing strong offspring is entirely dependent on his access to fertile females, and to the parental investment provided for his offspring by such females. So, the theory goes, we can expect this to be reflected in human behaviour.[11] What a man needs for optimal gene reproduction is access to many sexual partners; what a woman needs is access to a safe environment to raise her children to adulthood. These needs predispose men's and women's choice of mates and of mating strategies. Some evolutionary psychologists suggest that polygyny would have been the natural state in human evolutionary history as it is closer to the optimal social system than monogamy. Polygyny 'allows' men to impregnate many women in a secure setting without trespassing on the territory of other men and thus fuelling inter-male aggression. The males who out-produced other males in evolutionary history were precisely those who were willing and able to copulate with many females at the peak of fertility. And it is their genes that have continued down the generational line.

In the light of this evolutionary history we should not be surprised to find today that women are more highly selective in choosing mates who can provide status and security, and that men show less discernment in mating, other than to be drawn towards fertile women. Left to their own devices, men would propagate their genetic material as widely as possible. It is only the restraining influence of society, combined with the risks to paternity such philandering poses, that prevent them from doing this.[12] We would expect infidelity when social restraints are loosened or when benefits outweigh the risks. We would also expect men to be prepared to expend resources to obtain sex and be less inhibited than women about being involved in casual sex. Both prostitution and pornography thus hint back to our biological heritage. So does serial monogamy, which benefits the male more than the female, since it is predominantly men (usually of higher status) who marry, divorce and then remarry younger wives. 'Men who were incapable of becoming sexually stimulated by the physical features of young adult females are probably no one's evolutionary ancestors.'[13] Serial monogamy today gives particular men, in effect, monopoly over women's reproductive years. Throughout human history, psychological adaptations like these have been at work to ensure specific gene survival. The fact that the older, divorced wife usually suffers a drop in income and self-esteem, despite often having remained faithful to her spouse, is of no consequence. Sexual relations are about biology, not morality.

> Natural selection – the primary mechanism of evolution – simply prefers alleles that provide higher reproductive success in the current environment. Because selection is indifferent to moral standards and principles, it may produce adaptations for survival and reproduction that are antisocial.[14]

A new note is sounded here – 'antisocial'. Older evolutionists used to talk about natural selection favouring traits that were 'good' over those that were bad. These were not moral terms. A trait was 'good' in the sense of increasing an individual's reproductive success (which itself is different from ensuring group survival). If a trait failed to do this, it was eventually replaced by one more fitting. No connection exists between what is naturally selected and what is morally right or wrong. In fact some 'good' biological or adaptive traits might well be considered undesirable in ethical terms. In the statement above, the point is brought home by the word 'antisocial'. Antisocial behaviour is 'any aggressive, violent, criminal, or delinquent behaviour that benefits an actor at the expense of others'.[15] Rape and violent assault would come into this category.

Some theorists, therefore, do not shrink from explicitly including coercive sex as part of their evolutionary framework of explanation. Rape is not an aberration, but, as Glenn Wilson proposes, an alternative 'gene-promotion strategy', most likely to be adopted when access to legitimate, consenting sex is not available.[16] In many

other mammalian species a female's receptiveness is highly correlated with ovulation, but this is not so with human females. So
the human male, faced with 'the choice between force or genetic
extinction', will obviously go for force. Biologically speaking, there
is no reason to restrict his mating to receptive, consenting females.
'Non-receptive women can still get pregnant, so their protests are,
genetically speaking, irrelevant.'[17] Lee Ellis goes further, suggesting
that in the 'ancestral environment' males who under some circumstances employed force may have had 'greater reproductive success'
than other males who did not use force.[18] Rape might well be seen
therefore as an important potential reproductive strategy for males,
even when access to consenting females is available.

Rape, of course, is not the only form of violence against women.
We have spent many chapters looking at selective abortion, FGM,
domestic violence, honour killings, torture, and so on. How can
these fit into an evolutionary framework? Theorists are not at a
loss, however, in devising explanations which try to incorporate
some of these into the overall biological perspective. Intimate-
partner violence is the area most considered. Uppermost, here, are
appeals to jealousy and the fear of sexual infidelity.

Men's jealousy, it is argued, is likely to arise from fear of sexual
infidelity in their partners, rather than emotional infidelity, which
causes women distress. The fear is that someone else's genes
may be being passed on by an unfaithful partner. This problem of
'paternity uncertainty' present among our forebears has produced
adaptations which can account for intimate-partner violence today.
In one study using subject reporting, Goetz and Shackelford claimed
that there was a positive correlation between men's sexual coercion
and women's past and future likelihood of engaging in sexual
infidelity.[19] Three years later they had extended their work to other
forms of men's partner-directed violence, including insults, physical
violence and homicide. They concluded that although personality
traits played some part in triggering these behaviours in men,
suspicion of their partner's infidelity weighed more heavily.[20]

Male sexual jealousy is seen to be compatible with an evolutionary
psychological perspective, even in wife-killing. In situations where
jealousy is very strong it can apparently activate 'evolved mechanisms

associated with weighing the costs and benefits of homicide' to the extent that 'under certain circumstances, partner-killing by men might be the designed outcome'.[21] Wilson and Daly argue that occasional female-partner homicide allows threats of aggression to remain effective in the efforts of men to retain mates. Unless some men occasionally follow through these threats, they lose their effectiveness for all men.[22]

Evolutionary psychologists are not claiming the same kind of correlation between genes, past environment and present-day behaviour as sociobiologists. They insist that behaviour that was best suited for gene-promotion in the ancestral environment may not work today. Similarly, adaptations in the brain of our earliest forebears may not be relevant for understanding behaviour today. And this can also be true of adaptations in the brain. The question is whether these new emphases in evolutionary psychology can really resolve the problems inherent in sociobiology in explaining male violence against women.

So what's wrong with these theories?

I have tried to be as faithful as possible to the arguments presented by sociobiologists and evolutionary psychologists. But it has been difficult to avoid the accusation that they strain their explanatory frameworks way beyond what most others would regard as reasonable limits. The premises, methodologies, typology, gender-assumptions, conclusions and moral implications of these theories of male violence have all come under critical scrutiny. Allegations persist that the 'findings' of their research offer little more than gross stereotyping of men and women, in particular that women are naturally faithful; men are naturally promiscuous.[23] And even though genetic factors are not seen as *determining* behaviour, but as influencing how we act in response to specific cues or triggers, the inherent reductionism greatly limits the value of sociobiology. Evolutionary psychology's credibility is similarly dogged by the lack of real neurological evidence, especially in its assumptions about the brain and its evolution. One critic is not sparing in his dismissive summary: 'Evolutionary psychology is empirically unwarranted and conceptually incoherent to such an extent that it is a matter of professional sociological concern why it has come to achieve such a degree of popularity.'[24]

Lack of evidence and the stretch of imagination

When the concept of adaptation appears to be so elastic, absorbing almost every eventuality as we saw above, it needs careful empirical research to support the conclusions drawn about gender-based violence. Yet this evidence is undoubtedly scant, almost non-existent. For their notion that rape is an adaptive trait linked to gene-promotion strategies Thornhill and Palmer do offer something they call 'evidence'. They observe that women who are rape victims are most often of potential childbearing age; they also claim that rapists usually do not use more force than necessary, so avoiding physically thwarting the victim's chance of reproduction. They confidently assert:

> Rapists seldom engage in gratuitous violence; instead, they usually limit themselves to the force required to subdue or control their victims. A survey by one of us (Palmer), of volunteers at rape crisis centers, found that only 15 percent of the victims whom the volunteers had encountered reported having been beaten in excess of what was needed to accomplish the rape.[25]

Yet most social scientists would dismiss this flimsy 'empirical' research as somewhat ridiculous, and any visit to victims in Pakistan, Egypt or the Congo would immediately knock on the head the claim that rapists seldom use gratuitous violence. The suggestion that men choose fertile women to rape so they can maximize their genetic potential might sound plausible from this theoretical basis, but otherwise remains an unfounded interpretation of coercive sex. Other explanations seem much more obvious: women of childbearing years (rather than elderly women or children) are the ones most likely to be out and about unchaperoned, so they are obviously the ones more at risk; men behave aggressively because they see it as their entitlement to treat women as they wish. The idea that rape could have evolved as a genetically advantageous behavioural adaptation seems to have gained popularity despite manifest weaknesses in the hypothesis, and the very tentative, supposed link between rape and gene-promotion.

Even if the problems of explaining rape could be overcome, other aspects of gender-based violence are even harder to substantiate from an evolutionary perspective. There can hardly be any serious proposal that assault, torture, acid attacks or femicide were adaptations that provided genetic or biological advantage for our earliest ancestors. Killing the very mate who might otherwise be successfully passing on your genes is not a good strategy!

It makes little sense, either, to suggest that 'under certain circumstances, partner-killing by men might be the designed outcome'. What does this mean, other than supposing that 'adaptations in the mind' must suggest some benefits for the killer that we don't know about? An alternative second suggestion – the 'by-product hypothesis' – fares little better. Here, 'killing an intimate partner is not the product of evolved psychological mechanisms, but a by-product of mechanisms selected for their nonlethal outcomes'. In other words, the fact that the woman dies is an unfortunate error – to put it colloquially, a cock-up. Violence intended merely to control the partner (triggered presumably by the mechanism which brings gene-promotion and evolutionary advantage to the male) inadvertently resulted, instead, in her death.[26]

Perhaps the most plausible explanation presented by Thornhill and Palmer for lethal behaviour is what Richard Hamilton calls the 'misfit' hypothesis.[27] The argument is that where our cognitive architecture is not well suited to the present-day environment, it may well generate unacceptable behaviour if left unchecked. Such behaviour could include all the areas of vice, whether rape,[28] murder and domestic violence,[29] sexual jealousy[30] or sexual harassment.[31] In each case, the misfit hypothesis pinpoints the gap between the biological adaptations which evolved to meet the challenges facing our forebears, and the 'topsy-turvy contingencies we have created since the agricultural and industrial revolutions'.[32] The question remains, however, whether this really does offer any causal explanation, or simply admits a failure to explain!

Logical and methodological problems

Inadequate empirical evidence and spurious interpretations are only two of the problems which critics have identified in evolutionary accounts of male violence. Dogmatic leaps rather than logical coherence can be added to the list. The internal debates about how to explain mismatches between human observed behaviour and the genetic self-interest hypothesis do not hide the reality that the underlying premises retain the status of dogma. Thornhill and Palmer insist that, regardless of which hypothesis prevails, 'there is no doubt that rape has evolutionary – and thus genetic – origins'.[33] There is, in fact, plenty of doubt. The main logical problem with these assertions is that the dogmatic premises of the theories need to be accepted for any conclusions to make sense. So sociobiology requires the gene-centred view of evolution to be received as absolute; evolutionary psychology requires the acceptance of the notion of adaptations, or by-products of adaptations. Once we accept these assumptions, then we find that the conclusions drawn by the theorists are usually contained in the premises.

Although the arguments are often presented in a way that suggests a logical progression, the logic quickly disappears on examination. Reasoning often goes along lines like the following:

1   An evolutionary framework leads us to expect the manifestation of certain patterns – like a greater vulnerability of younger women to male violence, and likelihood that men will exhibit jealousy and fear of infidelity.
2   Younger women are more vulnerable to male violence, and men do exhibit jealousy and fear of infidelity.
3   Therefore, the evolutionary explanation is reliable.

Though oversimplified, this is no parody of the process of deduction. The clearly circular process does not progress the argument at all, and leaves the issue of real evidence untouched. Methodological problems which are even more undermining will become evident later.

Inbuilt naturalism and limited possibility for change

Evolutionary explanations of human relationships can plunge us into a cultural attitude akin to hopelessness. Kenan Malik warns that the pessimism of contemporary culture has cleared a space for a more naturalistic vision of humanity, and this is filled admirably by sociobiology. There is little room to acknowledge the independent existence of will, emotion, decision-making, values or economic analysis. Everything is ultimately related to the biological. According to Colin Blakemore,

> To choose a spouse, a job, a religious creed – or even to choose to rob a bank – is the peak of a causal chain that runs back to the origin of life and down to the nature of atoms and molecules.[34]

Consequently we are asked to believe that '[t]he social and the cultural are not alternatives to the biological. They are aspects of evolved human biology and, hence, they are the kinds of things to which evolutionary analysis can be properly applied.'[35] Gender-based violence, then, is merely one link in a causal, biological chain, which for the sociobiologist stretches back to our animal origins, and has nothing to do with will or deliberate intention. For 'will' is not real; 'decision to inflict pain' has no independent actuality. There is no other conscious aim or purpose at work in the act of rape. Yet this ploy to reduce all reality to biology fails to impress most critics. Those who are convinced that the human world is made up of elaborate, meaningful social interactions would argue that non-biological concepts are highly significant. In Mary Midgley's famous comment: 'toothache is as real as teeth or electrons, and debt as real as the house that was bought with it.'[36]

The promotion of the naturalistic viewpoint does more than turn (in Rob Foley's words) 'every large philosophical and meta-physical question into what are often straightforward and even boring technical ones'. It also produces sobering and depressing predictions for society.

> The idea that genes cause behaviours, and that society is the collection of all our individual sets of behaviours, lead[s] inextricably to the conclusion that the structures of society are just the indirect consequence (or extended phenotype, as Dawkins might term it) of the human genome – that we have the society we deserve, and there's no point in trying to do anything to change it. It robs us of our agency, and inspires inaction.[37]

Considering the urgent need to change the persistent and dehumanizing continuation of gender-based violence, this is very bad news. But despite evolutionary psychology's various protests to the contrary, if the problems lie deep in the different genetic predispositions of men and women, it can offer us little else. A laissez-faire response is apparently all we can hope for. At best we are left with mere shoulder-shrugging; at worst, we are presented with a dangerous biological and evolutionary justification for male violence.

Loss of moral responsibility

This opens up another accusation regularly levelled at these evolutionary explanations of human behaviour. They are 'amoral'. Amorality is inevitable when all moral concepts and moral awareness are themselves subsumed under the 'natural'. As Pinker asks, 'how did ought emerge from a universe of particles and planets, genes and bodies?'[38] Even though Pinker does not want to eliminate moral reasoning, he seems to find it incomprehensible. His arguments are also incomprehensible. He claims moral reasoning follows from our status as sentient beings: beings with self-consciousness and moral discernment. It is this sentience which 'underlies our certainty that torture is wrong and that disabling a robot is the destruction of property but disabling a person is murder'. This sounds reasonable enough, yet, from his theoretical framework, Pinker has no way of explaining why sentience exists. His conclusion is utterly inadequate: 'Our incomprehension of sentience does not impede our understanding of how our mind works in the least . . . [I]n the study of the mind, sentience floats in its own plane, high above the causal chains of psychology and neural science.'[39] Colin Blakemore at least has a more coherent response when he suggests that moral responsibility has no real meaning, but is a fiction we have created because otherwise society could not work.[40]

Since morality is not built anywhere into sociobiology, and is not integrated into evolutionary psychology, if it exists at all it has to be something manufactured by humans. If the concept can serve the best interests of gene preference and survival that is fine, but it has no independent meaning.

The position of the modern evolutionist . . . is that humans have an awareness of morality . . . because such an awareness is of biological worth. Morality is a biological adaptation no less than are hands and feet and teeth . . . Considered as a rationally justifiable set of claims about an objective something, ethics is illusory. I appreciate that when somebody says 'Love thy neighbor as thyself,' they think they are referring above and beyond themselves . . . Nevertheless . . . such reference is truly without foundation. Morality is just an aid to survival and reproduction . . . and any deeper meaning is illusory.[41]

However, if the meaning of morality is simply reduced to survival and reproduction, it is not, of course, morality at all; at least not in any sense in which the term has always been used. Morality is something we have to decide about, where we weigh up competing claims of good and bad, right and wrong, and make decisions that our consciences have to live with. The absence of these ethical realities within evolutionary psychology is serious enough, but it is left to Richard Dawkins to take the radical implications of this to their logical conclusion. What results is something so ethically vacuous that it leaves us morally stranded. Adopting a view more mechanistic than naturalistic, Dawkins simply assures us that we cannot be held responsible for what we do, because we are not intentional agents. He reminds us of the image of Basil Fawlty, in the sitcom *Fawlty Towers*, who ridiculously 'punishes' his defective car. We should show the same reaction towards a judge punishing a defective man – whether murderer or rapist – and that reaction should be to laugh at the judge's irrationality. For isn't the rapist 'just a machine with a defective component'? Dawkins hammers his point home:

> But doesn't a truly scientific, mechanistic view of the nervous system make nonsense of the very idea of responsibility, whether diminished or not? Any crime, however heinous, is in principle to be blamed on antecedent conditions acting through the accused's physiology, heredity and environment . . .
>
> Why is it that we humans find it almost impossible to accept such conclusions? Why do we vent such visceral hatred on child murderers, or on thuggish vandals, when we should simply regard

them as faulty units that need fixing or replacing? Presumably
because mental constructs like blame and responsibility, indeed evil
and good, are built into our brains by millennia of Darwinian
evolution.[42]

So human beings cannot be accountable for their actions. Violent
women-torturers are not responsible. They are not exercising any
choice about how to behave towards women, not intentionally
inflicting pain or treating them as objects. They are merely following through the effects of their 'antecedent conditions', and it is
irrational to think otherwise.

Of course, Dawkins' outburst itself strains the limits of logic.
Throughout, he is appealing to our 'rationality' as that which
should guide and rebuke our actions, and evaluate our responses.
Yet within his own framework there can be no such thing as
rationality. In order for it to be a measuring rod, reason would
have to exist independently of nature; it must be separate from
factors reduced to genes or mechanics. It cannot act as a guide to
anything if it is merely another mental construct 'built into our
brains by millennia of Darwinian evolution'. As Thomas Nagel
argues, 'One cannot embed all one's reasoning in a psychological
theory, including the reasonings that have led to that psychological theory. The epistemological buck must stop somewhere.'[43]
But with Dawkins, there are no buffers at the end of the line,
nowhere for the buck to stop; the circularity continues *ad infinitum*.
The whole hypothesis therefore implodes as there is no way of
making independent statements about it, no way of assessing ideas
or actions that are not in themselves reducible to evolutionary
processes. So Hamilton's summary is right: evolutionary theory
can have nothing interesting to say about reasons, nor can reasons
play any role in its explanations.

The possibility of any authentic morality, or indeed any independent route of evaluation or reasoning, now evaporates as the
full implications of evolutionary reductionism become evident.
The paradox is that not only does this leave us bereft of any way
of making judgements or of guidance on how to live; it also runs
counter to real people's experience. Every day, people go about
their lives making decisions, weighing up moral choices, often

struggling with a niggling conscience, exercising the will. Some of them will make choices which will enable those around them to flourish, and bring justice and freedom into previously broken situations. Others will rape women, throw acid in their faces, and traffic them into sex slavery. But evolutionary psychology can offer us very little in the way of explaining why. It offers even less in encouraging hope for the future.

The disappearance of the self

When we listen to women who have experienced gender-based violence, we often hear their sense of alienation. Many of those whose stories are in this book have related the problem of feeling cut off – both from other people and from themselves. In some cases they have even described it as 'annihilation', losing the identity which has shaped life up to this point. It is a deep emotional, often spiritual, sense of having lost their sense of self, of worth, and of God.

For all of us, this sense of self, of who we are, is part of our experience of being human. It is something formed throughout childhood and into adulthood. So many factors and experiences become building blocks to the self: our name, language, family milieu, faith, education, values, role models, interaction with others, social initiations, significant experiences – along with the broader social and cultural context of our lives. Our human identities – what we consider to be the common properties of our humanity – are shaped as much by our history as by our biology, and our history comprises many encounters with other selves. Yet, we do not simply acquire our habits and values from others. As Malik suggests, we are active agents: 'we also constantly innovate, transforming ourselves, individually and collectively, in the process.'[44]

Malik makes a critical point about evolutionary psychology in this regard. In seeking to erase the distinctions between humanity and nature, it is in danger of eliminating all that appears distinctive about human beings. Although animals are also cultural creatures, in that they live and interact in a social setting, there are huge differences between human and animal identities.

There is a fundamental difference between a process by which certain chimpanzees have learnt to crack open palm-nuts using two stones as 'hammer' and 'anvil', and a process through which humans have engineered the industrial revolution, unravelled the secrets of their own genome and developed the concept of universal rights.[45]

The failure to examine or understand the reality of the human self is an outstanding weakness of these theories. Without it, we cannot begin to understand any of the traumas involved in gender-based violence, or indeed in most other aspects of life. But it is not simply that the self lacks explanation; *the self is non-existent.* As Pinker states unequivocally: 'it is still tempting to think of the brain as ... the self, the soul, the ghost, the person, the "me." But cognitive neuroscience is showing that the self, too, is just another network of brain systems.'[46] This means that, along with moral value, freedom of action, or sentience, any meaning to personal identity vaporizes. The idea of self-consciousness becomes meaningless, because there is no self to be conscious. This in itself takes the lid off a heap of philosophical questions, and pushes their theories of the brain and mind to the limit.

Raymond Tallis points out that trying to construct a theory of the human mind while ignoring self-consciousness is a bit like 'trying to build a house by starting at the second floor'.[47] If thousands of 'modules' exist in the brain, each one responsible for some particular psychological characteristic – like reasoning, memory, choice, language, decision-making, and so on – how are they ever 'unified' into the experience of one person? And as Pinker himself muses, how can we talk about self-knowledge when none of us has access to our own brain?[48] John Searle's answer – that we need to postulate the self, but it is merely a formal postulation, not another entity in addition to the brain – is hardly reassuring.[49]

If there is no self who generates his or her own thinking or sensations, we are simply left with fragmented and atomized perceptions which belong to 'no one'. The result is one of the worst nightmares of science fiction:

We think we are in charge, but in reality there is no self that can take charge. There is simply the machinery of the brain churning away, thanks to a chain of causal links that goes back to the Big Bang itself.[50]

With so little to commend these theoretical approaches with regard to explaining human behaviour, we would search hard for any justification for accepting their analysis of violence against women. What is needed are explanations which will offer robust evidence, coherent arguments and ways forward which can help eradicate the atrocities we have been examining. It is time now to look at other explanations which might take us further in these directions.

11

Why gender-based violence? Power and patriarchy

———————

The root cause of violence lies in the unequal power relations between women and men, which ensure male dominance over women, and are a characteristic of human societies throughout the world.[1]

Men have been taught to relate to the world in terms of dominance and control, and they have been taught that violence is an acceptable method of maintaining control, resolving conflicts, and expressing anger.[2]

It is often said that where there is no strong social prohibition against it, men violate women simply because they can; some men regard it as their entitlement to subject women to brutal force or coercion. Though this might sound like an explanation, it simply raises further questions around the obvious one: 'But why?' In the last chapter we looked at biological explanations on offer. In this chapter I want to focus on the social sciences.

Other avenues – learning from the social scientists

Social scientists tackle almost every aspect of gendered violence, producing a welter of different approaches, which reflect the variety of disciplines involved. As with biological responses, their explanations embody many values and assumptions, mirrored in their choice of research projects, methodology and interpretation of findings. Even within a single discipline there are variations. In psychology, for example, behavioural psychologists differ from cognitive theorists and from systems analysts or social psychologists; the diverse interests of these scholars nuance their approach to the study of violence against women. In sociology, old arguments would be likely to re-emerge – between functionalists, conflict theorists, symbolic interactionists and phenomenologists, often exposing in their research different views about social reality, and motivations for human behaviour. Anthropologists or ethnologists would come to the problem through an inter-cultural lens, frequently informed through ethnographic research, and are more likely to focus on cultural similarities and divergences in the way violence is manifest. Beneath these varying approaches we are also likely to find distinctive concepts of human personhood.

Despite their divergence of approach and research methods, the social sciences have something fundamental in common. They recognize that human beings do not just behave; they *act*. And the way they act is significant, sometimes resulting from reflection and choice, sometimes not, but always in a cultural environment. The human sciences, therefore, recognize the crucial importance of *siting* the question. Without dismissing genetic factors, or minimizing the effects of physiology or hormones, social scientists are wary about reducing human actions to biology. Because interpersonal actions are located in social, psychological, cultural, economic or historical contexts, any study of gender-based violence inevitably involves understanding its location. The task is to unearth what goes on in these cultural environments, to unpack the traditions and roles, the structures and processes, the learning and socialization which shape and impact violence in human relationships.

Adopting a framework of analysis

Many people will recognize that my own approach in this book has been one which leans heavily on the social sciences. In particular it embraces a sociological outlook strongly influenced by a gender-aware standpoint. I want to spend most of this chapter outlining the history and implications of this approach. However, in analysing violence against women, this is not the only social science approach on offer, so it seems important to separate it from other (less promising) options. One theory, prominent in both anthropology and sociology with a very different take on violence, is functionalism.

Functionalism

Most functionalists see the meaning of human persons as deriving from their transient occupancy of social roles. Individuals are replaceable. Functionalism's concern is with society as a whole, and with the way social structures or processes contribute to the stability of the social order. It is through the good working, consensus and co-operation of various institutions and activities that the social system can function effectively. So a functionalist analysis of gender-based violence is very specific. It would look for the 'functions' violence performs in particular settings, and especially how it might operate to maintain the status quo and stability of the group or institution.

This task is not a difficult one, for such 'functions' are easy to find. For example, violence can be used as a way of reinforcing hierarchies, or maintaining gender protocols; fear of violence might curtail a woman's likelihood of opposing or humiliating her husband; threat of physical punishment or 'honour retaliation' might well ensure that family norms are upheld. From a functionalist view, violence thus acts as a deterrent against overthrowing protocols and practices regarded as essential for the equilibrium of the social order. It ensures that deviance from societal norms is resisted. And all are involved in this process. The finding that both women and men endorse 'honour killings' in societies where they are widely practised would come as no surprise to a functionalist theorist.

Functionalism presents itself as largely descriptive, observing how society holds together. But its implicit claims of value-freedom are beset with limitations. The idea of 'function', for example, often smuggles in the assumption that as long as a society is 'functioning', it is 'unproblematic'. But gendered violence, surely, *is* problematic, whether or not it enables society to 'function'. Furthermore, societies can 'function' in ways that might be draconian or complacent, discriminatory or unjust, and we need some way of understanding and measuring these aspects. Similarly, 'deviance' is almost always understood as deviance from the *status quo*, where maintaining the *status quo* is the assumed function of any institution in society. So, from this standpoint, as long as gendered violence is kept in check it need be no threat to the ultimate stability of the system; stability is threatened simply when violence is so brutal or overwhelming that it becomes dysfunctional and problematic.

Occasions which would meet these latter criteria would be violence in conflict situations where stability is fragile and the social order threatened with collapse. Yet, even here, the focus is on providing interventions that can address the destabilizing feature – the conflict. In such a context, functionalists are likely to perceive sexual violence as a problem that comes to the fore wholly because of the conflict situation. When interventions are found which work, and peace can restore the 'unproblematic status quo', the sexual violence will dissipate. Yet all this misses the point that the real problem might well be the status quo itself, which simply becomes exacerbated in a context of tension. As one critic notes: 'It is as if sexual violence in conflict has little if any connection with the pre-existing gender relations, social orientation and other forms of gendered violence *preceding* the descent into conflict.'[3]

All this indicates another significant weakness of functionalist theorists. They fail to accept as problematic the way processes are normalized, accepted, and incorporated into everyday behaviour. This needs careful investigation, but for that they would have to provide some bigger framework of analysis beyond the criterion of assessing social stability and functionality. Especially this is needed in trying to understand gender-based violence. Without conceptual categories that can identify unjust, pathological or problematic behaviour, there can be little real comprehension of what causes and maintains violence against women.

Family conflict theorists

A very different set of theories does focus on problematic behaviour and engages more critically with issues of violence. These theories adopt an institutional or family-based perspective. *Family conflict theorists* in the USA have been attempting to measure or quantify the prevalence of family violence there since the 1970s, with some success. With national surveys suggesting that partner aggression occurs in 12 per cent of US families,[4] and severe parent-to-child violence in 5 per cent of US families,[5] family sociologists and psychologists have set about identifying the factors that contribute to this pathology of intimate relationships. Some have focused research on psychological disturbances (low self-esteem, depression), or on substance abuse (alcohol, drugs),[6] or on interpersonal factors (poor parent–child attachment, neglect, intergenerational discord).[7] The 'systems' at work in families have also come under detailed scrutiny, for example punitive parenting, child maltreatment, parental conflict – all of which have been linked with hostile expectations of relationships in adulthood.[8] One area much studied has been the exposure of children to violence between parents; research evidence suggests young people can be led to assume that violence is an appropriate and effective means of resolving conflict with partners. Such exposure has also been found to increase the risk for aggressive behaviour not only in childhood, but throughout life.[9] Studies analysing the intergenerational transmission of family violence have noted a high correlation from one generation to another,[10] with particularly long-term effects found in a significant 20-year longitudinal research on child victims.[11]

Research which focused on men who, as children, had witnessed the normalizing of interpersonal violence revealed how difficult it then could be to find effective conflict-resolution strategies which were not themselves violent. Tactics of men in this group were likely to include insulting, swearing, sulking, refusal to talk, threatening, throwing, smashing, hitting or kicking. Such ineffective control methods also went along with a higher probability of those men engaging in wife-battering.[12] Volumes of research highlight the now well-accepted thesis that people raised in a home environment where aggression is the normal way of expressing anger are at greater risk of being aggressive throughout their adult life.

We should not underestimate the importance of these studies of salient psychological features of individuals and their families.

Careful research on childhood trauma, psychopathy or neurological dysfunction has uncovered vital insights into the significance of early learning and experiences. We can see how attitudes and behaviours, inculcated through exposure and habits, become part of normality in the lives of those who hold them. The findings uncovered have, in turn, fed into measures for treatment of individuals.[13]

The problem for us here is that these factors can hardly account for the vast incidence of gender-based violence that I have been confronting in the chapters of this book. Although intimate-partner abuse witnessed by a child may be highly significant in setting his persistent behaviour patterns, there are very many areas of violence which do not have this basis. What is more, the home is not the only context in which violence is learned. Cultural manifestations of violence as diverse as FGM, selective abortion, partner abuse, and rape as a weapon of war need much more extensive fieldwork and a bigger framework of explanation than family conflict theories provide.

Another problem emerges too. With their tendency to assume that violence between intimate partners is mutual and symmetrical, family conflict theorists have, quite rightly, come under criticism for having a *degendered* approach. The presumption has been that both partners have equal amounts of power and negotiating ability in the family, an oversight which misinterprets the violence within intimate relationships.[14] The underlying gendered basis of violence can remain hidden if it is not understood that women and men are differently located in society. Men's violence towards women and women's violence towards men are not the same; these acts occur 'within the historical, cultural, political, economic, and psychological contexts of gender'.[15] It is a sobering point that, in the way they are culturally interpreted, institutions such as marriage and the family may even support men's use of physical force against women. So, women and men are not influenced simply by what they are exposed to as children, but undergo years of learning in a variety of intensely influential cultural settings.[16] Inevitably, this process socializes people into attitudes and expectations which shape and reinforce gender roles.

A perceptive article on gender-based violence in Nigeria illustrates this well. It draws on a study which identifies a rigorous socialization process 'in which every member of the community is aware of what duties, responsibilities and roles are expected from them which is perceived as the correct order crucial for family and communal harmony'. An aspect of this 'correct order' is the accepted exercise of marital power. The female partner anticipates the position of the other, and defers to it, believing she has no power to resist, even fearing reprisals if she does. Psychologically, the systems of inequality mean that this partner cannot even conceive the possibility of having input in decision-making or using enabling strategies. So power imbalance significantly influences the experience of conflict in marital relations.[17]

The studies revealed that, cushioned in these attitudes towards power and the subsequent gender-role expectations, violence against women had simply become normalized as a way of expressing order and status. It was learned by both sexes, and then perpetuated, 'entrenched', as researchers saw it, 'in the strong patriarchal ideologies of control, subversion and subordination of women and girls'. Tracing the development of patriarchy through colonial systems and since independence, author Nkiru Igbelina-Igbokwe sees strong interconnections between its persistence and the violence meted out to women. Because efforts to resist the ideology have been mostly at individual level, such resistance made no strong challenge to patriarchy. For any kind of effective challenge to be mounted, the author argued that gender relations needed to be reappraised and relearned, socially and institutionally, and a more holistic model developed for reorientation which could release both women and men in Nigeria.[18]

The Nigerian study brings us back to the sort of analysis I have been suggesting throughout the earlier chapters of this book. It affirms that an analysis of family systems takes us only so far in understanding gender-based violence, and needs to be melded with a thorough probing of the effects of socialization, ideology and cultural variations. In contrast to both functionalism and family systems psychology, theories which embrace a more feminist perspective see gender-based violence as just one manifestation of the widespread oppression of women. Like other expressions of disadvantage, it grows out of the material, cultural and ideological conditions of women's lives. It is time to investigate how feminist theorists see the interlocking of these.

Feminist theorists

It is generally accepted now that reflection in the social sciences has been deeply engraved by feminism. Sociology in particular has faced a challenge to its 'complacency and comfort zones' with a solid exposure of its assumptions and 'stereotypical' subject matter. Now, few of the accepted understandings of gender remain unscathed by feminist critique.[19]

Feminist social science was deposited on the shores of Western academia during the second half of the twentieth century by the 'second wave' of feminism. The earliest feminist social scientists were largely *conflict theorists*, emerging out of, and ultimately away from, a Marxist–socialist analysis. They had little time for functionalism, positivism, or indeed for any of the value-free approaches to social science theory. Along with other post-positivist theorists they were convinced that scientific knowledge is not value-neutral but carries the assumptions and tenets of prevailing orthodoxies; they went further than Marxist theorists, however, in maintaining it was not gender-neutral either. Instead, they regarded much traditional analysis as male-biased or unconsciously gendered. Julia Bristor expresses this strongly: 'what has been assumed to be universal unbiased knowledge produced by an objective science, is actually knowledge about men and men's problems produced by a masculine science.'[20]

New methodologies in research, therefore, involved being explicit about the gender base and gender implications of social science exploration. New goals of research aimed to bring every aspect of women's lives into scholarly focus.

From the mid-1960s onwards, studies analysing women's work, domesticity, socio-economic relations, and reproduction poured out from this new interest in gender and social science. It was a period so fertile that prolific shoots growing from roots long dormant became visible everywhere. Just a few examples from the UK can illustrate the upsurge in this persistent unearthing of gender. Hannah Gavron's PhD study, 'The Captive Wife', published posthumously in 1966 after her suicide, provided a probing, sociological account of the dilemmas of housebound mothers. In that year also, Juliet Mitchell's feminist polemic 'Women: The Longest Revolution' came out in the *New Left Review*, offering an exposé and analysis of women's 'oppression'. In 1965 Olive Banks, who later was the first woman to hold a chair in sociology, co-authored with her husband, Joe, *Feminism and Family Planning*, challenging the assumption that Victorian feminists led the way to enthusiasm for contraception. She went on to open up and develop the whole field of sociology of education.[21]

In 1969 Sheila Rowbotham's pamphlet 'Women's Liberation and the New Politics' argued that academic study needed to consider the oppression of women in cultural as well as economic terms. The following year, Kate Millet's *Sexual Politics* and Shulamith Firestone's *The Dialectics of Sex* both attempted to identify the basis of gender oppression. In 1972 Anne Oakley wrote *Sex, Gender and Society*, followed by *The Sociology of Housework* and *Housewife*, putting women's unpaid hours of labour, previously ignored as sociologically insignificant, under careful scrutiny. In 1973 Rowbotham's *Hidden from History: 300 Years of Women's Oppression and the Fight against It*[22] broke any remaining silence on women's experience of class oppression and sexism. In 1974 a conference on 'Sexual Divisions' organized by feminist sociologist Diana Leonard, and others in the women's movement, was held by the British Sociological Association. The papers, collected and edited by Leonard and Sheila Allen, were published in two volumes in 1976 as *Sexual Divisions and Society, Process and Change* and *Dependence and Exploitation in Work and Marriage*. In 1976 also Anne Oakley and Juliet Mitchell produced together *The Rights and Wrongs of Women*. The list could continue . . .

The 1970s and 1980s were highly productive years for feminist scholars in the UK, USA and Europe. Many studies highly critical of 'androcentric research' toppled old orthodoxies. Authors of books like *Another Voice: Feminist Perspectives on Social Life and*

Social Science (Marcia Millman and Rosabeth Moss Kanter) were not content with critique, but committed to revising and rewriting the very knowledge base of their particular discipline. By the middle of the 1980s, writers had become keenly interested in how the control of sexuality was part of the deployment of gender against women; feminist studies on the family began to unwrap issues of domestic violence, rape and child abuse. Michèle Barrett and Mary McIntosh's polemic book *The Anti-Social Family* (1982) exposed the vulnerabilities faced by women in intimate relationships. Not only was the personal political; it could also be very violent. It was not long before the concept of 'gender-based violence' was coined to encompass rape, domestic assault, incest and harassment. I have tried to show in this book that now it has to include selective abortion, FGM, child brides, honour killings, trafficking, prostitution, war and femicide. Even this list is not exhaustive.

Beneath the outpouring of work, different types of feminism were becoming evident, with divergent interests. A task I set myself in 1985 was to outline the range of views held by liberal feminists, Marxist feminists and radical feminists,[23] adding postmodern feminists to this list in 2000.[24] As the decades have gone on, the list has grown longer, and the ideological underpinnings of feminism have been seen to vary very significantly.

Despite their differences, most feminists are still agreed on three points. The first is that the social constructions of gender are woven into the organization of human societies and are fundamental to a person's life experiences. The second is that these constructs are culturally varied: people *learn* how to be men and women in specific contexts. The third is that gender, as a political dynamic, works through ideology and structures to establish women in positions of vulnerability. It is in this combination of gender constructions, social expectations, and economic and cultural vulnerability that violence against women receives its meaning and explanation.

To understand these points, feminist sociologists, psychologists and anthropologists look not just at childhood attachment, or at conflict within family systems, but at all the cultural predictors which frame our expectations. We see how gender values and ideologies become inculcated through habits and protocols, until they are part of normality in the lives of those who hold them. Feminist scholars examine the characteristics which a functionalist might see as maintaining social stability – 'deference', 'worth', 'status', 'dress', 'protocols', 'rituals', 'communication' – and identify them, instead, as interweaving factors in the transmission of values, ideology and 'meanings'. They analyse how such meanings are transmitted through societal structures, passed on through simple everyday routines and patterns, or inculcated deliberately through teaching or even indoctrination.

Since its early focus on domesticity, feminist social science has provided a wealth of cross-cultural research to show that the link between gender, culture and sexuality operates in the discourses of the family, economics, politics, social structures, jurisprudence, the military, history and religion. The presence or absence of laws, the understanding of human rights, the establishment of hierarchies and privileges, the restrictions on movement or dress, the value accorded to women, and the interpretation of religious instruction are all pivotal in the gendering of social reality. Within this context, we can begin to see the way gender-based violence becomes shaped, framed and normalized.

The second area of agreement is reflected in the Nigerian study I mentioned earlier. It is that societies everywhere are *patriarchal* where male predominance is widely accepted and where decision-making, institutions and ideas largely emanate from men. Women's voices have been muted and women's experiences been interpreted by men, and patriarchal cultures have systematically overlooked, discounted or misinterpreted the concerns of half the human race.

The third area of agreement is how attitudes – about sexuality, pornography, stereotypes, power and resources – increase women's vulnerability and allow the structures of patriarchy to provide the basic building blocks on which the great edifice of violence against women can be built. For gender-based violence is not different in kind from any other kind of oppression or disadvantage suffered by women in patriarchy; it is simply more total, more intimate and closer to issues of identity. It is time, then, to unpack the concept of *patriarchy* to see what it offers us.

Patriarchy

Max Weber introduced the concept of patriarchy into sociology a century ago to describe domestic organization in which the father dominated an extended kinship network and controlled the production of the household.[25] Half a century later, Kate Millett's *Sexual Politics* offered the term to denote 'the rule of men' – an all-pervasive, universal power relationship that penetrates all other forms of social divisions and leaves women, in some way or another, always oppressed.[26] Later feminists have become uncomfortable with this 'trans-historical' description of the nature of male dominance, arguing that in this objectified form it leaves little hope for change.[27] Nevertheless, the concept of patriarchy itself has persisted.

Feminists have wanted to establish the origins of patriarchy to understand how it is produced and maintained. Only then can we know what might bring about change. Gerder Lerner attempts to trace it back to the ancient Near East and Greece in the period 3100 to 400 BC, unearthing statements by classical Greek writers on the virtues of male and female which delineate the superiority of the man and subordination of the woman.

> Let us take first the virtue of a man – he should know how to administer the state, and in the administration of it to benefit his friends and harm his enemies; and he must also be careful not to suffer harm himself. A woman's virtue, if you wish to know about that, may also be easily described: her duty is to order her house, and keep what is indoors, and obey her husband.
>
> Plato, *Meno* 71e–f

Lerner maintains that the power of patriarchy has persisted down the centuries. Reinforced by symbol-systems, class elites and perpetuation of male rule, it has been manifest in every culture. Structures of patriarchy grow through the entwining of significant cultural areas of discourse, constructing ideas of what is 'masculine' or 'feminine' which have lived-out implications in psychological, economic, social, legal, even religious life. Lerner's own thesis leads her nevertheless to cautious optimism. Since patriarchy is historical in origin, it can be ended by historical process.[28] Societies can develop in new directions. Carol Christ similarly rejects the belief that it is in the *nature* of men to dominate women through violence: 'Patriarchy is a system that originated in history, which means that it is neither eternal nor inevitable. Some women and some men have resisted patriarchy throughout its history. We can join together to resist it today.'[29]

Many feminist writers have been quick to pinpoint the part played by religion in constructing and reinforcing patriarchy, arguing that across the globe religions have institutionalized and upheld the authority of men over women; they have reinforced gender stereotypes to the detriment of women, and created structures of control over women's freedom. More than 40 years ago, Robin Morgan, in *Sisterhood Is Powerful*, wrote that 'every organised patriarchal religion works overtime to contribute its own brand of misogyny to the myth of woman-hate, woman-fear, and woman-evil.'[30] Radical, post-Christian American feminist Mary Daly concluded that '[p]atriarchy itself is the prevailing religion of the entire planet'.[31] Contemporary feminist writer Kamla Bhasin feels India must work on issues of religion 'because all of them justify patriarchy'.[32] Mehrdad Darvishpour sees a need to eliminate religion altogether, for '[s]ecularism is an unavoidable prerequisite in women's battle for liberation'.[33] And, as far as Cath Elliot is concerned, 'Wherever religion and its patriarchs rule, women's lives are in danger.'[34]

Often writers lump religions together generically, seeing the very process of seeking authorization from some higher authority as detrimental to cultural freedom, especially freedom for women. In many societies, when a belief or practice is imbued with patriarchal religious authority it needs no further justification. Kamla Bhasin objects,

> When you question something, you are told, '*yeh toh hamara sanskar hai, riwaaj hai* (this is our culture, our tradition)'. And when this is done, it means logic has ended, belief has come in. So how does one argue with belief?[35]

Yet religions are very different from each other, and what constitutes religious authority is not always entirely clear. Is it to be found in the sacred texts of a religion, or in the religious hierarchies that interpret those writings and structure how they should be applied? Is it in pre-existent cultural tenets linked to biology and procreation which religions have incorporated into their own practices? Is it in the precedents of religious history and tradition, or in the new reforming movements, which read ancient wisdom in the light of new challenges? In fact, the relationship between women, men and religious belief is a complex and intricate one, varying considerably from one religion to another. It is also true that in some religious traditions, women have experienced positive empowerment and liberation which they see as emanating from their relation with God. I shall be taking up some of these questions in the final chapters.

Ten years after Lerner wrote *The Creation of Patriarchy*, Sylvia Walby mapped a series of overlapping structures found in patriarchal systems. In each of them, strong gender demarcations pointed to the stratification of women and men. Women were less likely to have power, income and representation; they were more likely to be underpaid, misrepresented, sexually exploited and subjected to violence.[36] These characteristics were evident within the state, the household, the economy, sexuality, culture and media. Social scientists in many societies have since observed such patterns. The Nigerian study saw them as highly significant in the demography of violence.

> The incidence of GBV [gender-based violence] breeds essentially on the lower status of women. Subordination is the central weapon to exercise patriarchal control over women and girls in Nigeria. It is successfully perpetuated through cultural and religious socialization to the degree that most girls and adolescent women in Nigeria grow into adult women believing that these occurrences are natural and divinely ordered. As a result, most often change is resisted by such women themselves as they tend to perceive messages about gender equality as an aberrance to cultural dictates of appropriateness of behaviour for women and men.[37]

The last point is very significant. Years of socialization can mean that women uphold the structures of patriarchy, while men also suffer its impositions. Psychologist Terrence Real acknowledges this when he talks of patriarchy as 'the unacknowledged paradigm of relationships that has suffused Western civilization generation after generation, deforming both sexes and destroying the passionate bond between them'.[38] For Real, even though experiences of victimhood remain gendered, and feed on the subordination of women, both women and men are its victims.

This paradigm has suffused not only *Western* civilization. Surveying the epidemic of gender violence in Delhi, Kamla Bhasin points to the paradox that the men who carry out the rape know they will be caught. So why do they rape? She agrees that they too are 'victims'; coarsened, hardened by patriarchy which has corrupted men to the extent that unless they begin to change, their humanity will be destroyed. Rape is not just a female problem. 'Our men don't need to change to support women, but to save themselves from being brutalised by centuries of exposure to patriarchy.'[39]

Bhasin is linking arms with veteran US feminist bell hooks, long-standing critic of patriarchal rhetoric. Echoing the point that patriarchy is kept in place by both women and men, she also grieves that 'patriarchal ideology brainwashes men to believe that their domination of women is beneficial when it is not'.[40] Instead, patriarchy produces a system in which men are emotional cripples, denied access to real freedom of will, yet without true knowledge of the desperate state that they are in. 'As long as men are brainwashed to equate violent domination and abuse of women with privilege, they will have no understanding of the damage done to themselves or to others, and no motivation to change.'[41]

This is not to deny that the various systems of male dominance, whether economic, domestic, legal or educational, subordinate women in particular and leave them more susceptible to abuse than men. It is rather to affirm the view of patriarchy as a dangerous structure, in which both women and men participate and suffer damage. Terrence Real depicts it graphically, describing it as a 'dance of contempt . . . a perverse form of connection that replaces true intimacy with complex covert layers of dominance and submission, collusion and manipulation'.[42] Clearly, in this 'tortured value system', no one benefits. Men may hold the power over women, but they pay for that 'power' with their own humanity.

The discourse on patriarchy has thus become more nuanced over the years. The concept itself has lost the connotations it acquired in Kate Millett's *Sexual Politics* as an entire, self-subsisting 'form of truth', separated from any socio-historical context',[43] and has become what Rosemary Hennessy describes as a 'variable and historical social totality'. Now, although the structures which organize social relations continue to reinforce male dominance, they are varied and different and are themselves 'sites of social struggle'.[44]

We have come a long way from Weber's offer of 'patriarchy' as a descriptive term for work and domestic organization. There is no sense now that this is a value-neutral term; values are deeply embedded in both its development and conceptualization; it calls for a moral as well as an analytic assessment. Patriarchy has become an overriding but complex term for the processes by which male power is grasped and imposed, and the ideologies and practices which reinforce women's vulnerability. For feminist theorists, understanding patriarchy involves us in the need to recognize it as ubiquitous, name it as destructive and then reject it as a 'cultural given'. It might be variable, but it remains a 'social totality'. As a system it is pathological. If women and men are ever to flourish in a context of mutual freedom, justice and empowerment, we must travel beyond patriarchy into a new social order.

Those who have followed the argument so far may be feeling that despite its powerful rhetoric, there is an intrinsic problem with this kind of analysis. If both women and men are victims of patriarchy, who then are the culprits? Who is responsible for its development, its maintenance and power? 'Patriarchy' still seems to be a reified force, with a life of its own which is separate from the human agents who make it operate. In many theories it appears as a conceptual, linguistic embodiment of destructive and inhuman forces, which holds people in its grip. Yet these same theories do not relinquish their view of human beings as actual and responsive agents. Surely, then, it makes only partial sense to lay the blame at the feet of abstract structures or social-economic processes in society, for structures are built by human beings; processes are adopted by men and women. What shapes patriarchy if it is not the institutions, ideas and attitudes which are devised by human persons? And if human beings are the agents by which patriarchy comes into force and gains its power, what does this say about the shape and meaning of our human personhood?

The debates about human personhood are on the fringes of social sciences, but, without doubt, assumptions about human identity undergird theories and research. Whether our understanding of the person is developmental, behavioural, autonomous, formed by class, ethnicity, gender, ideology, history or social institutions, it directs the character of our investigations and the explanations we adopt. Because many of the social sciences started out in the post-Enlightenment drive for rational autonomy, and have grown through postmodern re-evaluations and relativism, these have also influenced the notions of what it means to be human. We have looked at the complex interaction between culture and ideology in constructing the kinds of systems that initiate and sustain gender-based violence. It is time now to look in more depth at religion.

12

Religion and women

———•◆•◆•———

Religion is uniquely powerful and not to address it when it is at the core of a problem is analytically and sociologically naïve . . . Religions that cannot admit and work to correct their lethal errors and flawed heroes do not deserve to survive.[1]

Religion, in many women's lives, has been a force, if not the primary force, in shaping our acceptance of abuse. And as such it has sustained violence against women.[2]

Women's bodies are the common battleground, symbols of all religions' authority and identity.[3]

The last chapter closed on the issues of human personhood, and the need to look more carefully at religion. It is probably true that most campaigners against gender-based violence are sceptical about the value of religion for women. But of the seven billion human beings living on our planet, more than five and a half billion identify with a religion, and at least half of these are women. Around 32 per cent of the world's population is Christian, 25 per cent Muslim, and 15 per cent Hindu.[4] One billion and a half of the rest (16.3 per cent of global population) are 'unaffiliated', but this does not mean they are people without 'faith'. People who are ostensibly religious and people who are not all have levels of faith, accepting, 'on trust', ideas and attitudes which may become the bedrock of their lives. Everyone holds values and views which involve some prior assumptions and commitments.

The values people give to 'being human' are influenced by religious or philosophical positions. Those values might be ethical: centred on issues about how we should live, or they might be ontological: concerned about the very nature of what it means to be a person. Either way, they will affect how we conduct our relationships and what we see to be the point of living. Most religious or ideological systems have well-articulated ethical and ontological views about human life. Those views provide much of the vision, drive and motivation for the shape of culture, and the rules that govern the polity of human societies.

The sense that we live our lives before a higher authority – usually understood as God – separates most religious from secular worldviews. It challenges the self-sufficiency of the human person or society; it appeals to norms and principles laid down by God in the very structure of creation, principles which point to respect for life and justice and which are embodied in almost universally acknowledged moral codes. It believes in interdependence. It accepts the significance of human freedom and choice but recognizes its boundaries and limitations. It recognizes too, that though people have a huge capacity for knowledge and understanding, they are also prone to getting things wrong.

Consequently, ideas about human personhood in most historic religions may be at odds with ideas which predominate in Western secular societies. Any view which challenges human autonomy and recognizes the spiritual nature of life does not fit comfortably with the prevailing climate of materialism and naturalism. It is not that religion is anti-materialist; Christianity, with its focus on Incarnation and Resurrection, has a very thorough concept of the importance of body and matter. It is rather that, along with many religious traditions, it resists the reducing of human life to materialist definitions and values.

Religions are more than philosophical and theological systems, however. They are given visibility in institutions which embody cultural practices, stratification, roles and rituals. Even within a single religion, the shape and structures of these institutions can vary enormously, with traditions and customs often vying with one another for status and authority. The question of what constitutes true religious authenticity is asked of almost all religions, and the answer can be given in terms of both theological beliefs and institutional embodiment.

Ordinary human stories often show that authentic religion can be transformative, and not only at momentous times when it draws human life beyond the 'mechanics' of existence to a bigger picture of reality.[5] It can encourage spiritual awareness, help people into a relationship with God, open up paths to forgiveness and healing, protect and empower the vulnerable. It can also give people a deeper understanding of relational responsibility, issuing prophetic challenges to injustice. Some of the world's most liberating movements have been (and are) shaped by faith in God, and driven by prayer.

Yet when religion manifests itself as a crude exercise of human will and control, it is anything but liberating. Freedom of choice and the dignity of women have both been casualties. In their bid to direct human societies along lines of 'divine approval', the world's religious systems have helped shape the structures of patriarchy, privileging the male and subordinating the female. It has often taken emancipating voices within to challenge this as spiritual blindness.

Religious power and gender control

Many writers have seen all religions as contributing indiscriminately to the process of gender control, where biological ideas of procreation and psychological notions of temperament or character have often melded with religious ideas about worth. These have served to hold women in check and left the door open for abuse. Gendered precepts and ideas, maintained by religious professionals through religious culture and ritual, have proved formidable in their strength and tenacity.

> Islam is interpreted in ways that justify women's inequality. Women's subordinate status is evident not only in the Islamic faith, but also within Buddhist culture, and in Hindu & Sikh ideologies. Just look at what happens to women in the poorer strata of societies in Bangladesh & India, Myanmar, Cambodia, Indonesia, even Malaysia, and the Philippines. What about Christianity? What does the abused woman hear when she turns to the scriptures? She is reminded of the Christian ideals of sacrificial love, acceptance of suffering, humility, meekness, turning the other cheek . . .[6]

The subtext here is that religion has provided both the institutional practice and the ideological underpinning for violence against women. Sacred texts themselves – the foundational documents of religious identity – have been used to justify harsh treatment of women. Whether we consider the ancient Hindu practice of *sati*, where the widow is immolated on her husband's funeral pyre (*Rig Veda Samhita* 10.18.7), the Qur'anic instruction to strike a troublesome wife (*Sura An-Nisa* 4.34), the labelling of women in Buddhist texts as uncontrolled, envious, irritable and greedy (*Anguttara Nikaya* section II.82.3), the gang rape and murder of a concubine in the Hebrew Scriptures (Judges 19), or submission for Christian women (Ephesians 5), gender inequality has been said to leave women vulnerable to male brutality. Research, undertaken both by secular social scientists and scholars from within religious traditions, has studied gender violence in relation to an array of religious expression and found that even in those religions reputed for non-violence, gender relations often follow predictable patterns of female oppression. Scholars have charged Sikh communities with treating girls like commodities, committing 'appalling crimes' against them,[7] accused Buddhism of being 'relentlessly misogynist',[8] and blamed Jainism for justifying domestic violence. One study found the high incidence of wife-beating among Jains to be 'startling'. It concludes:

> Religion, however much it sanctions nonviolence and requires strict adherence to peaceable ethics, does not inoculate individuals against woman abuse ... Although an overwhelming majority of Jain participants claimed they clung to the most significant code of their religion, active nonviolence, nearly 52% men and 18% women viewed violence as a satisfactory method of treating 'misbehaving' wives.[9]

In these and other religions there are vocal advocates and campaigners for changes in cultural practice, insisting that such practices are deviant, and must change to reflect more accurately the actual religious teaching. But there are also those who claim that it is the theology and teachings themselves that produce these disturbing patterns. To examine this, I will focus on just two religious traditions: the Muslim and the Judeo-Christian. Islam bears the reputation of producing woman-oppressive cultures, so I need to look at Islam and gender-based violence. I do so, however, as a sympathetic outsider, listening to others.

Islam and patriarchy

In an article on 'Recovering from Religious Patriarchy' an anonymous woman reflects on her experience of marriage as a Muslim:

> [T]he standards . . . of what a non-abusive marriage ought to be like didn't seem to be something that I could be justified in aspiring to. According to what we were taught, a man is supposed to be the head of the household, and a good wife obeys her husband. She does not have the right to work – or even to leave the house, in most cases – if he forbids her . . . If a husband reminds his wife to 'fear God' when she opposes him, or threatens to divorce her or to take another wife, or tells her that God will not be pleased with her if she does not do X, he would not be seen as abusive, but as living up to his God-given role . . . [P]eople would parse verses from the Qur'an, or hadiths, or the views of scholars past and present. Never was it presented to us in a larger context, as the ways and means that abusers the world over use against those they abuse.[10]

One of her readers who had left the Islamic faith responded with a snapshot of her own experience:

> Islam is anti-science, anti-woman, undemocratic, patriarchal, and downright vulgar . . . Being a Muslimah was a torturous experience. Always watched, always condemned, always lectured to, always criticized – why women think this is such a great experience, such a great lifestyle, so freeing!, is beyond my imagination . . . The happiest day of my life was when I left Islam. I took off the Hijab and when I felt the wind flowing through my hair, I realized how wonderful it is to be free from perpetual servitude and slavery to the opinions and regards of others.[11]

These are two of hundreds of public testimonies from women who found being a Muslim very restrictive. Social media have spread these messages across the world. The hijab in particular has been the focus of much passion. The image of feeling the wind flowing through unveiled hair has emboldened many young women to share their own search for freedom. One, Reem Abdel-Razek, believes that, for her, a whole associated identity change was needed:

> The only way I could take my life back was by unveiling, not only my hair but also my true nature. I would have to obliterate the persona that I was so carefully moulded into, in order to discover who I really was.[12]

Another expresses anger at her previous acceptance of disapproval: 'no matter how much I covered up, face veil and gloves and humiliation after humiliation. My husband was never happy with me.'[13] Another conforms outwardly but rebels internally:

> 'Your breast curves are showing. Your top is too tight. Cover it properly or else you will stay at home today.' They order me. I shut out my mind when they start preaching. I carry on with the rituals as their wish. I lie. I cheat. I fake. I don't question them anymore. I do as they say . . . Every morning, as I pin my hijab meticulously, I remind the girl in the mirror that she should not let her leash define her or constrain her.[14]

Many such despondent testimonies have been shared of women's struggles with identity and their need for wholeness. Yet, however painful, accounts of women's experiences of oppression within Islam do not automatically identify Islam itself as a misogynist religion. Background culture and religious mores can be very entangled and confused. As everywhere, context is important; in Western secular contexts some Muslim women have deliberately chosen to wear the hijab as a mark of their identity as women of faith.[15] For a broader judgement as to whether the Islamic religion is gender-oppressive, we need to reflect on its belief system, its structure, its intellectual traditions and how all these relate to its legacy and culture.

Islamic scholars often identify three quite different levels or 'strands' of Islam, each of which some might see as 'Islam proper'.[16] In its first and most fundamental level, Islam is based on its primary sources: the Qur'an, accepted by most Muslims as the revealed Word of Allah, and the *sunna*, the way of life, based on the normative sayings and activities of the Prophet Muhammad. From these primary sources comes a second strand – what has been called the 'complex, detailed Islamic intellectual legacy'. This forms a number of disciplines, for example: law (sharia), ethics, exegesis, dialectics, philosophy and aesthetics.[17] A third strand is the wide range of Muslim practices, lifestyles, activity, rules, drawn from the first two expressions of Islam. These are also likely to be nuanced by local culture, ethnicity and tradition, much of which might be less evidently related to Islam.

For many people, both within and outside Islam, these strands are not separated or distinctly identified. Many hold a conventional view of law (sharia) as central to Islamic identity, and see culture mandated to express respect for law. Some also insist that the Qur'an can be applied from its seventh-century Arabian origin directly into all and every culture today. Then there are those who know 'Islam' only from the media, and struggle to distinguish 'ordinary Muslims' who go about normal daily lives from 'Islamic militants' who make the headlines with their appalling atrocities. By and large, people's assumptions about the nature of Islam, gleaned from several varied sources, remain unchallenged. There is little recognition that there might be differences between the 'Islam' defined by cultural nuances, the 'Islam' legitimated by the (male) authorities of the intellectual legacy and the 'Islam' that reflects the primary sources. It is left to penetrating and radical scholars like Amina Wadud to ask the fundamental question, 'Is "Islam" what Muslims do, what governments establish, what the intellectual legacy says or what the primary sources imply?'[18]

That question is clearly a significant one, although few may be qualified to answer it. Wadud herself emphasizes the primary sources, but also insists that these must be read aright. Yet who does read them aright? In framing that question, we might look at the messages and signals that various strands emit about the value of women and justification of violence.

Intellectual legacy – whose voice counts?

Already in this book I have identified injustices to women, worryingly evident in Muslim-majority cultures, injustices like domestic violence, acid attacks, child brides, FGM, honour killing and femicide. These incidents in Islamic cultures are now reported very fully in the West, which has both positive and negative impacts. It is positive that injustice is being exposed, and international opinion mobilized, to put the elimination of violence against women firmly on the agenda across the world. It is negative when this exposure is then used as implicit justification for armed attack on countries perceived to be 'enemies of the West'.

Patriarchy is not the property of Islam alone. Some appalling practices towards women can be found in many cultures. In assessing whether Islam is irredeemably misogynist and how Islam actually values women, we do need to hear the authentic Islamic voice. Yet we return to the problem above. Is the authentic Islamic voice contained in the pronouncements of Muslim leaders, when they deliver their fatwas, and injunctions to kill? Is it in the activities of vigilante groups like Ansar-e-Hezbollah in Iran, whose members enforce social laws, pressuring women into dressing conservatively, and confronting unmarried couples seen together in public? Is it in the sermons of those clerics who have hit the headlines with their warped and twisted attitudes towards girls?

If it is any of these, it becomes very easy to understand the discontent and despair expressed by ex-Muslim women. Take the horrible story of Sheikh Fayhan al-Ghamdi, Islamic scholar and television preacher in Saudi Arabia, who killed his five-year-old daughter in 2012 after beating, torturing and allegedly raping her. His claim, that he was driven to this because of his fear that she had lost her virginity, combined with her inability to recite full verses from the Qur'an, shows both warped gender attitudes and his assumption of unquestionable authority over her life. Horrifyingly, the Saudi legal authorities seemed to concur, punishing him with a mere $50,000 fine. Only after international pressure was he given an eight-year prison sentence; then a few months later, in 2014, he was reported to have been released again.[19]

In 2013 another Saudi cleric, Sheikh Mohammed Al-Arefi, had issued a fatwa allowing jihadist militants in Syria to rape non-Sunni women – referring back to a Qur'anic provision for 'temporary marriage' (*nikā al-mut'ah*) which may last for only a few hours. He had previously insisted that a girl should not be alone with her father or dress in a way that might make her sexually attractive to him. This grim interpretation of the Islamic legacy offers little more than horror for non-Sunni women, and fear for growing Sunni girls.[20] Its view of fatherhood is far from the mature, loving care which Muslim girls have a right to expect. Yet another Saudi, Sheikh Abdullah Daoud, reinforced the fearful image when he insisted that all little girls, including newborn babies, must wear the burka to put them beyond male temptation.[21] Among many Muslims this sparked outrage, and prompted Mirna Yacob to suggest that male pronouncements which blame women for the sins of men show dogmatic weaknesses inherent in Islam itself.

> In Islamic dogma, these men (who molest their child daughters) are seen as the victims. A girl is a sexual creature. Hence it is her responsibility to spare men around her the agony of desire for if she does not, she will ultimately be responsible for her own molestation. The daughter is a sexual temptress in front of her father. The rapist is the victim of her wiles.
>
> In this universe of divine patriarchy, a female is defined by her eternal guilt, a shameful criminal responsible for her own violation and victimhood ... Exposing and opposing the injustice of this guilt and blame will bring down the house of Islamic patriarchy.[22]

We can understand the reactions from ex-Muslim women against the 'spirituality' 'which punishes females for being female'. One insists: 'this cannot possibly be from a Merciful Creator.'[23] The Islamic historical legacy is criticized for its overwhelming tendency to give men the right to tell women how to be women; to define, in Riffat Hassan's words, what constitutes the 'ontological, theoretical, sociological and eschatological status of Muslim women'. She believes that if women continue to be defined as theologically inferior, the battle for any political or economic rights will not go very far.[24]

However, Zohreh Abdekhodaie rejects the idea that Islam sees women as inferior, claiming 'the faith was initially a kind of feminist movement, especially when seen in its historical context'.[25] Certainly, when the implicit 'right to define' is publicly challenged by an authoritative and intelligent woman, wearing the hijab, it can be dramatic. We saw this in March 2015 when a London-based

Islamist scholar was interviewed on television by Lebanese presenter Rima Karaki. He had strayed from the subject of the interview, and she tried to bring him back to the point, but his anger erupted at not being allowed to say whatever he wished. In asserting his authority over hers, he told her to 'shut up' and that it was beneath him to be interviewed by her, a woman. Her swift response was to take him off mike, leaving him mouthing without sound, and countering his rudeness with her comment: 'either there is mutual respect or the conversation is over.' The video went viral, prompting thousands of supportive comments![26]

For an increasing number of faithful Muslims, these strident male clerics who define and decry the dignity of women, and blame them for the sexual waywardness of men, are definitely *not* the authentic voices of Islam. Their absolutist understandings of the Qur'an and *sunna* are used to discriminate against women and pressure communities and individuals to adhere to particular ways of life. Simply because such voices claim certainty, and appeal to intellectual legacy, does not confer on them the authority of being its guardians.

Sharia and its application

At the root of these kinds of attitudes from religious teachers lies sharia, believed by Muslims to be the divine law revealed in the Qur'an and *sunna*. Islamic jurisprudence (*fiqh*) defines the terms of the sharia, especially interpreting rules for morality, rituals and social legislation. Sharia is upheld throughout the Islamic world, even though different Islamic cultures may produce different interpretations; yet common throughout the Muslim legal tradition are different requirements legislated for women and men. The Qur'anic theological premise – that authority over women has been granted to men – is reflected in family law especially, producing judgments generally regarded as favouring males.

Different interpretations and different expressions of *fiqh* depend on which of the four schools of Islamic jurisprudence is being used. They also vary with the particular customs of the country. In Muslim-majority societies sharia is strongly integrated into their law codes; in Saudi Arabia it is the law of the land. But even when other systems of law exist alongside sharia, in almost all of these societies classical *fiqh* rulings will govern family affairs. Sharia courts also exist in non-Muslim countries to adjudicate family law for those of the faith, including in a number of Western countries. Wherever there is a conflict, laws claimed to be based on sharia will take precedence, at least in principle.

The conflicts, however, can be considerable. Under sharia, for example, though a woman may have only one husband, a man may have up to four wives (Sura 4.3). This, of course, is bigamy under most non-Muslim legal systems. In the implementation of sharia, also, women lack the equality built into most modern juridical systems. Their permission is not required for their husband to take other wives, they live under male guardianship, have limited rights of movement, occupy lower status as witnesses, can be divorced without their consent and are required to obey strict dress codes. In Saudi Arabia, women are not even allowed to drive.

There is plenty of scope, however, for different interpretations. The dress code is basically a requirement to dress 'modestly' – a perfectly reasonable prerequisite that most Muslim women choose to respect in most cultures. Dressing modestly is a mark of many religious traditions; witness the dress habits of Christian nuns or the plain attire of Amish women. Christian 'modesty' in the New Testament meant not wearing lots of jewellery or spending hours on appearance.[27] Modesty in many cultures means not showing excessive amounts of skin. However, in Muslim-majority countries it requires the complete covering of a woman's body, including hiding facial features behind the abaya, niqab or burka. No choice is offered for other interpretations; in countries like Iran, Sudan or Afghanistan, failure to comply with modesty laws can elicit violent responses from the authorities towards the women concerned. Even in non-Muslim countries women are at risk; in Italy a young Moroccan woman was attacked and beaten by two Moroccan men for 'offending Islam' when she refused to wear a headscarf.[28]

Dress codes are only one aspect of women's obligations under sharia. The male guardianship requirement places the married woman under submission to her husband, whose permission she needs even to leave the house. Staying single does not confer any independence, as she then comes under the supervision of her nearest male relative. Guardianship extends to the next generation also, as the custody of the father overrules that of the mother with regard to children. The former wife of Sheikh Fayhan al-Ghamdi lives with the tragic consequences of this for her daughter.

There seems little doubt that where sharia is strongly enforced it leaves less room for women's freedom, as generally understood in international law. It structures inequality into the everyday lives of women and men, which can leave women very vulnerable to abuse and violence. It's a problem articulated by legal anthropologist Ziba Mir-Hosseini, when she insists that the prevailing interpretations of the sharia do not reflect the core values of her faith and argues for a proper distinction between sharia and *fiqh*.[29] Men's 'unilateral rights' to divorce and polygyny are 'juristic constructs that follow from the way that early Muslim jurists conceptualized and defined marriage'. In other words, these 'rights' were 'not granted to them by God but by Muslim male jurists'.[30] Zainah Anwar agrees: 'Human engagement with the divine text produces laws that are fallible and open to change, given changing times and circumstances.'[31] For Amina Wadud, without women's engagement sharia is thoroughly patriarchal:

> You cannot legislate with regard to the well-being of women without women as agents of their own definition . . . Sharia was happy to legislate for women, even to define what is the proper role of women, and to do so without women as participants.[32]

Wadud cautions against re-implementing sharia law by taking decisions, conclusions and codes from the old system and applying them 'in situations that are absolutely incongruent with the original circumstances in which they were made'.[33] Her own envisaged re-implementation of sharia is one that wrestles the 'eternal system away from its contextual foundation' and expresses 'just and fair articulations of the divine will in our context'.[34] The wide consensus among these feminist scholars is that, though sharia is sacred, universal and eternal, *fiqh* is the interpretation of human minds and, like any other system of jurisprudence, subject to change.

The primary sources: Qur'an and sunna

Those who have left the Islamic faith usually leave behind also any confidence in the primary sources of Islamic law and theology: the Qur'an and *sunna*. The *sunna* – sayings and doings of Muhammad, recorded in *hadith*, now become the focus of critical rejection, rather than the way of life. The differences within Islam (not least between Sunni and Shia Muslims) as to what is regarded as authentic *hadith* collections are, of course significant, but for the committed Muslim, the *sunna* contains revealed divine will. Ex-Muslims, however, often cite the negative statements about women in well-known *hadiths*, including from Bukhari (d. 870), regarded as a reliable compiler. A few examples quickly make the point:

> The Prophet said, 'I looked at Paradise and found poor people forming the majority of its inhabitants; and I looked at Hell and saw that the majority of its inhabitants were women.'
> (Bukhari, Hadith 4.464)

> I heard the Prophet saying, 'Evil omen is in three things: The horse, the woman and the house.' (Bukhari, Hadith 4.110)

> If a man invites his wife to sleep with him and she refuses to come to him, then the angels send their curses on her till morning.
> (Bukhari, Hadith 7.62)

> The Prophet said, 'Isn't the witness of a woman equal to half of that of a man?' The women said, 'Yes.' He said, 'This is because of the deficiency of a woman's mind.' (Bukhari, Hadith 826)[35]

This *hadith* is often seen alongside the Qur'an in Sura 2.282 which says:

> And let two men from among you bear witness to all such documents [contracts of loans without interest]. But if two men be not available, there should be one man and two women to bear witness so that if one of the women forgets (anything), the other may remind her.[36]

Both *sunna* and Qur'an contain passages which present women as the sexual property of men, especially in allowing rape of slave girls, encouraging polygamy, condoning wife-beating (Sura 4.34) and endorsing child marriage (Qur'an in Sura 65.1, 4 – where rules are given for divorcing prepubescent wives). The Prophet himself was polygamous and, according to most reliable sources, one of his later wives, Aisha, was indeed a child: '[T]hen he [Muhammad] wrote the marriage (wedding) contract with Aisha when she was a girl of six years of age, and he consumed (consummated) that marriage when she was nine years old' (Bukhari, Volume 7, Hadith 62–4; see also Aisha's account in Sahih Al-Bukhari, Volume 5, Book 58, Hadith 234).

In one *hadith* the Prophet is said to encourage another man to do the same: 'Jabir also said: Allah's Apostle said, "Why didn't you marry a young girl so that you might play with her and she with you?' (Bukhari, Volume 7, Book 42, Hadith 17).

Critical discussions on the Prophet Muhammad remain off-limits in most commentaries, and the usual responses are to suggest that Aisha was older than it appears, she had an early puberty after which the marriage was consummated, and that she became herself a spiritual religious leader which puts the marriage in a different category.

There is more discussion, however, about the passage in the Qur'an, Sura 4.34. Although many interpretations work hard to soften the instructions on how to treat uncooperative wives, this sura remains, for many, a justification for domestic violence: 'If you fear high-handedness from your wives, remind them, then ignore them when you go to bed, then hit them.'

Many websites are now dedicated to refuting this reading.[37] Yet former Muslim Nonie Darwish deplores the refusal of Muslims to acknowledge that violence is the fruit of Qur'anic teaching:

> At least 5,000 reported honor killings happen annually in the name of Allah, but moderate Muslims insist that, too, has nothing to do with Islam, and is a hold-over tribal custom, despite the Sura and verses that are used to justify it [Qur'an 18:65–81].

For her, as long as both teachings and practice are not rebuked, atrocities against women will continue.[38] Qur'anic scholar Asma Barlas has a different approach. She insists that the Qur'an supports complete gender equality, but patriarchy has been read into

its teachings.[39] Younger scholar Zohreh Abdekhodaie offers uncon-
ditional commitment to the Qur'an, even rejecting the suggestion
that it might have absorbed a patriarchal outlook from the society
in which it was revealed. 'Rather, it influenced and influences the
society. Therefore, for me the Qur'ān is not only the Word of God,
but also it is a criterion that I can use as a tool.'[40]

Islamic feminism and reinterpretation

Islam and feminism have often been seen as utterly opposed. At the
1995 World Conference on Women in Beijing, neo-traditionalist
Muslim women contested the Convention on the Elimination
of All Forms of Discrimination Against Women (CEDAW) as
anti-Islamic. Amina Wadud linked this both to antipathy towards
the West, and failure to distinguish the Islamic primary sources
and contextual legal constructions. But many women have faced
a painful choice between their gender-justice awareness, and their
culturally prescribed identity as Muslims. In 1987 a group of women
lawyers in Malaysia had begun to meet around the question: if
God and Islam were just, why did laws and policies made in the
name of Islam create injustice? Becoming 'Sisters of Islam', they
discussed sharia family law implementation issues, held workshops
and published booklets on law and Qur'an.

Over the past decade, Muslim feminists have moved to the
forefront of advocacy both for Islam and women's rights, drawing on what they hold as the Qur'anic concept of the equality of
all human beings and the empowerment of women. Feminist
groups have grown, including the influential Malaysian initiative
in 2009, *Musawah*, 'Global Movement for Equality and Justice
in the Muslim Family', which stands firmly against the idea that
Islam mandates injustice. Zakia Salime made a careful sociological
study of very successful Islamist and feminist groups in Morocco,
showing how their organizational abilities, hopes and struggles
echo and inform one another.[41] Yet, as Ziba Mir-Hosseini explains,
even 'Islamic feminists' do not speak with one voice. While they
all seek gender justice and equality, they often disagree about what
constitutes justice or equality, or how it can be achieved. Inevitably,

like all feminist positions, they are 'local, diverse, multiple and evolving'.[42]

My focus here can only be on one main question: how feminist scholars resolve the 'patriarchal implications' in Islam's primary sources. Zainah Anwar gives a swift answer: 'we want to emphasize that everything we understand of Islam comes from human intervention with the word of God'.[43] Amina Wadud acknowledges the original articulation of Islam *is* patriarchal but sees the problem as a 'functional displacement' rather than an aspect of Islam's universality. Patriarchal interpretations of the Qur'an have, however, shaped Muslim societies so new engagement in Qur'anic hermeneutics must open up another direction.[44] When it becomes normal to read the text in context, to deconstruct patriarchal interpretations of the Qur'an and to make *fundamental* Qur'anic principles the basis for new reading, the divine intention towards women will be better understood. The move has to be from 'the text of the Qur'an to the heart of the Qur'an'.[45]

The Qur'an's call to justice is the suggested grid through which Muslims should approach the text, and override both its silence (as on slavery) and its androcentrism (as on gender). This has loud echoes of the 'hermeneutics of suspicion' employed in biblical scholarship by Catholic feminist Elisabeth Schüssler Fiorenza back in 1983. Rejecting the notion of objectivity of both the text and the scholar, Fiorenza addressed what she saw as their patriarchal and androcentric bias, then reconstructed Christian history to reclaim women's part in it.[46] Islamic feminists begin in a similar place, honouring the Qur'an, but rejecting the possibility of a non-subjective interpretation. For Barlas, 'to be human is to live a life that is politically, economically, sexually, culturally and historically situated'.[47] For Wadud, the Qur'anic text is a central means for transformation, 'provided the hermeneutical implications are accepted [and] . . . both the historical intellectual tradition and the current intellectual considerations are seen as integral . . . and prerequisites to actual social reforms'.[48]

Qur'anic feminism is clearly important work in progress. Wadud's own hermeneutics takes a postmodern direction, going far beyond the exegetical process of unearthing textual meaning through linguistics, etymology, syntax, cross-referencing and grammar. Having already argued for a framework of egalitarianism as the interpretative construct, she now gives more authority to the human readers to 'dance the delicate dance between text and agency to assert a movement of complete gender justice'. We are the makers of textual meaning. The results of meaning-making is the reality we establish from those meanings to human experiences and social justice.[49]

The Qur'an is given, but its meaning is in our hands. It is a brave assertion, yet one heavily contested, even by younger Islamic women scholars, since 'the best source of exegesis for the Qur'an is the Qur'an itself, because of its infallibility and consistency'.[50] The gap between Wadud's 'Islam' and that of the prevailing systems remains wide.

Changes to Islamic gender culture will have to come through its Qur'anic sages, young and established, as they challenge the authenticity of a monolithic, aggressive, global Islam. We need thoughtful scholars to pursue their gender-justice hermeneutics, and feminist Muslims to help lead the eradication of violence against women. At the same time, ISIS continues its relentless barbarism and bloodshed, Boko Haram keeps hundreds of Nigerian girls in captivity, Islamic regimes enact oppressive laws, and honour killings continue across the world. Culture is powerful. The battle for justice and righteousness may be long and hard. Yet the witness of thousands of peace-seeking Muslims across the world, who honour their faith, love their families and work tirelessly for the common good, brings optimism and hope.

13

Christianity and gender: a fuller picture

―――――•◦•―――――

At its most repugnant, the belief that women must be subjugated to the wishes of men excuses slavery, violence, forced prostitution, genital mutilation and national laws that omit rape as a crime.[1]

Human life possesses an intrinsic dignity and value because it is created by God in his own image for the distinctive destiny of sharing in God's own life.[2]

As a Christian this may be the most difficult chapter for me to write. Both an insider and an observer of a tradition which spans centuries, I have a responsibility to listen to critics, especially critics who tell the truth. Feminists have been pointing out for 50 years that the patriarchy afflicting all religions is evident in Christianity's long history. They are right. In gender attitudes, family roles, institutional structures, church history, religious hierarchies, authorship and theological interpretations the evidence is there.

It's easy to see the strong, set lines of patriarchy in the public face of the Church. Centuries of male popes, patriarchs, cardinals, archbishops, bishops, priests, clergy, elders, overseers and theologians have led the flock, exegeted the Scriptures, written the agendas and preached the sermons. Authority has been often subtly transferred from the Scriptures to the magisteria (of whatever denomination). Inerrancy has been built into papal edicts. Biblical interpretations of gender inequality have been elevated as a mark of orthodoxy. From early in church history, men have defined women's sexuality, and presented it as a problem. Anxiety about its tempting allure drove celibate monks into the desert;[3] fear of its potency led to the persecution of ordinary women as witches.[4] The need to control women's sexuality has therefore shaped policies of church and family governance, reinforcing female submission to male authority.[5] The strange and silly comments issued by church 'Fathers' show not only that fear was mixed with contempt, but also that their gender attitudes owed more to pagan Greek philosophy than the Christian gospel.[6] A few examples make the point:

> Every woman should be filled with shame at the thought that she is a woman . . . the consciousness of their own nature must evoke feelings of shame.
>
> St Clement of Alexandria (*c*.150–*c*.215), *Paedagogus*

> You are the devil's gateway . . . The image of God, the man Adam, you broke him, it was child's play to you. You deserved death, and it was the son of God who had to die.   Tertullian (160–223)

> It does not profit a man to marry. For what is a woman but an enemy of friendship, an inescapable punishment, a necessary evil, a natural temptation, a domestic danger, delectable mischief, a fault in nature, painted with beautiful colours? . . . The whole of her body is nothing less than phlegm, blood, bile, rheum and the fluid of digested food . . .   St John Chrysostom (*c*.347–407)

> There is something not good in the number two . . . while scripture on the first, third fourth and sixth days relates that having finished the works of each God saw that it was good, on the second day He omitted this altogether, leaving us to understand that two is not a good number because it prefigures the marriage contract.
>
> St Jerome (342–420)

> To embrace a woman is to embrace a sack of dung.
>
> Odo of Cluny (*c*.878–942), *Patralogia Latina*

> Woman is a misbegotten man . . . What she cannot get, she seeks to obtain through lying and diabolical deceptions . . . [S]o one must be on one's guard with every woman, as if she were a poisonous snake and the horned devil . . .   St Albertus Magnus (*c*.1200–80)

These much-quoted comments show what some early church leaders thought about women and helped produce generations of bigotry, yet, we must note, they have no theological status. They are simply offensive, misogynous noises. As a Catholic ethicist has pointed out: 'Fathers of the church and great scholastic doctors not only at times uncritically repeat the sexist truisms inherited from the secular culture of their day, but sometimes interpret the theological tradition in light of those assumptions.'[7] That is probably why Pope John Paul II felt it necessary to issue an abject apology for his spiritual forebears! His words were very welcome: 'If objective blame [for offences against the dignity of women], especially in particular historical contexts, has belonged to not just a few members of the Church, for this I am truly sorry.'[8]

The apology is important, not just to acknowledge and rebuff centuries of gratuitous rudeness, but because gender inequality and misogyny often lie at the base of violence against women.

Gender inequality in the Church today

Christianity has not been involved in many of the forms of gender-based violence which we looked at in earlier chapters. Selective abortion, honour killings, acid attacks, bride burning and trafficking are abhorrent to humanity and rarely, if ever, encountered in Christian contexts. Approval of child marriage does occur within some communities, but is limited to countries like Ethiopia. Yet there is widespread evidence for intimate-partner violence. Destructive abuse in Christian families echoes the same pathological human brokenness seen throughout this book, even though hidden from public view. It often goes with an overt or subconscious belief in male privilege and entitlement, by which men assume rights to freedom, status and opinions not applicable to their partner. We don't hear about it, because much of the abuse of women in 'Christian' homes is not brought under the searchlight of the Christian faith; it stays hidden and unrecognized, sometimes even by victims. The work of Nancy Nason-Clark and Catherine Clark Kroeger opens up some of the reasons why.[9] They also identify why many women victims feel disappointed when they do seek help from the Church. In their study, 83.2 per cent of pastors had counselled an abused woman yet only 8 per cent of them felt equipped to respond to domestic violence.[10] Ninety-five per cent of church women reported they had never heard any sermon preached against abuse.[11]

Kiara's story reflects many others. A Christian victim of intimate-partner abuse, she did not identify it as such, because anger attacks from her well-respected husband were verbal and emotional; his bursts of temper were spasmodic. Yet immediately following their wedding, his Jekyll and Hyde characters emerged:

> [He would be] incredibly sweet one moment, and explosive the next. I never knew what would set him off, and walked on eggshells constantly. He was extremely verbally abusive, manipulative, and played head games, often making me feel crazy . . . But I continued to stay, always praying, always hoping that he would change back into the man I had known before we were married. I thought, he hasn't hit me, so it's not that bad, I can stay.

From then on, all the classic symptoms of denial and blame became manifest:

> He said the problems in our marriage were because of me, that he didn't have a problem . . . if I would just be better, [then] he wouldn't have to get angry. So I fixed his favourite gourmet meals, cleaned the house, said the right things and tried to change myself, thinking he would stop being angry. But he always found something else to be angry about.

If she had hoped for understanding from church members, she got none. Their 'pious' attitudes reinforced her vulnerability and left him free to heap spiritual abuse on her, gravely damaging her own faith.

> I also spoke with people in the church about what was going on and the response was always to pray about it and try to be more 'submissive'. During this time I slipped further and further into depression, often feeling suicidal, and also shared this with people in the church. Again, they just prayed, and said God would work it out. This was another area where he was abusive, spiritually, often saying, 'Why would God answer you? Look at you! You're so horrible, God wouldn't talk to you. You're in sin and God won't bless you. He blesses and uses me all the time.' For some time this destroyed my faith and relationship with God to the point where I stopped praying or trying. I started to believe that God saw me this way and that I must deserve his (my husband's) abuse since I'm a 'bad person'.

One day, five years into marriage, when the abuse had become physical, she reached out and dialled the police. Her husband backed off instantly, and she put the phone down, but the police traced her and turned up within 15 minutes. Seeing the evidence through their eyes was a revelation: her bruises, her trauma, his damage to walls and furnishings, and the police's immediate decision to arrest him all enabled her to recognize the truth of her situation.

Now divorced, with protection from her former husband, Kiara has got her life back. She moved church, away from those who criticized her for not 'trusting God' and not giving the abuser another chance; and she regained her faith. She was eventually able to thank God for the arrest: 'I believe in God and know that He kept me through this and directed [the outcome]. He doesn't want anyone in an abusive relationship. I know this now.'[12]

This is one story of so many across the globe: stories of public humiliation, threats, control, violence and manipulation from 'respected Christian men' who quote Scripture about submission, love and forgiveness. Prevalent in the USA as in Africa or Asia,[13] it continues despite widely held Christian insistence that there is no justification for it.[14] The question is not whether this problem exists, but why. Could it be linked to an immutable authoritarian theology where '*someone* needs to be in charge, *someone* needs to have the final authority' and that *someone* is the man?[15] Or have overriding cultural views validating heavy-handed male authority been superimposed on the Christian faith, reinforcing Mary Daly's allegation: '(p)atriarchy is itself the prevailing religion of the entire planet'?[16] For misogyny is certainly no stranger to Christianity.

Feminism, theology and the Bible

These issues began to be unravelled in the feminist upsurge in the second half of the twentieth century. Theology, as well as social science, was impacted. Feminist groups, like the Catholic Women's Network and the US Evangelical Women's Caucus, debated not just structures and practice, but doctrine and interpretation. Christian Women's Resource Centres – in London, Oxford (CWIRES) and Massachusetts – amassed libraries of theological material. Newsletters, conferences and publications swept through feminist Christian circles. Some feminists called for 're-imagining' – a reworking of God and gender – which would be truly liberational in the lives of women. Others advocated leaving the faith, convinced that gender abuse is supported by theology, and leaves no space for authentic women.

It was no longer enough to absorb a few women into leadership structures. Nothing but an uprooting of centuries of patriarchy would be sufficient. For that, language, worship, authority and soteriology all had to be revisited and the 'complex interlocking set of religious symbols that have sanctified the integral system of patriarchy' dismantled.[17] These included not just the image of God as Male, but those that associate divinity with violence and bloodshed.[18] Scottish post-Christian feminist Daphne Hampson rejected Christianity as 'a brilliant, subtle, elaborate, male cultural projection, calculated to legitimise a patriarchal world and to enable men to find their way within it'.[19] Post-colonial feminist Kwok Pui Lan challenged traditional Christology as the colonizers' imposition of a 'white Jesus'.[20] American post-Christian Mary Daly insisted that the depiction of Christ's crucifixion idealized victim qualities of 'sacrificial love, passive acceptance of suffering, humility, meekness . . .', thus reinforcing the 'scapegoat syndrome' for women.[21] Womanist theologian Delores Williams doubted whether any theology of atonement helped women: 'I don't think we need folks hanging on crosses, and blood dripping, and weird stuff.'[22]

'Texts of terror'

Biblical depictions of women fared particularly badly: victims of violence and abuse were unearthed from the texts. The dreadful abandonment of Hagar by Abraham and Sarah (Genesis 21), the violation of Dinah by Shechem, son of a local leader (Genesis 34), the brutal gang rape and murder of a concubine (Judges 19), the incestuous attack by Amnon on his half-sister Tamar (2 Samuel 13), the appalling sacrifice of his beloved daughter by Jephthah after a ridiculous vow (Judges 11) – stories summarized by Phyllis Trible as 'texts of terror'[23] – all make one's hair stand on end. Along with passages which advocated stoning adulterous women, and the capturing of Midianite virgins as wives or concubines, they offered post-Christian feminists further justification for leaving the Hebrew Scriptures behind them.

Peter, Paul and women

The New Testament letters to the early churches were seen to compound the Bible's 'patriarchal bias', for example, St Peter's insistence that women were 'the weaker partner' who should be 'submissive' to their husbands (1 Peter 3.1, 7). St Paul's judgements: 'women must be silent in the churches' (1 Corinthians 14.34–35), 'I do not permit a woman to teach or to have authority' (1 Timothy 2.12), 'the head of the woman is man' (1 Corinthians 11.3), 'the husband is the head of the wife' (Ephesians 5.23) seemed evidence of entrenched inequality, with 'headship' for the man and obedience from the woman. This inequality was reflected in church order, admission to ordained ministry, and family structure. The result was seen not only in a male priestly hierarchy, but also in the subjection of wives to husbands. (While visiting churches in different cultures, I have been told by some Christian men, in all seriousness, that using physical violence was sometimes 'necessary to enforce the obedience' owed by their wives.)

How to respond to the distorted gendered nature of 'biblical revelation' thus became a key issue. Should Scripture be read more in cultural context, should we focus on better hermeneutics or should biblical authority itself be deconstructed? Christian feminists were soon in debate and even conflict, reflecting a wide spectrum of perspectives and worldviews – from biblical feminism, liberation feminism, eco-feminism and goddess spirituality to post-Christian feminism. Virginia Mollenkott, Nancy Hardesty and Letha Scanzoni offered biblical paradigms for liberating textual understanding,[24] Letty Russell affirmed that the biblical tradition witnessed to the 'presence of God in Jesus Christ and in our lives'.[25] Biblical scholar Catherine Clark Kroeger melded a conservative view of Scripture with radical hermeneutics.[26] Other writers suggested various forms of canonical revision to relocate the weight and meaning of authority. Elisabeth Schüssler Fiorenza developed her 'hermeneutics of suspicion'. Rosemary Radford Ruether proposed a 'canon within the canon' with the prophetic messianic tradition as the authoritative core.[27] Many, like Carter Heyward and Chung Hyun Kyung, transferred authority away from external revelation to women's own experience.[28] Disagreements grew sharp. While post-Christian Daphne Hampson and Mary Daly rejected the 'biblical God' as utterly destructive to women,[29] Phyllis Trible urged careful biblical exegesis, believing that the Bible could be 'liberated from patriarchy'.[30] Mary Daly speculated on the probable length of a 'depatriarchalized' Bible, suggesting there might be 'enough salvageable material to comprise an interesting pamphlet'.[31]

Since those early days, feminists have nuanced the debate in every continent.[32] The relationship between Christian theology, patriarchy and the oppression of women has been raised in synods and seminaries, in conferences and lectures.[33] Yet the central allegation from post-Christian feminists – that Christianity constructs a divinity who has written gender oppression and male licence into a universal, cosmic order – has made few ripples. Despite their own failings, most Christians around the world believe in a different God, compassionate and loving, who abhors injustice to women.

But if post-Christian feminism failed to inspire and encourage widespread response, can the global Church find in its own theology the resources both to understand and eliminate violence against women? Can the Spirit of this compassionate God impart enough wisdom and move enough hearts to turn people from unawareness and complacency to become advocates for gender justice? It is time to look at a different reading of history and biblical theology.

A global faith

Christianity is a global movement which has persisted through diverse political regimes, cultural threats, natural disasters and brutal persecutions and continues its growth today in many parts of the world. This is despite the fact that, on average, a staggering 100,000 Christians have been martyred annually since AD 2000, with Orthodox communities particularly targeted.[34] Contrary to popular myth, the majority of Christians today are not white

American or European, but oriental, African and Latin American; they worship in more than 43,000 different denominations and organizations[35] – unsurprising since authentic faith is always expressed in the culture of the people.

The Bible, originally written in Hebrew, Aramaic and Greek over thousands of years, has been translated in its entirety into more than 530 languages, with New Testament portions in almost 3,000 languages. Such translation is undertaken, on low budgets, by Christians committed to enabling neighbours across the world to read the gospel for themselves.[36] Organizations like the World Council of Churches draw Christians together from every language, tradition and culture, to hear one another, share faith together, and work co-operatively for peace, truth and justice. Yet in this diverse, expanding, global Church, real unity of vision has to come from shared faith and spiritual resources. A united commitment for gender justice can only be born from spiritual conviction, and experience of God's love.

Patriarchal attitudes have left their mark, yet radical liberation for women is evident in Christianity too, both in history and today. We see it in women prophets and sages, respect and mutuality in marriage, strong female leadership, gifts of teaching and directing, women's spiritual authority, and the fundamental union of male and female in biblical metaphors of the 'image of God' and the 'body of Christ'. Disrespect or violation of women undermines the fundamental values of the gospel. Yet, where it occurs, it calls for repentance and change, not an abandonment of faith.

Women and the Church

Movements in the church, such as those of the Quakers and Levellers, reflected Christianity's liberating power for women in their own structures. A challenge not to 'pervert the Apostle's words' and discriminate against women was issued in 1666 by Quaker leader Margaret Fell.[37] Women in mainstream denominations, excluded from church office, often took other options for service. Some entered Catholic religious orders, serving in all-women communities; some became active pamphleteers and reformers during the early Reformation; some were Scottish Covenanters in the seventeenth century, often martyred for their religious–political protests; and many threw themselves into philanthropy, reform, and Protestant mission in the eighteenth and nineteenth centuries. Pioneering girls' education, addressing health issues, and challenging abuses like infanticide, foot binding and FGM brought European and American Christian women into close relationship with Africans, Asians and Latin Americans.

For 150 years women have been moving into church leadership. The Salvation Army, founded in 1865, affirmed women leaders from the start. By the 1920s women were ordained into the Church of the Nazarene, Methodist Church, Mennonites, Assemblies of God and some Baptist churches. The Anglican Communion ordained its first woman, Florence Li Tim-Oi, in 1942, followed by the Czechoslovak Hussites in 1947 and the Danish Evangelical Lutherans in 1948. Movements for women's ordination flourished. By the end of the twentieth century ordained women served in churches throughout the world.

Women Christian reformers, often feminists, carried the vision of liberation for women into social and political spheres. British and American nineteenth-century social reform was strongly supported by evangelical feminists. In 1911 the Catholic Women's Suffrage Society joined the British women's suffrage movement and blazed a trail for women's emancipation. A decade later it became St Joan's International Alliance, leading the advocacy for women in education, health, professions, family, and reproductive safety; it continues today in the battle against FGM, hunger, poverty and violence. Over the past 40 years Christian women's initiatives – from Men, Women and God and Christians for Biblical Equality, to the Circle of Concerned African Women Theologians, and the Indian Christian Women's Movement – have moved the Church towards a stronger biblical vision. Theological scholars have scrutinized issues of biblical interpretation and hermeneutics on gender. Hundreds of publications and commentaries offer exegeses different from those just outlined, maintaining that the biblical texts support neither male supremacy nor gender-based violence.

Another look at the Bible

The Bible is more of a library than a two-volume tome. It incorporates diverse genres of literature and includes multiple human authors. Books of law, genealogy, history, census records, war annals, poetry, song, proverbs, prophecy, dream analysis, biography, early church history, instruction and letters are all embraced in the canonical text and offered to readers as the 'Word of God'. The Bible's texts are best read in their genre-appropriate way: it's much harder to understand the psalms if we read them like law books, or St Paul's letters if we read them as Old Testament prophecies. Within this diversity of genres, the Bible opens up key themes of God, creation and human personhood; it speaks of past history and future hope, of God's forgiveness, salvation and healing. The unity of the biblical revelation prevails as the story unfolds.

We read the Bible aware also of the cultural attitudes of the time. We notice these particularly in tribal customs, genealogies and legal prescriptions. Punishments prescribed in the Torah were severe, but although penalties were often gender-specific, they were not biased against women: taboos surrounding menstruation, for example, went alongside taboos concerning sperm ejaculation. Grabbing the genitals of a man, even to protect her husband, would put a woman at risk of losing her hand (Deuteronomy 25.11–12), yet not providing offspring to a brother's childless widow could cost a man his life (Genesis 38.3–10). Adultery was punishable by death, but that applied to both men and women offenders. Rape was considered equal to murder and also punishable by taking life (Deuteronomy 22.26) but, in this case, the rapist's (indicating a greater recognition of the seriousness of rape for women than found in some cultures today). Many other punishable offences now seem insignificant. Wearing clothes made of two different types of thread (Deuteronomy 22.11), sowing different kinds of seed in the same field (Leviticus 19.19), refraining from certain foods (Leviticus 11), touching the carcass of a pig (Deuteronomy 14), dressing in clothing appropriate to the other sex (Deuteronomy 22) and celebrating certain holidays (Leviticus 23) are now regarded as specific to those people of Israel, rather than as universal laws.

Even in the transition from Hebrew Scriptures to New Testament the level of law-observance changes. St Paul, himself a Jew, outlines what receiving Christ's forgiveness implies in relation to law and judgement: 'Therefore do not let anyone judge you by what you eat or drink, or with regard to a religious festival, a New Moon celebration or a Sabbath day' (Colossians 2.16).

'Texts of terror' revisited

We need, therefore, to read all Scripture in context, including the 'texts of terror'. Especially, we need to recognize that those passages are *narrative*, not *instructional*. They are horror stories to shock us, certainly not examples of how people should live. Behind Hagar's banishment to the desert was not Abraham's violence but problems of polygamy and Sarah's jealousy. Dinah's brothers avenged the rape of their sister by brutally killing the entire male population of the city. Amnon's actions breached the strict *biblical prohibition against incest and violation* of women, and his own later murder can be seen as the consequence. The Levitical law forbade human sacrifices, yet Jephthah's daughter became a willing sacrifice to protect her father. The whole period of the judges was a period of appalling ignorance and sin, when 'every man did what was right in the sight of his own eyes', including gang rape. The results were barbarous and wretched, the incidents recorded as a dire warning to the people. Nothing in them offers any approval of violence against women.

These stories also need to be seen alongside those in the Hebrew Scriptures where women were protected from harm. God shielded Sarah when her husband, Abraham, lied to the Egyptians that she was his sister. His son Isaac tried exactly the same ruse with his wife Rebecca, with a similar outcome! (Genesis 26) The biblical text hardly covers these 'great men' in glory; maybe their pathetic cowardice is exposed (as one commentator charitably suggests) 'to extol the heroines as most beautiful and show that the Patriarchs were under the special protection of the Deity'![38] Rare stories also show women being commended for aggression. A 'wise woman' saved a town from destruction by arranging the beheading of an offender (2 Samuel 20.14–22). A non-Israelite woman, Jael, killed General Sisera, enemy of Israel, by hammering a tent peg through his temple (Judges 4.17–22). Blood and guts everywhere; these were violent times![39]

Elsewhere in the Hebrew Scriptures, we see the authority of women in mature leadership in Israel. Miriam saves her baby brother, Moses, and later becomes a prophetic leader in her own right. Deborah, the judge, is commended for her wisdom and justice; Huldah is a prophet with acute spiritual insight, consulted even by King Josiah and his high priest to interpret the newly discovered book of the law.[40] Women are lauded for bravery and peace-bringing; Shiprah and Puah, Hebrew midwives, defy Pharaoh, and deliver live male babies,[41] Abigail overrules the stupidity of her husband and averts bloodshed by diplomacy,[42] Queen Esther courageously exposes a high court official and saves her people,[43] and tenacious in-laws Naomi and Ruth give us a glimpse of God's faithfulness through the eyes of migrant women.[44] These and other accounts are all foretastes of Joel's prophecy that the Spirit of God is no respecter of gender, and will empower women and men, young and old with spiritual insight and authority – a prophecy fulfilled strikingly in the early Church after Pentecost.[45]

Peter, Paul and women revisited

The New Testament epistles are significant documents. Written to men and women followers of Christ, from different ethnic backgrounds, education and cultures, they teach about God, about living as Christian minorities, and urge good relationships in the 'body of Christ' (a metaphor Paul employs many times[46]). So, Christians are frequently asked to seek one another's interests rather than their own. Wives are *not* asked to 'obey' but to 'submit' – a voluntary act, relinquishing self-interest for the other. For Peter this means the husband must recognize and protect the vulnerability of the woman (very evident in a patriarchal culture). Paul is more radical, stressing *mutual* submission to one another (Ephesians 5.21) and detailing the husband's daily, caring and sacrificial love for his wife (Ephesians 5.25–28). Paul's brief summary affirms reciprocal marriage – men should love their wives and women should respect their husbands (v. 33).[47] So any action 'disciplining' a wife completely distorts the apostles' concept of marital love, and repudiates Paul's teaching on radical equality.[48]

The theme of certain passages is also important. Instruction to be 'silent' (1 Corinthians 14.34: better translated 'quiet') comes when Paul is pleading for order in worship, and the elimination of excess noise or banality. It is probably a requirement not to disrupt worship by chattering (*lalein*) or talking across to husbands. The other controversial passage (1 Corinthians 11) is about dress and worship, not hierarchy, as often misunderstood. Women were to wear a head covering when they spoke prophetically or prayed in church (so obviously they were not 'silent'). This is accepted now as a historical–cultural requirement (possibly to distinguish Christian from pagan worship), not some universal rule. 'Head' (*kephale*) both in this verse and in Ephesians 5 is clearly a metaphor, and needs to be understood in relation to Christ's initiating and enabling 'headship' of the Church (Colossians 1.18).[49] We must be careful also not to separate Paul's teachings from his practice. Women were clearly permitted to teach. Priscilla taught Apollos (Acts 18.26) and was a co-worker with Paul (Acts 18.18; Romans 16.3); Phoebe had authority as a deacon and Junia was spoken of as an 'apostle'. Paul affirms and commends the ministry of many other women in the early Church (Romans 16) so the remark about denying women 'authority' (1 Timothy 2) needs to be interpreted in a specific local context.

New Testament scholars commonly acknowledge that, far from reinforcing the patriarchy of his age, Paul advocates dismantling those barriers which privilege some and penalize others. His urge is for Christians to recognize the freedom from cultural bondage that true faith brings, and experience unity and equality in the body of Christ. It is a recurrent theme, expressed most powerfully in the well-known passage: 'There is neither Jew nor Greek, slave nor free, male nor female, for you are all one in Christ Jesus'[50] (Galatians 3.28).

None of this affirms women's subservience or, even remotely, validates gender violence. It repudiates it, and urges a far better way of living. But does it bring us any closer to *understanding* violence against women, or why it happens, even in Christian circles? This question has been left hanging since our excursion into evolutionary psychology and the social sciences. So it is important to know if biblical concepts offer any better explanatory power than 'biology' or 'patriarchy', or help us identify a firmer starting point for an answer.

Christian theology and human personhood

To explore that, we need to return to the question of human personhood, and address it from a perspective derived from biblical theology. The biblical story defines us as *persons-in-relationship* – to God, the world and each other, and the central dynamic of all our relationships is summed up in the single word 'love'. 'Love' is given magnetic shape and content – it is truthful, patient, kind, faithful, committed, generous, trusting, protective, hopeful, peaceful. It keeps no score of wrongs, leaves no space for bitterness, shuns self-centredness and violence, and returns good for evil.[51] With all our needs of intimacy, growth, work and rest, we are created to reflect the love of God; our self-love to be replicated in neighbour-love, which seeks well-being and justice for others. As co-inhabitants of creation, we are also given loving guardianship of the world, with all the ecological implications this entails. These characteristics can be seen in all kinds of people who give their lives to making the world a better place.

But biblical theology also identifies the great gap between all we are created to be, and the way most of us actually live. The consequences of that failure hang over much of history and international relations: institutionalized in structures of exploitation and greed, entombed in militarism and war. They are also manifest, as we have seen throughout this book, in atrocities against women. And a theology of human personhood identifies our failure as the product of 'sin' – a word that really has little to do with sex, and everything to do with human responsibility. Sin is described in biblical language as 'transgression', or 'rebellion against God'. In more simple terms it is a violation of our calling to live within the moral contours of love, which emanates from God.

Sin breaks the integrity of our human identity as persons in relationship. Its complexity affects so much of our lives. Sin is alienating – cuts us off from others, ourselves and God. It is destructive – tears down and devastates, never builds up. It is distortive – changes truth into half-truth, untruth and complete lies, so we don't know what to believe. Sin is delusory; we live with denial, fool ourselves, and learn self-justification. It is addictive, gripping our lives, creating destructive habits which we cannot do without. It is generational, passing down the lines to third and fourth generation. It is societal, embedding itself in political, economic and social structures which hold sway over others. When sin corrupts those who have power, the effects on the powerless can be overwhelming, leaving them dehumanized and objectified. The Congolese woman whose sexual organs were mutilated by her gun-touting rapist described the attack as one of 'hatred'. She was right. The Bangladeshi woman, hit by the police for not going back to the husband who threw acid on her, said it was 'evil'. She was right too. Sin eliminates love, and fuels loathing. Unless we recognize its power we cannot repel it. As Aleksandr Solzhenitsyn observed in *The Gulag Archipelago*, the line 'dividing good and evil cuts through the heart of every human being'. Sin's unleashed power destroys those who wield it, as well as those who are its victims. Like Bhasin's comment about rape, there are no winners. But the losses are incalculable.

At a far deeper level than either 'biology' or 'culture', then, 'sin' helps us explain the ubiquity of violence against women. We are responsible. Patriarchal structures are a product of human choice and attitudes; oppression and brutality are rooted in the power sin exercises in human communities. A Christian theology of sin places accountability for attitudes, culture and actions firmly on human shoulders; we have to own what we create.

Thankfully, this doesn't leave us with the hopelessness of a doomed humanity. The Christian faith is built on the solid conviction that sin does not have the last word. We are not stuck forever in a defeating spiral of abuse and violence. A theology of human personhood moves beyond sin to a theology of redemption. In biblical terms redemption is brought by Christ's defeat of evil through God's love: Christ faces the injustice of the world, the brutality of the human race, and dies for sin. To human minds it is unfathomable. Its reality comes home in our own experiences of forgiveness and resurrection.

This means there is always hope for those struggling with oppression and violation. Lives can be restored, pain healed, bondage broken, the past left behind. Repentance and change can transform even repressive structures. Redemptive living affects gender relations as it affects everything else. This was true even in the earliest times. The Gospels give us a glimpse of how Jesus cuts open cultural norms, hierarchies, stereotypes, and the low status of women, and injects the reality of equal significance before God. A woman is about to be stoned for having illicit sex (not her partner, although the Torah rule includes them both), Jesus challenges her prosecutors about their own sins, and she is freed. He heals a woman struggling with menstrual problems, who touches his clothing, in direct defiance of the laws of menstrual hygiene. She makes him ritually 'unclean', yet he ignores that and commends her faith (Luke 8). Jesus asks a despised and much-divorced Samaritan woman at the well for a drink and discloses to her his identity as Messiah (John 4). He accepts tears and kisses from a former prostitute who perfumes his feet and dries them with her hair in gratitude for her own new freedom, and rebukes the poor hospitality of his hosts (Luke 7). He banters with a Canaanite woman about the primacy of the Jews, and heals her daughter (Mark 7). He brings life to a widow's only son, recognizing her social vulnerability as well as her devastation at his loss (Luke 7). He notices a struggling spondylitis victim and heals her, defying legalist authorities (Luke 13).

Women are included among Jesus' closest friends and followers: Joanna, the wife of Herod's household manager, Susanna, Mary Magdalene, whom he releases from a life of emotional turmoil, Mary and Martha whose home he visits regularly. His stories often relate to women's domestic lives – sweeping rooms, baking bread, looking for lost coins, being pregnant, facing authorities and seeking justice. He points out the generosity of a poor widow and affirms mothers who bring their children to be blessed, despite his impatient disciples. When dying in great pain, he commits the care of his mother to John, his disciple. His women disciples come to anoint his body and are heralded as the first witnesses of his resurrection.[52] It is not surprising that, through the centuries, women have found their own identity and significance in following Christ. As both victims and advocates, they draw inspiration from the Gospels to fight injustice and bring transformation.

Seeing signs of hope

Many Christian initiatives show both the challenges and effectiveness of redemptive love. In Goma, DRC, Heal Africa has refused to let the power of evil and hatred obliterate the intrinsic worth of vulnerable people. Rape survivors find hope and healing; war victims are saved. I was there when Jo Lusi worked all night, his skill as a surgeon tested to its utmost on the body of a child mutilated by a grenade attack. In Mexico City, the Armonia Community carries its holistic vision into all areas of community life; a single mother, formerly abused and destitute, showed me with tearful pride her literacy graduation certificate. In Ecuador, Peru and Bolivia, Paz y Esperanza runs courses 'from violence to tenderness', sharing the implications of gender equality with churches and communities. 'It was like a light switched on,' said a woman who had endured a 30-year violent marriage.

In Madhya Pradesh, India, a remote missionary hospital made history when, with few initial resources, they delivered, then separated conjoined twin girls, left behind by their family. For Drs Rajiv and Deepa Choudrie, it was a prayerful, joyous statement of their own Christian value of the girl child. In Uganda, the participatory Evaluation Project, run by the Pentecostal Assemblies of God (PAG) churches, develops community living on neighbour-love and gender-empowerment. Women HIV & AIDS survivors hugged me and told how warmly their local community had welcomed them and shared resources. In Paraguay, the Santa Maria Education Fund, founded and developed by Catholic writer and feminist Margaret Hebblethwaite,[53] puts the reality of love and equality into practice in its vision and provision of tertiary education for poor youngsters. In Durban, South Africa, the Phesipha Movement set up by HIV and sexual violence worker Veena O'Sullivan helps survivors reclaim their lives. In UK, Restored works internationally to further the message of redemptive relationships, and First Man Standing invites men into the fight against women's abuse and violation. In Delhi, Asha brings hope to thousands in slum colonies, especially in empowering and educating vulnerable young girls.

Others are many: Tearfund, Micah, CAFOD, Christian Aid, World Vision, Boaz Trust, CAP (Christians Against Poverty), Spark, Speak, ICAP, 28 Too Many, ACET (AIDS Care, Education and Training), Mothers' Union, Women at Risk, Ethiopia, PASCH (Peace And Safety in the Christian Home), Not For Sale, Netherlands, Oasis, A Rocha, Netzwerk Gegen, Care International, Beyond the Streets, World YWCA, Girls in ICT, Christians for Biblical Equality, Siam Care, Nightlight International, Open Doors. The list could go on: the Anglican Communion collaborates in Silent No More to bring the resources of the worldwide Anglican Church to help eliminate violence against women. Some groups cannot be named because they work quietly with women at risk, and we would not want to endanger their lives. But the consensus from all would be that, far from underwriting violence and abuse, the Christian faith offers a biblical framework for understanding it and the power of God's love to combat it.

An ongoing challenge

Alyse Nelson of Vital Voices Global Partnership has called gender-based violence 'the great unfinished business of our time', and we cannot underestimate the walls that must be dismantled before it can be brought to an end. It will need the combined support of the Christian Church, Islam, Judaism, Hinduism and all faith communities, especially in those areas where religion and oppression of women co-exist. But the elimination of all the areas of violence covered in this book is a task which stretches beyond creeds, nations and gender. It is a global humanitarian project, which asks us all to move beyond our comfort zones, complacency and cultural limitations to support actively the initiatives which bring change. Campaigning, advocating, funding, media exposure, broadcasting, legislating, healing, counselling, educating and praying will all have to be undertaken if the fight against abuse and injustice is to be won. But we cannot allow these violations against millions of women to continue. We cannot ignore their suffering or condone this assault on our humanness.

Ending the violence is urgent. The scars across humanity are deep. It is time to join the healing and the work of restorative justice.

Notes

1 A global pandemic

1 LeVine, Mark, 'The Revolution, Back in Black', Al Jazeera, 2 February 2013.

2 FIDH report: *Egypt: Keeping Women Out: Sexual Violence against Women in the Public Sphere*, FIDH (Fédération internationale des ligues des droits de l'Homme), April 2014: <http://www.fidh.org/IMG/pdf/egypt_sexual_violence_uk-webfinal.pdf>.

3 Iaccino, Ludovica, 'Women after Arab Spring: "Rape, Like Bombs, Used as War Weapon"', *International Business Times*, 11 June 2014: <http://www.ibtimes.co.uk/women-after-arab-spring-rape-like-bombs-used-war-weapon-1452189>.

4 Eltahawy, Diana, 'Sexual Attacks on Women in Egypt', Livewire, Amnesty International's global human rights blog, 1 February 2013.

5 Shalaby, Ethar, 'A Woman's Permanent Scar', *Daily News Egypt*, 12 September 2012.

6 'Once Again . . . Women Speak out: Results of a Field Research on Violence against Women in Egypt', El Nadim Center for Rehabilitation of Victims of Violence, Ramses, Cairo, Egypt, 2009.

7 United Nations Secretary-General's study: *Ending Violence against Women: From Words to Action*, 9 October 2006: <http://www.un.org/womenwatch/daw/vaw/launch/english/v.a.w-exeE-use.pdf>.

8 United Nations Population Fund (UNFPA), *State of the World Population 2005: The Promise of Equality: Gender Equity, Reproductive Health and the Millennium Development Goals*, UNFPA, 2005, p. 65.

9 United Nations Secretary-General's report: *In-depth Study on All Forms of Violence against Women*, United Nations General Assembly, sixty-first session, item 60.

10 Sen, Purna and Kelly, Liz, *Violence against Women: Shadow Thematic Report* for the Committee for the Elimination of all Forms of Discrimination Against Women in the UK (CEDAW), 2007.

11 Scottish Government publication: *Equally Safe: Scotland's Strategy for Preventing and Eradicating Violence against Women and Girls*, 25 June 2014, p. 18: <http://www.scotland.gov.uk/Resource/0045/00454152.pdf>.

12 See Kutchinsky, Serena, 'Violence against Women Is Europe's Secret Shame', *Prospect*, 21 March 2014: <http://www.prospectmagazine.co.uk/blogs/serena-kutchinsky>.

13 Peacewomen fact sheet: 'Philippines: Laws Protecting Women Bring Down Abuse Cases', March 2011.

14 UN Department of Economics and Social Affairs, *Handbook for Legislation on Violence against Women*, New York, July 2010.

15 United Nations Assistance Mission in Afghanistan, *Still a Long Way to Go: Implementation of the Law on Elimination of Violence against Women in Afghanistan*, Kabul, Afghanistan, December 2012, p. 2.

16 'Afghan MPs Block Divisive Women's Rights Law', Al Jazeera, 18 May 2013.

17 Graham-Harrison, Emma, 'New Afghanistan Law to Silence Victims of Violence against Women', *The Guardian*, 4 February 2014: <http://www.theguardian.com/world/2014/feb/04/afghanistan-law-victims-violence-women>.

18 Walsh, Declan, 'Taliban Gun Down Girl Who Spoke Up for Rights', *New York Times*, 9 October 2012.

19 Brickell, Katherine, 'Violence against Women: Legal Reform Is No Silver Bullet', *The Guardian*, 15 March 2013.

20 Tran, Mark, 'UN Women's Lakshmi Puri Urges Global Action to End Violence against Women', *The Guardian*, 12 November 2012.

21 Tran, 'Lakshmi Puri Urges Global Action'.

22 Tran, 'Lakshmi Puri Urges Global Action'.

23 Tran, 'Lakshmi Puri Urges Global Action'.

24 Rhine, Sarah, 'Violence against Women Common in Psychiatric Hospitals', *Baltimore Sun*, 4 October 2010.

25 Thompsons Solicitors, 'Vigilance Needed to Avoid Sexual Attacks on Health Workers', 28 December 2011: <http://www.thompsons.law.co.uk/personal-injury/vigilance-needed-sexual-assaults-health-workers.htm>.

26 UN Secretary-General's study: *Ending Violence against Women*.

27 'The Rape of the Sabine Women': Even though the Roman historian Livy assumed that 'rape' meant 'abduction' and that no sexual assault took place, it is clear that the women were being kidnapped to procreate and were not willing victims. See Livy, *The Early History of Rome*, Books 1–5, trans. Aubrey de Sélincourt, London, Penguin Classics, 2002, p. 45.

28 Obaid, Thoraya Ahmed, 'United Nations Agencies Forward Together in the Response to Violence Against Women', *UN Chronicle*, February 2010.

2 Violence begins before birth: selective abortion and infanticide

1 George, Sabu, 'The Need for Action against Female Feticide in India': <http://aidindia.org/aipsn/health/feticide.html>.

2 Prasad, Raekha and Ramesh, Randeep, 'India's Missing Girls', *The Guardian*, 28 February 2007.

3 Bhalla, Nita, 'Rise in India's Female Feticide May Spark Crisis', Reuters, 31 August 2007: <www.reuters.com/article/healthNews/idUSDEL22936620070831>.

4 Anderson, Siwan and Ray, Debraj, 'The Age Distribution of Missing Women in India', *Economic and Political Weekly* 47(47–8), 1 December 2012.

5 Wright, Rusty and Korpi, Meg, 'India's Missing Girls and the Right to Choose', The Amy Foundation: <http://www.amyfound.org/writing_resources/amy_internet_syndicate/articles/rusty_wright/rw65.html>.

6 Leidl, Patricia, 'Silent Spring: The Tragedy of India's Never-born Girls', United Nations Population Fund, 2005: quoted in: <http://patricialeidl.com/writing/gender-equity-and-reproductive-health/>.

7 CRIN (Child Rights International Network), 'A Girl's Right to Live: Female Foeticide and Girl Infanticide', Working Group on the Girl Child NGO, Committee on the Status of Women, 2007: <http://www.ngocsw-geneva.ch/tag/female-foeticide/>.

8 Leidl, quoted in Dowling, Patrick, '"We as a Society Cannot Continue Killing Girls": The Fate of India's Children under the Spectre of Foeticide': <http://www.legalaidboard.ie/lab/publishing.nsf/Content/The_Researcher_June_2008_Article_8>.

9 The Medical Termination of Pregnancy Act no. 34, 1971, as amended by The Medical Termination of Pregnancy Act no. 64, 2002.

10 Nehra, Krishan S., Senior Foreign Law Specialist, *Sex Selection and Abortion: India*, The Law Library of Congress, US Government, June 2009: <www.loc.gov/law/help/sex-selection/india.php>.

11 Prasad and Ramesh, 'India's Missing Girls'.

12 George, Sabu and Karat, Brinda, 'Don't Trash This Law; the Fault Lies in Non-implementation', *The Hindu*, 4 February 2012. See also Ramesh, Randeep, 'Foetuses Aborted and Dumped Secretly as India Shuns Baby Girls', *The Guardian*, 28 July 2007: <www.guardian.co.uk/world/2007/jul/28/india.randeepramesh/print>.

13 Siwal, B. R., 'Preventive Measures for Elimination of Female Foeticide', 2005: <http://www.eldis.org/go/home&id=18526&type=Document#.Vfhr6WRViko>.

14 Sinha, Kounteya, 'Govt Mulls Ban on Portable Ultrasound Machines', *The Times of India*, 7 January 2012.

15 Quoted in Dowling, Patrick, 'We as a Society Cannot Continue Killing Girls', *The Researcher* 3(2), June 2008, Refugee Documentation Centre, Dublin, p. 26.

16 George and Karat, 'Don't Trash This Law'.

17 Nanda, Bijayalaxmi, 'The Real Truth behind Sex-selective Abortions', *OneWorld, South Asia*, 6 June 2012: <http://southasia.oneworld.net>.

18 George and Karat, 'Don't Trash This Law'.

19 See Ministry of Women and Child Development, sub-group report: *Girl Child in the Eleventh Five Year Plan*, 2007–12.

20 Virmani, Priya, 'Dowry Deaths Are the Hidden Curse of the Big Fat Indian Wedding', *The Guardian*, 28 May 2012.

21 Prasad and Ramesh, 'India's Missing Girls'.

22 Virmani, 'Dowry Deaths Are the Hidden Curse'.

23 'Dowry Deaths: One Woman Dies Every Hour', *The Times of India*, 1 September 2013.

24 Virmani, 'Dowry Deaths Are the Hidden Curse'.

25 Wadhwa, Lakita, 'Dr Mitu Khurana Is an Epitome of Social Justice When It Comes to Killing Daughters', MaStyle Care, Delhi, 21 April 2015: <http://www.mastylecare.org/mothers-day/dr-mitu-khurana-india-daughters/>.

26 CIA, The World Factbook: <https://www/cia/gov/library/publications/the-world-factbook>.

27 Estimates of sex ratios at birth based on data from the Sample Registration System put the ratio at 902 from 2008 to 2010.

28 Office of the Registrar General and Census Commissioner, Census of India 2011, 2012, quoted in Barot, Sneha, 'A Problem-and-Solution Mismatch: Son Preference and Sex-Selective Abortion Bans', *Guttmacher Policy Review* 15(2), Spring 2012: <https://www.guttmacher.org/pubs/gpr/15/2/gpr150218.html>.

29 The situation in Kerala is complex, and Moly Kuruvilla attempts to unravel it in the book *Discrimination against Girl Child: The Trajectory of Missing Girls*, New Delhi, Gyan Publishing House, 2011.

30 Prasad and Ramesh, 'India's Missing Girls'.

31 'Census of India 2011: Child Sex Ratio Drops to Lowest since Independence', *Economic Times*, 31 March 2011.

32 Jacob, K. S., 'Sex Ratio, Patriarchy and Ethics', *The Hindu*, Opinion, 29 April 2011.

33 Hudson, Valerie M. and Boer, Andrea M. den, *Bare Branches: The Security Implications of Asia's Surplus Male Population*, Boston, MIT Press, 2005.

34 'Bare Branches, Redundant Males', *The Economist*, 18 April 2015.

35 UNFPA, *State of World Population 2005*.

36 Sharma, Kalpana, 'The Other Half: Where Have All the Girls Gone?' *The Hindu*, 17 April 2011.

37 George and Karat, 'Don't Trash This Law'.

38 Quoted in MacAskill, Andrew and Pradhan, Bibhudatta, 'Delhi Assaults on Women Rise as Verdict Due in Fatal Rape', *Bloomberg*, 24 July 2013.

39 Nanda, 'The Real Truth behind Sex-selective Abortions'.

3 Cut for purity: female genital mutilation

1 Woman in her thirties, O-K Project, Norway, quoted by Saeveras, Elin Finnseth in *Female Genital Mutilation: Understanding the Issues*, Oslo, Norwegian Church Aid, 2003, p. 9.

2 Mohammed, Halima, 'Female Genital Mutilation, Marriage and Delivery', *World Pulse*, 1 December 2012: <http://worldpulse.com/mode/61985>.

3 UNICEF report, quoted in Mohammed, 'Female Genital Mutilation'.

4 HM Government, *Multi-Agency Practice Guidelines: Female Genital Mutilation*: <https://www.gov.uk/government/uploads/system/uploads/attachment_data/file/380125/MultiAgencyPracticeGuidelinesNov14.pdf>, with figures from Macfarlane, A. J. and Dorkenoo, E., *Female Genital Mutilation in England and Wales*, London, City University, 2014.

5 'Sierra Leone: The Political Battle on FGM/C', IRIN Humanitarian News and Analysis, UN Co-ordination of Humanitarian Affairs, Freetown, 2012.

6 Mohammed, 'Female Genital Mutilation'.

7 Mohammed, 'Female Genital Mutilation'.

8 See Knight, Mary, 'Curing Cut or Ritual Mutilation? Some Remarks on the Practice of Female and Male Circumcision in Graeco-Roman Egypt', *Isis* 92(2), June 2001, pp. 317–38.

9 Seligman, Charles G., 'Aspects of the Hamitic Problems in the Anglo-Egyptian Sudan', *Journal of the Royal Anthropological Institute of Great Britain and Ireland* 40(3), 1913, pp. 593–705.

10 The Bristol Peer Review, Principal Researcher Dr Eiman Hussein, 'Women's Experiences, Perceptions and Attitudes of Female Genital Mutilation', Foundation for Women's Health Research and Development, 2010.

11 Gill, Aisha K., 'How Do We Bring FGM to an End in Britain?' *New Statesman*, 6 February 2015: <http://www.newstatesman.com/politics/2015/02/how-do-we-bring-fgm-end-britain>.

12 Toubia, Nahid in a BBC World Service programme: 'Changing Attitudes to Female Circumcision', April 2002.

13 Barnes, Virginia Lee and Boddy, Janice, *Aman: The Story of a Somali Girl*, London, Bloomsbury, 1995.

14 Bristol Peer Review, 'Women's Experiences', p. 12.

15 Bristol Peer Review, 'Women's Experiences', p. 13.

16 Bristol Peer Review, 'Women's Experiences', p. 15.

17 Bristol Peer Review, 'Women's Experiences', p. 21.

18 Ali, Nimco, quoted in Dzerins, Natalie, 'Female Genital Mutilation Might Be Illegal, but It Still Takes Place in the UK', *The Independent*, 14 May 2012.

19 Health and Social Care Information Centre: <http://www.hscic.gov.uk/catalogue/PUB16773/>.

20 Willsher, Kim, 'France's Tough Stand on FGM Is Working, Say Campaigners', *The Guardian*, 10 February 2014: <http://www.theguardian.com/society/2014/feb/10/france-tough-stance-female-genital-mutilation-fgm>.

21 Quoted in Strayer, Robert W., *The Making of Mission Communities in East Africa*, London, Heinemann Educational, 1978, p. 137.

22 Strayer, *Making of Mission Communities*, p. 137.

23 Reported in the *Daily Sentinel*, Rome/New York, 6 January 1930.

24 Mufaka, Kenneth, 'Scottish Missionaries and the Circumcision Controversy in Kenya, 1900–1960', *International Review of Scottish Studies* 28, 2003.

25 Strayer, *Making of Mission Communities*, p. 137.

26 United Nations Population Fund press release: 'Fewer Girls Threatened by Female Mutilation', February 2013: <www.unfpa.org/public/home/news/pid/12684>.

27 Nashipae Nkadori, Evelyn, 'FGM: Maasai Women Speak Out', *Cultural Survival 40 Years 1972–2012*, Cambridge, MA, May 2010.

28 United Nations, *Report of the International Conference on Population and Development*, Cairo, New York, 1994.

29 United Nations, *Report of the Fourth World Conference on Women*, New York, 1995.

30 Toubia, Nahid, *Female Genital Mutilation: A Call for Global Action*, New York, Women Ink, 1993.

31 Imam Ali, Afroz, 'Mutilating Facts: Setting the Record Straight about Female Circumcision and Genital Mutilation', 26 April 2012, on his website: http://seekershub.org/blog/2012/04/mutilating-facts-setting-the-record-straight-about-female-circumcision-genital-mutilation/>.

32 Baxendale, Rachel, 'Female Circumcision Is a Right, Says Imam', *The Australian*, 24 December 2012.

33 Hathout, Hassan, 'Female Circumcision: Ask a Shari'ah and Medical Expert', Islamonline live dialogue: <http://drhassanhathout.org/medicals/female_circumcision.html>.

34 The Muslim Women's League, 'Female Genital Mutilation', Los Angeles, January 1999: <http://www.mwlusa.org/topics/violence&harrassment/fgm.html>.

35 Beach, Alastair, 'Egypt's Terrible FGM Death', *Daily Beast*, June 2013: *Newsweek* online magazine: <http://www.thedailybeast.com/newsweek.html>.

36 Manson, Katrina, 'Women Fight Africa's Taboo', *The Independent*, 27 February 2009.

37 Hill, Amelia, 'Female Genital Mutilation Campaigners Face Death Threats and Intimidation', *The Guardian*, 8 May 2013.

38 Equality Now, 'Egypt: Enforce FGM Law and Prosecute Those Responsible for Soheir al Batea's Death', New York, Nairobi, London, 2 July 2013: <http://www.equalitynow.org/take_action/egypt_action383>.

39 World Health Organization factsheet no. 241, February 2013.

40 28 Too Many is a charity dedicated to researching and campaigning to end FGM in the 28 countries where it is traditionally practised and worldwide: <http://28toomany.org>.

41 <http://www.npwj.org/GHR/BAN-FGM-CAMPAIGN.html>.

4 Early and enforced marriage: child abuse by another name

 1 Plan UK children's charity; quoted in Anderson, Lisa, 'Child Marriage a Scourge for Millions of Girls', TrustLaw, Thomas Reuters Foundation, 4 August 2011.

 2 United Nations press release, New York, 7 March 2014; figures taken from United Nations Population Fund (UNFPA), *Marrying Too Young: End Child Marriage*, New York, UNFPA, 2012, p. 6: <http://www.unicef.org>; <http://www.unfpa.org/child-marriage>.

 3 UNFPA, *Marrying Too Young*, p. 6.

 4 Gumbonzvanda, Nyaradzayi, 'Statement to the Human Rights Council High Level Panel on Preventing and Eliminating Child, Early and Forced Marriage', Geneva, 23 June 2014.

5 Too Young to Wed: http://tooyoungtowed.org/blog/tag/unicef/.

6 Al-Haj, Ahmad, '"Yemeni Bride Was Tied up, Raped", Says Mom', Associated Press, 4 October 2010.

7 UNFPA, *Marrying Too Young*, p. 48. Najood's story became a film in 2015.

8 UNFPA, *Marrying Too Young*, p. 27. The bulk of data on child marriage was collected through household surveys – the Demographic and Health Survey (DHS) and the Multiple Indicators Cluster Survey (MICS) 26 – conducted in close collaboration with national counterparts: national statistics offices or ministries of health.

9 Quoted in Iaccino, Ludovica, 'Child Marriage in 2013: Third of Women in Developing World Married before 18', 20 January 2014: <http://www.ibtimes.co.uk/child-marriage-2013-third-women-developing-world-married-before-18-1433070>.

10 UNFPA Asia and the Pacific, joint press release: 'Child Marriages: 39,000 Every Day', New York, 7 March 2013: <http://asiapacific.unfpa.org/public/cache/offonce/ChildMarriages39000EveryDay>.

11 Osotimehin, Babatunde, 'Don't Forget the Girls', UNFPA, *Opinion*, 19 April 2012: <http://www.unfpa.org/public/home/news/pid/10516>.

12 Quoted in Anderson, 'Child Marriage a Scourge'.

13 UNICEF press release: 'Child Marriages: 39,000 Every Day: More Than 140 Million Girls Will Marry between 2011 and 2020', September 2013.

14 Gumbonzvanda, 'Preventing and Eliminating Child, Early and Forced Marriage'.

15 Keane, Fergal, 'Big Money for Niger's Child Brides', BBC News, 29 May 2014.

16 Keane, 'Big Money'.

17 <http://tooyoungtowed.org/blog/tag/unicef/>.

18 Khan, Wajahat S. and Austin, Henry, 'Girls "Treated as Cattle": Child Brides Divide Pakistan', NBC News, 29 March 2014.

19 Cook, Kathy, *Stolen Angels: The Kidnapped Girls of Uganda*, Penguin Global, 2009 (an account of the 1996 abduction by Lord's Resistance Army (LRA) leader Joseph Kony of 30 Ugandan schoolgirls, subsequently exploited as child soldiers and sex slaves).

20 UNICEF, *State of the World's Children 2014 in Numbers: Every Child Counts*, New York, January 2014, p. 81: <http://www.unicef.org/sowc2014/numbers/documents/english/SOWC2014_In%20Numbers_28%20Jan.pdf>.

21 Khan and Austin, 'Girls "Treated as Cattle"'.

22 Murphy, Caryle, 'Child Marriage Case Showcases Deep Split in Saudi Society', *Global Post*, 16 April 2009: <http://www.globalpost.com/dispatch/saudi-arabia/090416/child-marriage-case-showcases-deep-splits-saudi-society>.

23 Allison, Simon, 'Amina Filali: A Story of Rape, Suicide and the Society Searching for Its Soul', *Daily Maverick*, 20 March 2012: <http://www.dailymaverick.co.za/article/2012-03-20-amina-filali-a-story-of-rape-suicide-and-the-society-searching-for-its-soul/#.U-gtaIBdVxs>.

24 Li, Kevin, 'Iraq's New Jafaari Marriage Law Permits Marital Rape, Child Brides and Polygamy: Men Granted Right to Sex, Authority to Marry Multiple Girls as Young as 9': <http://www.latinpost.com/articles/10859/20140421/iraqs-new-jaafari-marriage-law-permits-marital-rape-child-brides-and-polygamy-men-granted-right-to-sex-authority-to-marry-multiple-girls-as-young-as-9>.

25 Fordham, Alice, 'Iraq Debates Law That Would Allow Men to Marry 9 Year Old Girls', *Parallels*, 13 May 2014: <http://www.npr.org/blogs/parallels/2014/05/13/312160466/iraq-debates-law-that-would-allow-men-to-marry-9-year-old-girls>.

26 Nelson, Sarah C., 'Spoon in Underwear Helps Prevent Forced Marriages', *Huffington Post*, 15 October 2013. See also: <http://www.karmanirvana.org.uk/>.

27 See World Young Women's Christian Association (YWCA), 'High Level Panel: Preventing and Eliminating Child, Early and Forced Marriage', 25 June 2014: <http://www.worldywca.org/Events/UN-Human-Rights-Council/HRC-2014/High-Level-Panel-Preventing-and-Eliminating-Child-Early-and-Forced-Marriage>.

28 Ban Ki-moon, March 2013; quoted in: <http://tooyoungtowed.org/blog/today-is-a-big-day-for-child-marriage/>.

29 Video: 'Melka Stands Up for Early Marriage': <http://www.care.org/country/ethiopia>.

30 <http://www.carebangladesh.org/shouhardoII/human_story/WomenWomenStoryChallengingPovertyEKATA.pdf>.

5 Whose 'honour'? Killings and femicide as reprisals for shame

1 <http://www.dailymail.co.uk/news/article-2115984/Is-Britains-white-honour-killing-victim-The-happy-headstrong-girl-17-love-racial-divide-tragic-end.html#ixzz2pA4MxHVl>.

2 Statements from the judge at Chester Crown Court, BBC News report, 2 August 2012.

3 Published too late to include in this chapter is the study in Gill, Aisha K., *'Honour' Killing and Violence*, London, Palgrave Macmillan, 2014.

4 Gill, *'Honour' Killing*.

5 Chesler, Phyllis, 'Worldwide Trends in Honor Killings', *Middle East Quarterly* 27(2), Spring 2010: <http://www.meforum.org/2646/worldwide-trends-in-honor-killings>.

6 <http://globalhumanrights.awardspace.com/Pakistan.swf>.

7 Hassan, Yasmeen, 'The Fate of Pakistani Women', *New York Times*, 25 March 1999.

8 'Nearly 1000 Pakistani Women "Killed for Honour"', Al Arabiya News, 22 March 2012: <http://english.alarabiya.net/articles/2012/03/22/202385.html>.

9 Goldenberg, Suzanne, 'A Question of Honour', *The Guardian*, 27 May 1999.

10 Goldenberg, 'Question of Honour'.

11 'Pakistan: Honour Killings of Women and Girls': quoted in <http://www.csmonitor.com/2007/0306/p06s01-wosc.html>.

12 Taufeeq, Nighat, quoted in 'Culture of Discrimination: A Fact Sheet on Honor Killings': <http://www.amnestyusa.org> (retrieved 1 October 2011).

13 Boom, Jon, 'Pregnant Woman Beaten to Death by Family outside Pakistani Court', *The Guardian*, 28 May 2014.

14 Boom, 'Pregnant Woman Beaten to Death'.

15 Khan, M. Ilyas, 'Kohistan "Honour" Killing: Pakistani Woman Rukhsana Bibi Relives Horror', BBC News, 7 January 2014; <http://www.bbc.co.uk/news/world-asia-24540073>.

16 Hassan, 'Fate of Pakistani Women'.

17 Khan, Tahira Shahid, 'Chained to Custom', *The Review*, 4–10 March 1999, p. 9.

18 Saleem, Sana of the *Bolo Bhi* ('Speak Up') rights group, quoted in Crilly, Bob, '1000 Pakistani Women and Girls Honour Killing Victims', Islamabad, 22 March 2012.

19 Constable, Pamela, 'The Price of Honour', *The Gazette*, Montreal, 22 May 2000.

20 Amnesty International report, quoted by BBC World Service: <http://www.bbc.co.uk/worldservice/people/features/ihavearightto/four_b/b_right_2.shtml>.

21 Boom, 'Pregnant Woman Beaten to Death'.

22 Tait, Robert, 'Turkish Girl, 16, Buried Alive "for Talking to Boys"', *The Guardian*, 4 February 2010: <www.guardian.co.uk/world/2010/feb/04/girl-buried-alive-turkey>.

23 Ammar, Manar, 'Egypt: Honor Killing Hits Alexandria', *Bikyamasr*, 29 September 2010: <http://bikyamasr.com/wordpress/?p=17594>.

24 Winter, Michael, 'Bangladeshi Teen Dies from Sharia Lashing after Reportedly Being Raped', *USA Today*, 2 February 2011: <http://content. usatoday.com/communities/ondeadline/post/2011/02/bangladeshi-teen-dies-from-sharia-lashing-after-reportedly-being-raped/1#. VaqVrSpViko>; Ethirajan, Anbarasan, 'Four Arrested after Bangladesh Girl "Lashed to Death"', BBC News, 2 February 2011: <http://www. bbc.co.uk/news/world-south-asia-12344959>.

25 'Yemeni "Burns Daughter to Death for Contacting Fiancé"', BBC News, 23 October 2013: <http://www.bbc.co.uk/news/world-middle-east-24638059>.

26 Equality Now, 'Honor Killings', Spotlight: Speaking Out against Global Violence: <http://www.feminist.com/violence/spot/honor. html>.

27 Neharnet Newsdesk: 'Lebanese Man Impregnates His Sister, Kills Her in Honour Crime', Voice of Lebanon Radio, 8 February 2013.

28 Quoted in Kiener, Robert, 'Honor Killings', *Global Researcher* 5(8), April 2011, p. 191: <http://www.cqpress.com/product/CQ-Global-Researcher-Honor-Killings-v5.html>.

29 Quoted in Kiener, Robert, 'Honor Killings', p. 191.

30 Reported in the *Chicago Tribune*, 1 September 2000.

31 Ghuneim, L. and Eisner, M., 'Honour Killing Attitudes among Teenagers in Amman, Jordan', *Aggressive Behaviour* 39(5), Sept.–Oct. 2013, pp. 405–17; DOI: 10.1002/ab.21485. Epub 6 June 2013, Wiley Publications.

32 Hundal, Sunny, 'The Left Cannot Remain Silent over Honour Killings', *New Statesman*, London, 4 August 2012.

33 Butt, Riazat, '"You Are Not My Mother Any More" Shouted Samaira. Then Her Family Killed Her', *The Guardian*, 15 July 2006.

34 'Teenager Is White Victim of Honour Killing', *Daily Telegraph*, 17 March 2012: <http://www.telegraph.co.uk/news/uknews/crime/9149929/Teenager-is-first-white-victim-of-honour-killing.html>.

35 'Crimes of Honour', *Panorama*, BBC 1, 12 March 2012.

36 <http://www.change.org/en-GB/petitions/number10gov-david-cameron-introduce-a-day-to-remember-britainslostwomen>.

37 'Honour Violence: A Threat to Immigrant Women', *Yle Uutiset*, 19 October 2009: <http://yle.fi/uutiset/quothonour_violencequot>.

38 Corbin, Jane, 'Is This Britain's First White Honour Killing?' *Mail Online*, 15 March 2012.

39 Hilderbrandt, Johanne, 'Honour Killing in Sweden Silences Courageous Voice on Ethnic Integration', *The Guardian*, 31 January 2002: <http://www.theguardian.com/theguardian/2002/jan/31/guardianweekly>.

40 'Jail for Denmark "Honour" Killing', BBC News, 29 June 2006: <http://news.bbc.co.uk/1/hi/world/europe/5128206.stm>.

41 Biehl, Jody K., 'The Death of a Muslim Woman: The Whore Lived Like a German', *Spiegel Online International*, March 2005.

42 Mir, Meritxell, 'Dad Killed Daughter in Brutal Axe Murder', *The Local: Switzerland's News in English*, 13 January 2012: <http://www.thelocal.ch/20120113/2278>.

43 'Justice Story: Die, My Daughter, Die!', *New York Daily News*, 10 November 2013: <http://www.nydailynews.com/news/justice-story/justice-story-honor-killing-article-1.1510125#ixzz2pe36Yseo>.

44 '"Honour" Attack Numbers Revealed by UK Police Force', BBC News, 3 December 2011: <http://www.bbc.co.uk/news/uk-16014368>.

45 Khan, 'Rukhsana Bibi Relives Horror' and Taufeeq, 'Culture of Discrimination'.

6 Nowhere to run, nowhere to hide: violence in the home

1 Brody, Liz, 'Relationship Violence: The Secret That Kills 4 Women a Day', *Glamour*, June 2011.

2 Turley, Sarah, 'Ending Violence against Women: Crucial to Global Development', *The Guardian*, 29 June 2011.

3 National Center for Injury Prevention and Control, 'Understanding Intimate Partner Violence', factsheet 2006: <http://www.cdc.gov/violenceprevention/pdf/ipv-factsheet-a.pdf>.

4 Bureau of Justice statistics selected findings: 'Female Victims of Violence', September 2009: <http://www.bjs.gov/content/pub/pdf/fvv.pdf>.

5 Acid Survivors Foundation, Dhaka, Bangladesh, 2005.

6 WomenSafe, 'Statistics on Partner Violence: Domestic Violence': <http://www.womensafe.org/statistics-on-partner-violence/>.

7 Bachelet, Michelle, UN Women's Executive Director, press release, 12 November 2012.

8 United Nations Statistics Division, *The World's Women 2010: Trends and Statistics*, United Nations Publication ST/ESA/STAT/SER.K/19, 2010, p. 131.

9 Garcia-Moreno, C. et al., 'Multi-country Study on Domestic Violence and Violence against Women', Geneva, World Health Organization, 2005.

10 Council of Europe, 'Recommendation of the Committee of Ministers to Member States on the Protection of Women against Violence',

adopted on 30 April 2002; and Explanatory Memorandum, Council of Europe, Strasbourg.

11 Turkish Republic Ministry Directorate General on the Status of Women, 'National Research on Domestic Violence Against Women in Turkey 2008', Hacettepe University Institute of Population Studies, January 2009, Figure 4 in the summary report: <http://www.hips.hacettepe. edu.tr/eng/dokumanlar/2008-TDVAW_Main_Report.pdf>.

12 Human Rights Watch report: *'He Loves You, He Beats You': Family Violence in Turkey and Access to Protection*, 2011.

13 'Milestone Women Act Passed by Turkish Parliament', *Hurriyet Daily News*, Ankara, 9 March 2012. The law also introduced new restraining orders.

14 Bayraktar, Bora, 'Violence against Women', Euronews, Turkey, March 2012.

15 Krug, Etienne G., Dahlberg, Linda L., Mercy, James A., Zwi, Anthony B. and Lozano, Rafael (eds), *World Report on Violence and Health*, Geneva, World Health Organization, 2002, p. 97.

16 United Nations Secretary-General's Campaign, UNiTE to End Violence Against Women: <http://endviolence.un.org/situation.shtml>.

17 Mental Health Europe, 'Putting an End to Domestic Violence Needs Commitment, Legislation and Funds': <http://www.epha.org/a/ 5032>.

18 See many examples of these in survivors' stories told on the Hidden Hurt website: <http://www.hiddenhurt.co.uk/domestic_violence_ stories.html>.

19 Krug et al. (eds), *World Report on Violence and Health*.

20 Browne, Angela, *When Battered Women Kill*, New York, The Free Press, 1987.

21 Ingala Smith, Karen, 'Sex Differences and Domestic Violence Murders': http://kareningalasmith.com/2015/03/14/sex-differences-and-domestic-violence-murders/>.

22 Buckley, Amy R., 'Questions No Victim of Domestic Violence Should Have to Answer', *Relevant* magazine, 17 September 2014: <http:// www.relevantmagazine.com/current/>.

23 Ahmed, Syed Masud, 'Intimate Partner Violence against Women: Experiences from a Woman-focussed Development Programme in Matlab, Bangladesh', *Journal of Health, Population and Nutrition* 23, 1 March 2005.

24 United Nations Development Programme, the Gender Inequality Index 2014: <http://hdr.undp.org/en/content/table-4-gender-inequality-index>.

25 Directorate General on the Status of Women, 'Status of Women in Turkey', 2010, p. 10, in Turkish: <http://www.ksgm.gov.tr/Pdf/ trde_kadinin_durumu_2011_subat.pdf> (accessed 4 March 2011) and reported on in English: Prime Minister Office's Directorate General on the Status of Women, 'National Research on Domestic Violence against Women in Turkey', Ankara, 2008; quoted in Cizre, Ümit: <http://www.hurriyetdailynews.com/n.php?n=nearly-4-million-turkish-women-illiterate-2011-02-01> (accessed 4 March 2011).

26 The index is based on a series of factors that indicate the status of women in a society, including: maternal mortality rates, adolescent fertility rates, antenatal care, women in parliament, labour force participation, secondary education.

27 *Gulf Times*, 2008, quoted in Salhi, Zahia Smail (ed.), *Gender and Violence in Islamic Societies: Patriarchy, Islamism and Politics in the Middle East and North Africa*, London, I. B. Tauris, 2013, p. 44.

28 Zambarakji, Angie, 'Analysis: Lebanon Debates Laws Protecting Women from Domestic Violence', *Bureau of Investigative Journalism*, City University, London, 8 March 2012.

29 'Domestic Violence in Rural Uganda: Evidence from a Community-based Study', *Bulletin of the World Health Organization* 81(1), January 2003.

30 All Africa, 'Man Kills Wife over HIV Infection': <www.allafrica.com/ stories/200808150469.html>.

31 Ahmed, 'Intimate Partner Violence against Women', p. 97.

32 Koenig, M. A., Ahmed, S., Hossain, M. B., Khorshed, Alam and Mozumder, A. B., 'Women's Status and Domestic Violence in Rural Bangladesh: Individual and Community-level Effects', *Demography*, Baltimore, MD, Johns Hopkins University, 2003.

33 Home Office Statistics Bulletin: *Crime in England and Wales 2010/11*, London, July 2011. See also: Home Office Violent Crime Unit, *Developing Domestic Violence Strategies – A Guide for Partnerships*, London, December 2004.

34 Walby, Sylvia and Allen, Jonathan, *Domestic Violence, Sexual Assault and Stalking: Findings from the British Crime Survey*, London, Home Office, 2004.

35 Walby and Allen, *Domestic Violence*.

36 Home Office Violent Crime Unit, *Developing Domestic Violence Strategies*.

37 <http://www.patient.co.uk/health/domestic-violence-leaflet>.

38 Barter, Christine, McCarry, Melanie, Berridge, David and Evans, Kathy, *Partner Exploitation and Violence in Teenage Intimate Relationships*, London, NSPCC, 2009, pp. 55, 65.

39 Barter et al., *Partner Exploitation*, p. 196.

40 Brody, 'Relationship Violence'.

41 Barter et al., *Partner Exploitation*, p. 139.

42 Brody, 'Relationship Violence'.

43 Brody, 'Relationship Violence'.

44 Rojas, John Paul Ford, 'Jean Say Murdered Children to Spite Estranged Wife', *The Telegraph*, 8 December 2011.

45 Parashar, Archana, 'Gender Equality and Religious Personal Laws in India', *The Brown Journal of World Affairs* 14(2), Spring–Summer 2008, p. 107.

46 Parashar, 'Gender Equality', p. 108.

47 Directorate General on the Status of Women, 'Status of Women in Turkey', p. 10.

48 Viner, Katharine, 'A Year of Killing', *The Guardian*, 10 December 2005.

49 See a well-researched analysis in Manckton-Smith, Jane, *Murder, Gender and the Media: Narratives of Dangerous Love*, London, Palgrave Macmillan, 2013.

50 Williams, Rob, 'US Judge Prompts Outrage . . .', *The Independent*, London, 14 December 2012.

7 Money, sex and violence: trafficking and prostitution

1 'Women and Exploitation': <http://www.csun.edu/~sm60012/WS_300/OLD%20Group%20Projects/Women%20and%20Exploitation%20Project.htm>.

2 Barton, Cat, 'Brides for Sale: Vietnamese Women Trafficked to China', AFP, 25 June 2014: <http://news.yahoo.com/brides-sale-vietnamese-women-trafficked-china-045146327.html>.

3 UN Protocol 2000, quoted in United Nations Office on Drugs and Crime, *Global Report on Trafficking in Persons 2012*, Vienna, p. 16. See also the updated *Global Report on Trafficking in Persons 2014*: <https://www.unodc.org/documents/data-and-analysis/glotip/GLOTIP_2014_full_report.pdf>.

4 The Global Slavery Index 2013 Walk Free Foundation: <http://www.ungift.org/doc/knowledgehub/resource-centre/2013/GlobalSlaveryIndex_2013_Download_WEB1.pdf>, p. 10.

5 United Nations Office on Drugs and Crime, *Global Report on Trafficking in Persons 2014*, p. 7.

6 <http://www.ilo.org/global/topics/forced-labour/publications/WCMS_181953/lang–en/index.htm>.

7 <http://www.globalslaveryindex.org/>.

8 Forst, Michael, 'Report of the Independent Expert on the Situation of Human Rights in Haiti', *United Nations General Assembly Human Rights Council*, 7 February 2013, p. 13: <http://www.ledevoir.com/documents/pdf/global_slavery.pdf>, p. 37.

9 Shelley, Louise, *Human Trafficking: A Global Perspective*, Cambridge, Cambridge University Press, 2010, p. 16.

10 ECPAT (Ending Child Prostitution And Trafficking), *Global Monitoring Report on the Status of Action against Commercial Sexual Exploitation of Children – Ethiopia*, 2007, p. 11, available at: <http://www.ecpat.net/sites/default/files/Global_Monitoring_Report-ETHIOPIA.pdf> (accessed 22 April 2014).

11 Letsche, Constanze, 'Syria's Refugees: Fears of Abuse Grow as Turkish Men Snap Up Wives', *The Guardian*, 8 September 2014: <http://www.theguardian.com/world/2014/sep/08/syrian-refugee-brides-turkish-husbands-marriage>.

12 'UNIAP: The Human Trafficking Situation in China', *2011 US Department of State Trafficking in Persons Report*: <http://www.state.gov/j/tip/rls/tiprpt/2011/164231.htm>.

13 Central Body for the Suppression of Trafficking in Persons, Burma, quoted in: <http://www.dvb.no/news/brides-to-china-trafficking-ring-uncovered-in-shan-state-burma-myanmar/42375>.

14 'UNIAP: The Human Trafficking Situation in China'.

15 'Brides for Sale: Trafficked Vietnamese Girls Sold into Marriage in China', *The Guardian*, 29 June 2014: <http://www.theguardian.com/global-development/2014/jun/29/brides-for-sale-trafficked-vietnamese-girls-sold-marriage-china>.

16 <http://www.bluedragon.org/about/the-team/>.

17 'UNIAP: The Human Trafficking Situation in China'.

18 Siddarth, Kara, *Sex Trafficking: Inside the Business of Modern Slavery*, New York, Columbia University Press, 2009, p. 37.

19 Cho, Seo-Young, Dreher, Axel and Neumayer, Eric, 'Does Legalized Prostitution Increase Human Trafficking?', *World Development* 41, 2013, pp. 67–82: <http://www.lse.ac.uk/geographyAndEnvironment/whosWho/profiles/neumayer/pdf/Article-for-World-Development-_prostitution_-anonymous-REVISED.pdf>, p. 75.

20 Shelley, *Human Trafficking*, p. 83.

21 United Nations Office on Drugs and Crime, *Global Report on Trafficking in Persons 2012*, p. 28.

22 Shelley, *Human Trafficking*, p. 17, quoting Sheldon, X., Zhang, Ko-lin and Millar, Jody, 'Women's Participation in Transnational Human Smuggling: A Gendered Market Perspective', *Criminology* 45(3), August 2007, p. 699.

23 Shelley, *Human Trafficking*, p. 17.

24 Shelley, *Human Trafficking*, p. 29.

25 <http://www.equalitynow.org/survivorstories/trisha>.

26 Shelley, *Human Trafficking*, p. 39.

27 United Nations Office on Drugs and Crime, *Global Report on Trafficking in Persons 2012*, p. 36.

28 Jarvinen, Justine, Kail, Angela and Miller, Iona, *Hard Knock Life: Violence against Women*, New Philanthropy Capital, London, April 2008, p. 100.

29 See studies: Herman, J. L., 'Introduction: Hidden in Plain Sight: Clinical Observations on Prostitution', in Farley, M. (ed.), *Prostitution, Trafficking and Traumatic Stress*, Binghamton, NY, Haworth Press, 2003, pp. 1–13, and <http://www.psychiatrictimes.com/sexual-offenses/prostitution-sexual-violence/page/0/2#sthash.cBm0eFvv.dpuf>.

30 United Nations, *Protocol to Prevent, Suppress and Punish Trafficking in Persons, Especially Women and Children*, 2000.

31 United Nations Office on Drugs and Crime, *Global Report on Trafficking in Persons 2012*, p. 17.

32 Da Costa, Kate, 'Nigeria: 250 Trafficked Nigerian Girls Rescued in Ghana', *Daily Trust*, 22 September 2014: <http://allafrica.com/stories/201409221598.html>.

33 <http://www.irinnews.org/Report/95013/UGANDA-Women-trafficked-into-sex-work>.

34 <http://www.beyondthestreets.org.uk/index.php/news/#sthash.G7GdR6pw.dpuf>.

35 Cessou, Sabine, 'Prostitution in the Netherlands: "Paying for Sex? It's Strictly Business"', *The Guardian*, 11 December 2013.

36 'Unprotected: How Legalizing Prostitution Has Failed', *Spiegel Online International*, 30 May 2013: <http://www.spiegel.de/international/germany/human-trafficking-persists-despite-legality-of-prostitution-in-germany-a-902533.html>.

37 'Unprotected'.

38 Schwarzer, Alice, *Der kleine Unterschied und seine großen Folgen* was published in 11 languages to become a feminist handbook.

39 Cho et al., 'Does Legalized Prostitution Increase Human Trafficking?', p. 75.

40 Owen, R., 'Italy Divided over Plan to Bring Back Brothels', 9 May 2002: <http://www.timesonline.co.uk/article/0,,3-290855,OO.html>.

41 German Federal Ministry for Family Affairs, Senior Citizens, Women and Youth, *Report by the Federal Government on the Impact of the Act Regulating the Legal Situation of Prostitutes* (Prostitution Act), July 2007, p. 79.

42 'Unprotected'.

43 Leidholt, Dorchen, 'Prostitution: A Violation of Women's Human Rights', *Cardoza Women's Law Journal*, 1993–4, p. 135.

44 EVAW submission to Amnesty International, March 2014.

45 O'Connor, Monica and Healey, Grainne, 'The Links between Prostitution and Sex Trafficking: A Briefing Handbook', 2006: <http://blog.lib.umn.edu/globerem/main/Handbook%20excerpt.pdf>.

46 Ekberg, Gunilla, 'The Swedish Law That Prohibits the Purchase of Sexual Services: Best Practices for Prevention of Prostitution and Trafficking in Human Beings', *Violence Against Women* 10(10), October 2004.

47 Ekberg, 'The Swedish Law', pp. 1188–9.

48 <http://www.government.se/sb/d/13420/a/151488>.

49 Schofield, Hugh, 'Will France Make Paying for Sex a Crime?', BBC News, Paris, 11 November 2013: <http://www.bbc.co.uk/news/world-europe-24852978>.

50 EVAW statement, 2014: <http://www.endviolenceagainstwomen.org.uk/evaw-s-position-on-prostitution>.

51 Shelley, *Human Trafficking*, p. 57.

52 <http://www.dailymail.co.uk/debate/article-1282092/Bradford-prostitute-murders-Horror-victims-hear-about.html#ixzz3CSy6IFvC>.

53 Farley, Melissa, 'Prostitution Is Sexual Violence', *Psychiatric Times*, 1 October 2004: <http://www.psychiatrictimes.com/prostitution-sexual-violence#sthash.4ab16lcI.dpuf>.

54 Farley, 'Prostitution Is Sexual Violence'.

55 Farley, M., Cotton, A., Lynne, J. et al., 'Prostitution and Trafficking in Nine Countries: An Update on Violence and Posttraumatic Stress Disorder', in Farley (ed.), *Prostitution, Trafficking and Traumatic Stress*, pp. 33–74. See more at: <http://www.psychiatrictimes.com/sexual-offenses/prostitution-sexual-violence/page/0/2#sthash.cBm0eFvv.dpuf>.

56 <http://www.equalitynow.org/survivorstories/ayesha>.

8 Rape

1 Jones, Owen, 'Sexual Violence Is Not a Cultural Phenomenon in India – It Is Endemic Everywhere', *The Independent*, 30 December 2012.

2 Naqvi, Muneeza, 'Journalist Gang-raped in Mumbai', New Delhi, Associated Press, 23 August 2013.

3 National Center for Injury Prevention and Control, 'The 2011 National Intimate Partner and Sexual Violence Survey', p. 20: <www.cdc.gov/violenceprevention/nisvs/>, p. 20.

4 Osborn, Sarah, 'Violent and Sexual Crime', in Chaplin, Rupert, Flatley, John and Smith, Kevin (eds), Home Office Statistical Bulletin: *Crime in England and Wales 2010–2011*, pp. 56–68: <https://gov.uk/government/uploads/system/uploads/attachment_data/file/116417/hosb1011.pdf>. See also 'Forging the Links: Rape Investigation and Prosecution', a joint review by Her Majesty's Inspectorate of Constabulary/Her Majesty's Crown Prosecution Service Inspectorate (HMIC/HMCPSI), 2012.

5 Aggregated data from the Crime Survey for England and Wales (CSEW) across the years 2009/10, 2010/11 and 2011/12 suggests that 0.5 per cent of women over age 16 were victims of the most serious offences of rape or sexual assault in the previous 12 months, equivalent to around 85,000 victims on average per year. Four hundred thousand women are estimated to be sexually assaulted annually. See: <http://www.theguardian.com/uk/2013/jan/10/sex-crimes-analysis-england-wales>.

6 Johnston, Chris, 'Iran Executes Reyhaneh Jabbari Despite Global Appeals for Retrial', *The Guardian*, 25 October 2014: <http://www.theguardian.com/world/2014/oct/25/iran-reyhaneh-jabbari-executes-appeals>.

7 Dodd, Vikram, 'Metropolitan Police's Handling of Rape Allegations to Be Reviewed', *The Guardian*, 9 June 2014: <http://www.theguardian.com/uk-news/2014/jun/09/metropolitan-police-handling-rape-allegations-review-scotland-yard>.

8 Newman, Melanie, 'The Toll of Rape and the Lack of Conviction', *Open Security*, 7 March 2014: <https://www.opendemocracy.net/opensecurity/melanie-newman/toll-of-rape-and-lack-of-conviction>; Jarvinen, Justine, Kail, Angela and Miller, Iona, *Hard Knock Life: Violence against Women*, New Philanthropy Capital, London, April 2008, Appendix 2.

9 Professor Betsy Stanko, Assistant Director of Planning and Portfolio, Metropolitan Police, quoted in Newman, 'The Toll of Rape'.

10 BBC News, 19 February 2014: <http://www.bbc.co.uk/news/uk-england-birmingham-26254639>.

11 International Federation of Journalists, 'Supreme Court Upholds Conviction and Sentence in Nepalese Journalist Rape Case', 22 December 2014: <http://www.ifj.org/nc/news-single-view/backpid/1/article/supreme-court-upholds-conviction-and-sentence-in-nepalese-journalist-rape-case/>.

12 Eichler, Leah, 'Domestic Violence: Rape Hurts Our Economy Too', *Huffington Post Canada*, 16 April 2013. For a study of cost of gender-based violence in the European Union published in 2014, see: <https://www.academia.edu/11673634/Estimating_the_Costs_of_Gender-Based_Violence_in_the_European_Union?auto=download&campaign=weekly_digest>.

13 Jarvinen et al., *Hard Knock Life*, p. 11.

14 Eichler, 'Domestic Violence'. See also Center for Disease Control (CDC), 'Sexual and Reproductive Health of Persons Aged 10–24 Years – United States 2002–2007', *Morbidity and Mortality Weekly Report* 58(6), 2009, pp. 1–58: <www.cdc.gov/mmwr/preview/mmwrhtml/ss5806a1.htm>.

15 Jarvinen et al., *Hard Knock Life*, p. 120; see also Walby, S., *The Cost of Domestic Violence*, London, Women and Equality Unit, 2004: <http://paladinservice.co.uk/wp-content/uploads/2013/07/cost_of_dv_research_summary-Walby-2004.pdf>.

16 Smith, S. G. and Breiding, M. J., 'Chronic Disease and Health Behaviours Linked to Experiences of Non-consensual Sex among Women and Men', *Public Health 2011* 125, pp. 653–9.

17 Walby, *Cost of Domestic Violence*; quoted in Jarvinen et al., *Hard Knock Life*, p. 54.

18 <http://www.cdc.gov/violenceprevention/pdf/nisvs_report2010-a.pdf>.

19 '2011 National Intimate Partner and Sexual Violence Survey', p. 20.

20 See: <http://www.ncbi.nlm.nih.gov/pubmed/23738545>.

21 Koenen, Karestan C., 'Fallout: How Rape Has Affected the Women I Study, and My Life', Women Under Siege project: <www.womenundersiegeproject.org/author/profile/karestan-c.-koenen>.

22 'Rape Culture', Marshall University Women's Center, Huntington, WV: <www.marshall.edu>.

23 Bale, A. J., 'Rape Victim Cries Every Day and Sleeps in Clothes', *The Times*, 10 March 2006.

24 Herman, Judith Lewis, *Trauma and Recovery*, New York, Basic Books, 1997, p. 56.

25 Picoult, Jodi, *The Tenth Circle*, New York, Atria Books, Simon & Schuster, 2006, p. 184.

26 'The Story of a Rape Victim: My Thoughts and More 2004–2011': <http://here4victims.tripod.com/rape/id4.html>.

27 Barter, Christine, McCarry, Melanie, Berridge, David and Evans, Kathy, *Partner Exploitation and Violence in Teenage Intimate Relationships*, London, NSPCC, 2009: <http://www.nspcc.org.uk/Inform/research/findings/partner_exploitation_and_violence_report_wdf70129.pdf>.

28 Picq, Manuela, 'A Much Needed International Day of the Girl', Al Jazeera, 11 October 2012: <http://www.aljazeera.com/indepth/opinion/2012/10/20121010614437332.html>.

29 Serafini, Natalie, 'On the Offensive', The Other Press, 31 July 2012: <http://theotherpress.ca/on-the-offensive>.

30 'Rape Is No Joke: Campaigning for Comedy without Misogyny': <http://rapeisnojoke.com/about/>.

31 Peck, Tom, 'Women Mobilise for First British "Slutwalk" Rally', *The Independent*, 10 May 2011.

32 Diton, Sarah, 'Comment Is Free', *The Guardian*, 28 September 2012.

33 Dines, Gail and Murphy, Wendy J., 'Slutwalk Is Not Sexual Liberation', *The Guardian*, 8 May 2011: <http://www.blackwomensblueprint. org/2011/09/23/an-open-letter-from-black-women-to-the-slutwalk>.

34 Black Women's Blueprint 2011, quoted in Mendes, Kaitlynn, *SlutWalk: Feminism, Activism and Media*, London, Palgrave Macmillan, 2015, and *Huffington Post*, 27 September 2011: <http://www.huffingtonpost. com/susan-brison/slutwalk-black-women_b_980215.html>.

35 For example, in *I Know Why the Caged Bird Sings*, *God Help the Child* and *The Color Purple*.

36 Halawi, Dana, 'Activists Urge Lebanon to Make Marital Rape Illegal', Thomson Reuters Foundation, 23 March 2015: <http://www.trust. org/item/20150323070027-qyd4o/>.

37 Hunt, Helen, 'Merseyside's Rape Victims' Stories, Hidden in Two Fridges', *Liverpool Echo*, 4 May 2014.

9 War and sexual violence

1 Townsend, Mark, 'Raped, Plundered, Ignored: Central Africa State Where Only Killers Thrive', *The Observer*, London, 27 July 2013.

2 Amnesty International, 'Women, Peace and Security': <www.amnestyusa. org/our-work/issues/women-s-rights/women-peace-and-security>.

3 Herman, Judith Lewis, *Trauma and Recovery*, New York, Basic Books, 1997, p. 61.

4 de Brouwer, Anne-Marie and Chu, Sandra Ka Hon (eds), *The Men Who Killed Me: Rwandan Survivors of Sexual Violence*, Vancouver, Douglas and McIntyre, 2009.

5 Magwaro, Cleopatra, 'Syria War: Rape Is a Weapon of War', April 2013: <http://mic.com/articles/34007/syria-war-rape-is-a-weapon-of-war>.

6 UN Women, *Gender-Based Violence and Child Protection amongst Syrian Refugees in Jordan with a Focus on Early Marriage*, New York, 2014.

7 Mason, Jamie, 'Sexual Violence against Women in War Should Be Classified as Terrorist Acts', *National Catholic Reporter*, Kansas City, 10 October 2014.

8 Felden, Esther, 'Former Comfort Woman Tells Uncomforting Story', *Deutsche Welle*, Asia, September 2013.

9 United Nations Security Council Resolution 1325 on Women and Peace and Security, 2000: <http://physiciansforhumanrights.org/library/reports/nowhere-to-turn.html>.

10 Physicians for Human Rights report: *Nowhere to Turn: Failure to Protect, Support and Assure Justice for Darfuri Women*: <https://s3.amazonaws.com/PHR_Reports/nowhere-to-turn.pdf>; <http://physiciansforhumanrights.org/library/reports/nowhere-to-turn.html>.

11 Médecins Sans Frontières (MSF) briefing paper: *The Crushing Burden of Rape: Sexual Violence in Darfur*, Amsterdam, March 2005.

12 <http://www.amnesty.org/en/library/info/AFR54/076/2004/en>.

13 Crncevic, Jovana, 'Women under Siege: Burma', The Women's Media Center, 17 December 2012: <http://www.womenundersiegeproject.org/conflicts/profile/burma>.

14 Lwambo, Desiree, *'Before the War I Was a Man': Men and Masculinities in Eastern Congo*, Goma, Heal Africa Publication, 2011, in partnership with Harvard Humanitarian Initiative, Cambridge, MA, 2009, p. 52.

15 Physicians for Human Rights, *Nowhere to Turn*.

16 MSF, *Crushing Burden of Rape*.

17 Smith-Spark, Laura, 'In Depth: How Did Rape Become a Weapon of War?', BBC News, 8 December 2004 (retrieved 4 March 2010).

18 Shapiro, Danielle, 'Mothers in Congo Get Help Raising Children of Rape', *Christian Science Monitor*, 9 May 2012.

19 Quoted in Hirsch, Michele Lent and Wolfe, Lauren, 'Women under Siege: Democratic Republic of the Congo', The Women's Media Center, 8 February 2012: <http://www.womenundersiegeproject.org/conflicts/profile/democratic-republic-of-congo>.

20 'Human Rights Watch interview, Bukavu, October 17, 2001', in *The War within the War: Sexual Violence against Women and Girls in Eastern Congo*, New York, Human Rights Watch, 2002, p. 54.

21 Eriksson Baaz, Maria and Stern, Maria, 'Making Sense of Violence: Voices of Soldiers in the Congo (DRC)', *Journal of Modern African Studies* 46(1), 2008, pp. 57–86.

22 For more background see: <http://www.healafrica.org/history>.

23 Quoted in Dieu-Donné Wedi Djamba, 'We Want Our Dignity Back', *Pambazuka News* 312, July 2007: <www.pambazuka.org>.

24 Nduwimana, Françoise, *The Right to Survive: Sexual Violence, Women and HIV/AIDS*, Quebec, Rights and Democracy, 2004, p. 74.

25 Green, Llezlie, 'Gender-Hate Propaganda and Sexual Violence in the Rwandan Genocide: An Argument for Intersectionality in International Law', *Columbia Human Rights Law Review* 33(733), 2002.

26 Elbe, Stefan, 'HIV/AIDS and the Changing Landscape of War in Africa', *International Security* 27(2), Fall 2002, pp. 159–77.

27 United Nations High Commissioner for Refugees (UNHCR), *Global Trends Report*, 2013.

28 Quoted in Greenwood, Phoebe, 'Rape and Domestic Violence Follow Syrian Women into Refugee Camps', *The Guardian*, 25 July 2013.

29 Bindel, Julie, 'Women Come Last in Syrian Refugee Camps', *Standpoint* magazine, UN Refugee Agency, April 2013.

30 'Somalia Rape on the Rise amid "Climate of Fear" in Mogadishu IDP Camps', Nairobi, IRIN News, 22 December 2011; IRIN is a service of the UN Office for the Coordination of Humanitarian Affairs.

31 UN Women, *Gender-Based Violence and Child Protection*, p. 25.

32 MSF, *Crushing Burden of Rape*.

33 Wolfe, Lauren, 'Will There Ever Be Justice for Syria's Rape Survivors?', *The Nation*, 14 May 2014: <www.thenation.com/article/179843/will-there-ever-be-justice-syrias-rape-survivors>.

34 Wolfe, Lauren, 'Syria Has a Massive Rape Crisis', *The Atlantic*, 2 April 2013.

35 UN Women, *Gender-Based Violence and Child Protection*, p. 24.

36 Jones, Ann, 'The War against Women: A Dispatch from the West Africa Front', February 2008: <www.tomdispatch.com/post/174895>. See also Jones, Ann, *War Is Not Over When It's Over: Women Speak Out from the Ruins of War*, New York, Metropolitan Books, Henry Holt, 2010.

37 *Report of the United Nations Commissioner for Human Rights on the Human Rights Situation and the Activities of Her Office in the Democratic*

Republic of the Congo, UN General Assembly, September 2014, Human Rights Council, twenty-seventh session, Agenda items 2 and 10.

38 Amnesty International, 'Women, Peace and Security'.

39 See Storkey, Alan, *War or Peace?*, Cambridge, Christian Studies Press, 2015.

10 Why gender-based violence? It's in our genes: exploring our evolutionary heritage

1 Goetz, Aaron T., 'The Evolutionary Psychology of Violence', *Psicothema* 22(1), 2010, pp. 16, 18: <http://www.academia.edu/1077393/The_Evolutionary_Psychology_of_Violence>.

2 See Johnson, Kirsten, et al., 'Association of Sexual Violence and Human Rights Violations with Physical and Mental Health in Territories of the Eastern Democratic Republic of the Congo', *Journal of the American Medical Association*, 4 August 2010.

3 Heise, L. L., 'Violence against Women: An Integrated Ecological Framework', *Violence Against Women* 4(3), June 1998, pp. 262–90.

4 Simpson, G. G., 'The Biological Nature of Man', *Science* 152, April 1966, p. 472.

5 See Thornhill, Randy and Palmer, Craig T., *A Natural History of Rape: Biological Bases of Sexual Coercion*, Cambridge, MA, Bradford Books, MIT Press, 2001, p. 4.

6 Van Vugt, M., De Cremer, D. and Janssen, D., 'Gender Differences in Cooperation and Competition: The Male-Warrior Hypothesis', *Psychological Science* 18(1), 2007, pp. 19–23; DOI: 10.1111/j.1467-9280.2007.01842.x.

7 Thornhill and Palmer, *Natural History of Rape*, p. xiii.

8 Thornhill and Palmer, *Natural History of Rape*, p. xii.

9 Wilson, Edward O., *Sociobiology: The New Synthesis*, Cambridge, MA, Harvard University Press, 1975.

10 Dawkins, Richard, *The Selfish Gene*, New York, Oxford University Press, 1976.

11 Dawkins, *Selfish Gene*, p. 35.

12 Buss, D. M., *The Evolution of Desire: Strategies of Human Mating*, New York, Perseus/Basic Books, 1994.

13 Thornhill and Palmer, *Natural History of Rape*, p. 41.

14 Goetz, 'Evolutionary Psychology of Violence', pp. 15–16.

15 Goetz, 'Evolutionary Psychology of Violence', p. 16.

16 Wilson, Glenn, *The Great Sex Divide*, London, Peter Owen, 1989, pp. 128–31; Washington DC, Scott-Townsend, 1992.

17 Alexander, R. D. and Noonan, K. M., 'Concealment of Ovulation, Parental Care, and Human Social Evolution', in Chagnon, N. A. and Irons, W. (eds), *Evolutionary Biology and Human Social Behavior*, North Scitute, MA, Duxbury Press, 1979, pp. 436–53; quoted by Wilson, *Great Sex Divide*, pp. 128–31. See also, however, Steven, W. and Thornhill, Randy, 'Human Oestrus', *Proceedings of the Royal Society, Biological Sciences* 275(1638), 7 May 2008, pp. 991–1000, which claims evidence for women's pre-fertile period.

18 Ellis, Lee, *Theories of Rape: Inquiries into the Causes of Sexual Aggression*, Washington, DC, Hemisphere Pub. Corp., 1989.

19 Goetz, A. T. and Shackelford, T. K., 'Sexual Coercion and Forced In-pair Copulation as Sperm Competition Tactics in Humans', *Human Nature* 17, 2006, pp. 265–82.

20 Kaighobadi, F., Goetz, A. T. and Shackelford, T. K., 'From Mate Retention to Murder: Evolutionary Psychological Perspectives on Men's Partner-Directed Violence', *Review of General Psychology* 13(4), 2009, pp. 327–34.

21 Goetz, 'Evolutionary Psychology of Violence', p. 19, quoting Buss, David M., *The Murderer Next Door*, New York, Penguin, 2005.

22 Wilson, M. I. and Daly, M., 'Male Sexual Proprietariness and Violence against Wives', *Current Directions in Psychological Science* 5, 1996, p. 5.

23 Symons, D., *The Evolution of Human Sexuality*, New York, Oxford University Press, 1979.

24 Hamilton, R., 'The Darwinian Cage: Evolutionary Psychology as Moral Science', *Theory, Culture and Society* 25(2), 2008, pp. 105–25: <http://doi.org/10.1177/0263276407086793>.

25 Thornhill, Randy and Palmer, Craig T., 'Why Men Rape', New York Academy of Sciences, January/February 2000, p. 25.

26 Thornhill and Palmer, 'Why Men Rape', p. 19.

27 Hamilton, 'Darwinian Cage', p. 109.

28 Thornhill and Palmer, 'Why Men Rape'.

29 Daly, M. and Wilson, M., *Homicide*, New York, Aldine De Gruyter, 1988.

30 Buss, D. M. (2000), *The Dangerous Passion: Why Jealousy Is as Necessary as Love and Sex*, New York, Simon & Schuster, 2000. See also his article 'Sexual Jealousy', *Psychological Topics* 22(2), 2013, pp. 155–82.

31 Browne, Kingsley R., 'An Evolutionary Perspective on Sexual Harassment: Seeking Roots in Biology Rather Than Ideology', *Journal of Contemporary Legal Issues* 8, 1997, pp. 5–7.

32 Pinker, S., *How the Mind Works*, London, Allen Lane/Penguin, 1997, p. 207.

33 Thornhill and Palmer, 'Why Men Rape', p. 25.

34 Blakemore, Colin, *The Mind Machine*, London, BBC, 1988.

35 Symons, D., 'On the Use and Misuse of Darwinism in the Study of Human Behaviour', in Barkow, J., Cosmides, L. and Tooby, J. (eds), *The Adapted Mind: Evolutionary Psychology and the Generation of Culture*, New York, Oxford University Press, 1992, pp. 137–59.

36 Midgley, Mary, *Science and Poetry*, London, Routledge Classics, 2006, p. 141.

37 Bennet, Neil, 'Biology and Ideology: The Case against Biological Determinism', *Frontline* 2(8), December 2008: <http://www.redflag.org.uk/frontline/dec08/evolution.html>.

38 Pinker, *How the Mind Works*, p. 559.

39 Pinker, *How the Mind Works*, pp. 147–8.

40 Blakemore, Colin, quoted by Malik, Kenan, 'What Science Can and Cannot Tell Us about Human Nature', in Headlam Wells, Robin and McFadden, Johnjoe (eds), *Human Nature: Fact and Fiction: Literature, Science and Human Nature*, London, Bloomsbury Continuum, 2006, p. 178.

41 Taylor, Richard, *Ethics, Faith and Reason*, Englewood Cliffs, NJ, Prentice-Hall, 1985, pp. 2–3.

42 Dawkins, Richard, 'Let's All Stop Beating Basil's Car', Edge Foundation, 2008: <http://www.edge.org/q2006/q06_9.html>.

43 Nagel, Thomas, *The Last Word*, New York, Oxford University Press, 2001, pp. 136–7.

44 Malik, 'What Science Can and Cannot Tell Us', p. 178.

45 Malik, 'What Science Can and Cannot Tell Us', p. 178.

46 Pinker, S., *The Blank Slate: The Modern Denial of Human Nature*, London, BCA, 2002, p. 42.

47 Tallis, Raymond, *The Explicit Animal: A Defence of Human Consciousness*, London, Macmillan, 1991.

48 Pinker, *Blank Slate*.

49 Searle, John, 'Putting Consciousness Back into the Brain' – reply to Bennett and Hacker in Bennett, M., Dennett, D., Hacker, P. and Searle, J. (eds), *Neuroscience and Philosophy: Body, Mind and Language*, New York, Columbia University Press, 2007, pp. 97–126.

50 Malik, Kenan, 'In Defence of Human Agency', 2002: <http://www.kenanmalik.com/papers/engelsberg_nature.html>.

11 Why gender-based violence? Power and patriarchy

1 Minnesota Advocates for Human Rights, 'Causes and Effects of Gender-based Violence': <http://www.stopvaw.org>.

2 'Toward an Understanding of Male Violence against Women': <http://www.feminist.com/resources/ourbodies/viol_toward.html>.

3 Ayiera, Eve, 'Sexual Violence in Conflict: A Problematic International Discourse', *Feminist Africa*, Nairobi, Urgent Action Fund, p. 14: <http://agi.ac.za/sites/agi.ac.za/files/3._fa_14_-_feature_article_eva_ayiera.pdf>.

4 Straus, M. A. and Gelles, R. (eds), *Physical Violence in American Families: Risk Factors and Adaptations to Violence in 8,145 Families*, New Brunswick, NJ, Transaction Publishers, 1990.

5 Straus and Gelles (eds), *Physical Violence in American Families*. See also Straus, M. A., Hamby, S. L., Finkelhorn, D., Moore, D. W. and Runyan, D., 'Identification of Child Maltreatment with the Parent–Child Conflict Tactics Scales: Development and Psychometric Data for a National Sample of American Parents', *Child Abuse and Neglect* 22, 1998, pp. 249–70.

6 Dutton, D. G. and Nicholls, T. L., 'The Gender Paradigm in Domestic Violence Research and Theory: Part 1 – The Conflict of Theory and Data', *Aggression and Violent Behavior* 10, 2005, pp. 680–714.

7 Alexander, Pamela C., *Intergenerational Cycles of Trauma and Violence: An Attachment and Family Systems Perspective*, London, W. W. Norton and Co., 2014.

8 Gould, Jonathan W. and Martindale, David A., *The Art and Science of Child Custody Evaluations*, New York, The Guildford Press, 2009, pp. 207–9.

9 Dodge, K. A., Bates, J. E. and Pettit, G. S., 'Mechanisms in the Cycle of Violence', *Science* 250, 1990, pp. 1678–83.

10 Cappell, C. and Heiner, R. B., 'The Intergenerational Transmission of Family Aggression', *Journal of Family Violence* 5(2), 1990, pp. 135–52. See also Straus, M. A., 'Ordinary Violence, Child Abuse and Wife Beating: What Do They Have in Common?', in Straus and Gelles (eds), *Physical Violence in American Families*.

11 Ehrensaft, Miriam K., Cohen, Patricia, Brown, Jocelyn, Smailes, Elizabeth, Chen, Henian and Johnson, Jeffrey G., 'Intergenerational Transmission of Partner Violence: A 20-Year Prospective Study', *Journal of Consulting and Clinical Psychology* 71(4), 2003, pp. 741–53.

12 Choice, P., Lamke, L. K. and Pittman, J. F., 'Conflict Resolution Strategies and Marital Distress as Mediating Factors in the Link between

Witnessing Interparental Violence and Wife Battering', *Violence and Victims* 10(2), 1995, pp. 107–19.

13 See Briken, Peer, Habermann, Niels, Berner, Wolfgang and Hill, Andreas, 'The Influence of Brain Abnormalities on Psychosocial Development, Criminal History and Paraphilias in Sexual Murderers', *Journal of Forensic Science* 50(5), September 2005, Paper ID JFS2004472: <http://www.astm.org/industry/forensics-journals.html>.

14 Currie, D. H., 'Violent Men or Violent Women? Whose Definition Counts?', in Bergen, R. K. (ed.), *Issues in Intimate Partner Violence*, Thousand Oaks, CA, Sage, 1998, pp. 97–111.

15 Loseke, D. R. and Kurz, D., 'Men's Violence toward Women Is the Serious Social Problem', in Loseke, D. R., Gelles, R. J. and Cavanaugh, M. M. (eds), *Current Controversies on Family Violence*, 2nd edn, Thousand Oaks, CA, Sage, 2005, p. 84.

16 See Nixon, Kendra L., 'The Construction of Intimate Partner Woman Abuse in Alberta's Child Protection Policy and the Impact on Abused Mothers and Their Children', PhD dissertation, University of Calgary, 2009: <http://research4children.com/data/documents/TheConstructionof IntimatePartnerViolenceinAlbertasChildProtectionPolicypdf.pdf>.

17 In Wamue-Ngare, G. and Njoroge, E. N., 'Gender Paradigm Shift within the Family Structure in Kiambu, Kenya', *African Journal of Social Sciences* 1(3), 2011, pp. 10–20.

18 Igbelina-Igbokwe, Nkiru, 'Contextualizing Gender-Based Violence within Patriarchy in Nigeria', *Pambuzuka News*, 30 May 2013, <http:// www.pambazuka.net/en/category/features/87597/print>, quoting from Wamue-Ngare et al., 'Gender Paradigm Shift within the Family Structure', p. 14.

19 Skeggs, Beverley, 'The Dirty History of Feminism and Sociology: Or the War of Conceptual Attrition', *Sociological Review*, 2008: <http:// www.academia.edu/5136812/The_dirty_history_of_feminism_and_ sociology_or_the_war_of_conceptual_attrition>.

20 Bristor, Julia M., 'Insider Versus Outsider: Reflections on a Feminist Consumer', *Advances in Consumer Research* 19, 1992, pp. 843–4: <http://www.acrwebsite.org/search/view-conference-proceedings. aspx?Id=7400>.

21 See Banks, Olive, *Parity and Prestige in English Secondary Education*, London, Routledge, 1955.

22 Rowbotham, Sheila, *Hidden from History: 300 Years of Women's Oppression and the Fight against It*, London, Pluto, 1973.

23 Storkey, Elaine, *What's Right with Feminism*, London, SPCK, 1985. See also Storkey, Elaine, 'The Production of Social Divisions', *Society and the Social Sciences*, Open University, 1987.

24 Storkey, Elaine, *Created or Constructed? The Great Gender Debate*, Carlisle, Paternoster Press, 2000.

25 Weber, Max, *Economy and Society*, revd edn, Oakland, CA, University of California Press, 2013 (1922).

26 Millett, Kate, *Sexual Politics*, London, Shere, 1971.

27 Rosbech, Malise, 'What Is Patriarchy?', New Left Project, 20 September 2013: <http://www.newleftproject.org/index.php/site/article_comments/what_is_patriarchy>.

28 Lerner, Gerder, *The Creation of Patriarchy*, Oxford, Oxford University Press, 1987.

29 Christ, Carol, 'Patriarchy as a System of Male Dominance', *Religion and Feminism*, 18 February 2013: <http://feminismandreligion.com/2013/02/18/patriarchy-as-an-integral-system-of-male-dominance-created-at-the-intersection-of-the-control-of-women-private-property-and-war-part-1-by-carol-p-christ/#comments>.

30 Morgan, Robin, *Sisterhood Is Powerful*, New York, Random House, 1973.

31 Daly, Mary, *Gyn/Ecology: The Meta-ethics of Radical Feminism*, Boston, Beacon Press, 1978, p. 39.

32 Pisharoty, Sangeeta Barooah, 'She Lives It!', *The Hindu*, 13 April 2006: <http://www.thehindu.com/todays-paper/tp-features/tp-metroplus/gender-bender/article4674863.ece>.

33 Darvishpour, Mehrdad, '"Islamic Feminism": Compromise or Challenge to Feminism?', *Iran Bulletin – Middle East Forum*, Summer 2003, pp. 55–8: <http://www.iran-bulletin.org/political_islam/islamfeminismedited2.html>.

34 Elliot, Cath, 'The Patriarchy Made Flesh', *The Guardian*, 25 March 2009: <http://www.theguardian.com/commentisfree/belief/2009/mar/24/sobrinho-abortion-catholic>.

35 Pisharoty, 'She Lives It!'

36 Walby, Sylvia, *Theorizing Patriarchy*, Cambridge, Polity Press, 1997.

37 Igbelina-Igbokwe, 'Contextualizing Gender-Based Violence'.

38 Real, Terrence, *How Can I Get Through to You? Reconnecting Men and Women*, New York, Simon & Schuster, 2010, p. 18.

39 Pisharoty, 'She Lives It!'

40 hooks, bell, 'Understanding Patriarchy', in *The Will to Change: Men, Masculinity and Love*, New York, Simon & Schuster, 2004, p. 27.

41 hooks, bell, *Will to Change*, p. 27.

42 Quoted in hooks, bell, *Will to Change*, p. 33.

43 Barrett, Michèle, *Woman's Oppression Today: Problems in Marxist Feminist Analysis*, London, Verso, 1980, p. 14.

44 Hennessy, Rosemary, *Profit and Pleasure: Sexual Identities in Late Capitalism*, New York/London, Routledge, 2000, p. 23.

12 Religion and women

1 Maguire, Daniel C., 'Violence against Women: Roots and Cures in World Religions': <http://www.religiousconsultation.org/violence_vs_women_roots_and_cures_in_world_religions.htm>.

2 Tang, Susan, 'Ending Impunity against Women', Free Community Church Sermon, 11 March 2007: <http://www.amplifyproject.net/05-110307.htm>.

3 Toynbee, Polly, 'Sex and Death Lie at the Poisoned Heart of Religion', *The Guardian*, 14 October 2010.

4 The Pew Forum on Religion and Public Life, 'The Global Religious Landscape', Pew Research Center, 18 December 2012.

5 Ogbonnaya, Joseph, *Lonergan, Social Transformation, and Sustainable Human Development*, African Christian Studies, Eugene, OR, Pickwick, 2013, p. 122.

6 Tang, 'Ending Impunity against Women'.

7 Metropolitan Police Sikh Association (MPSA), *A Brief Guide to Honour Based Violence*, MPSA, 2010, pp. 1, 17: <http://www.sikhpolice.org/MPSA%20Repository/Articles/Honour_Violence_Booklet.pdf>.

8 Faure, Bernard, 'Introduction', *The Power of Denial: Buddhism, Purity, and Gender*, Princeton, NJ, Princeton University Press, 2003, p. 3. See also Shaw, Miranda, *Passionate Enlightenment: Women in Tantric Buddhism*, Princeton, NJ, Princeton University Press, 1994, p. 27, with particular reference to the fourth-century Bodhisattvabhūmi.

9 Dasgupta, Shamita Das and Jain, Shashi, 'Ahimsa and the Jain Community', in Dasgupta, Shamita Das and Jain, Shashi (eds), *Body Evidence: Intimate Violence against South Asian Women in America*, New Brunswick, NJ, Rutgers University Press, 2007, p. 162.

10 Anon., 'A Sober Second Look: Recovering from Religious Patriarchy': <https://sobersecondlook.wordpress.com/recovering-from-religious-patriarchy/>.

11 'Louise', August 2012, in 'A Sober Second Look'.

12 Abdel-Razek, Reem, 'Unveiled: Three Former Muslim Women Look Back on the Hijab': http://valerietarico.com/2014/03/18/unveiled-three-former-muslim-women-look-back-on-the-hijab-part-3-reem-abdel-razek/>.

13 #3, April 2014, in 'A Sober Second Look'.

14 Ex-Muslim Blogs: <http://www.exmuslimblogs.com/chistascontemplation/blog/2014/04/05/like-closet-ex-muslim-woman/>.

15 A much fuller discussion in Mernissi, Fatema, *Beyond the Veil: Male–Female Dynamics in Modern Muslim Society*, London, Saqi Books, 2011 (1975) and Ahmed, Leila, *A Quiet Revolution: The Veil's Resurgence from the Middle East to America*, New Haven, CT, Yale University Press, 2011.

16 See, for example, conservative Islamic scholar Shaykh Yusuf al-Qaradawi, *Islamic Awakening between Rejection and Extremism* (English edn ed. Al Shaikh-Ali, A. S. and Wasty, Mohamed B. E.), Riyadh, International Islamic Publishing House, 1995.

17 Wadud, Amina, 'Alternative Qu'ranic Interpretation and the Status of Muslim Women', in Webb, Gisela (ed.), *Windows of Faith: Muslim Women Scholar-Activists in North America*, Syracuse, NY, Syracuse University Press, 2000, p. 4.

18 Wadud, 'Alternative Qu'ranic Interpretation'.

19 Iaccino, Ludovica, 'Saudi Preacher Fayhan al-Ghamdi Released after Raping and Killing Daughter Because He "Doubted Her Virginity"', *International Business Times*, 10 March 2014: http://www.ibtimes.co.uk/saudi-preacher-fayhan-al-ghamdi-released-after-raping-killing-daughter-because-he-doubted-her-1439657>.

20 'Sunni Saudi Wahabi Preacher Issues Fatwa Allowing Jihadis to Rape Syrian Women and Girls . . .', *The Muslim Issue*, 3 July 2013: <https://themuslimissue.wordpress.com/2013/07/03/sunni-saudi-wahabi-preacher-issues-fatwa-allowing-jihadis-to-rape-syrian-women-and-girls>.

21 Alyousei, Mohammad, '"Burkas for Babies": Saudi Cleric's New Fatwa Causes Controversy', Al Arabiya News, February 2013: <http://english.alarabiya.net/articles/2013/02/03/264031.html>.

22 Yacob, Mirna, 'Sexual Perversion in Patriarchy', 26 June 2013: <http://www.councilofexmuslims.com/index.php?topic=24432.0>.

23 <http://www.exmuslimblogs.com>.

24 See Cooey, Paula M., Eakin, William R. and McDaniel, John B., *After Patriarchy: Feminist Transformations of the World Religions*, New Delhi, Sri Satguru Publications, 1991, p. 41.

25 Abdekhodaie, Zohreh, 'Letty Russell: Insights and Challenges of Christian Feminism', MA thesis, University of Waterloo, Canada, 2008, p. 117.

26 See: <http://www.theguardian.com/world/2015/mar/09/lebanese-tv-presenter-cuts-short-interview-with-sexist-islamist-scholar>. See also: <http://qz.com/360949/360949/>.

27 1 Peter 3.3–4: 'Your beauty should not come from outward adornment, such as braided hair and the wearing of gold jewellery and fine clothes. Instead, it should be that of your inner self, the unfading beauty of a gentle and quiet spirit, which is of great worth in God's sight.'

28 Pew Research 2015: <http://www.pewresearch.org/fact-tank/2015/02/ 27/5-facts-about-religious-hostilities-in-europe/>. This research indicates that in 19 out of 45 countries in Europe women were harassed over dress codes – by both Muslims for violation, and non-Muslims for observation. This proportion of countries is roughly the same as in the Middle East and North Africa, but double the global rate.

29 Mir-Hosseini, Ziba, 'Muslim Women's Quest for Equality: Between Islamic Law and Feminism', *Critical Enquiry*, Summer 2006, Amherst Education.

30 Mir-Hosseini, 'Muslim Women's Quest for Equality'.

31 Quoted in Segram, Elizabeth, 'The Rise of the Islamic Feminists', *The Nation*, December 2013.

32 Interview with Amina Wadud in March 2002: <http://www.peacethrujustice. org/wadudInterview.htm>.

33 <http://www.peacethrujustice.org/wadudInterview.htm>.

34 <http://www.peacethrujustice.org/wadudInterview.htm>.

35 In Mushim Khan's translation of Bukhari, Sahih – vol. 3, section XVII, on Witnesses.

36 Maududi, Sayyid Abul A'la, *The Meaning of the Qur'an*, vol. 1, Chicago, Kazi Publications, 1999, p. 205.

37 <http://www.islamswomen.com/marriage/fiqh_of_marriage_8.php>.

38 Darwish, Nonie, <http://www.gatestoneinstitute.org/3681/muslim-family-next-door>; see also *The Devil We Don't Know: The Dark Side of Revolutions in the Middle East*, Hoboken, NJ, John Wiley and Sons, 2012. She is President of Former Muslims United: <http:// formermuslimsunited.org/>.

39 Barlas, Asma, *Believing Women in Islam: Unreading Patriarchal Interpretations of the Qur'an*, Austin, TX, University of Texas Press, 2002.

40 Abdekhodaie, 'Letty Russell', p. 126.

41 Salime, Zakia, *Between Feminism and Islam: Human Rights and Sharia Law in Morocco*, Minneapolis, University of Minnesota Press, 2011.

42 Mir-Hosseini, 'Muslim Women's Quest'.

43 Quoted in Segram, 'Rise of the Islamic Feminists'.

44 Barlas, Asma, 'Still Quarrelling over the Qur'an: Five Theses on Interpretation and Authority', Religious Authority in Practice Conference,

Institute for the Study of Islam in the Modern World, Amsterdam, 24 June 2007.

45 Prado, Abdennur, 'Qur'anic Feminism: The Makers of Textual Meaning', in Keccia, Ali et al. (eds), *A Jihad for Justice*: http://www.bu.edu/religion/files/2010/03/A-Jihad-for-Justice-for-Amina-Wadud-2012-1.pdf.

46 Schüssler Fiorenza, Elisabeth, *In Memory of Her: A Feminist Reconstruction of Christian Origins*, New York, Crossroad, 1985.

47 See also the writings of Asma Barlas, Sa'diyya Shaikh, Riffat Hassan, Azizah al-Hibri, Ali Asghar Engineer, Na-eem Jennah, Musdah Mulia, Khalid Masud, Fatema Mernissi.

48 Wadud, Amina, *Inside the Gender Jihad*, London, Oneworld, 2007, p. 188.

49 Wadud, *Inside the Gender Jihad*, p. 204.

50 See Abdekhodaie, 'Letty Russell', p. 122.

13 Christianity and gender: a fuller picture

1 Former US President Jimmy Carter, 'Losing My Religion for Equality', *The Age: Federal Politics*, 15 July 2009: <http://www.theage.com.au/federal-politics/losing-my-religion-forequality-20090714-dk0v.html>.

2 See Ogbonnaya, Joseph, *Lonergan, Social Transformation, and Sustainable Human Development*, African Christian Studies, Eugene, OR, Pickwick, 2013.

3 Barr, Jane, 'The Influence of St Jerome on Mediaeval Attitudes towards Women', in Soskice, Janet Martin (ed.), *After Eve*, London, Marshall Pickering, 1990.

4 See Storkey, Elaine, 'Nuns, Witches and Patriarchy', *Anvil*, 1989.

5 See Christenson, Larry, *The Christian Family*, Minneapolis, Bethany House, 1970.

6 Greek dualism with its 'form–matter' dichotomy often projected 'matter' on to woman and 'rational form' on to men. See Freeland, Cynthia, 'Nourishing Speculation: A Feminist Reading of Aristotelian Science', in Bar On, Bat-Ami (ed.), *Engendering Origins: Critical Feminist Readings in Plato and Aristotle*, Albany, NY, State University of New York Press, 1994, pp. 145–6.

7 Kaczor, Christopher, 'Does the Catholic Church Hate Women?', Catholic Education Resource Centre, 2011: <http://www.catholiceducation.org/en/religion-and-philosophy/apologetics/does-the-catholic-church-hate-women.html>.

8 Pope John Paul, Letter to Women 3, 1995, quoted in Kaczor, 'Does the Catholic Church Hate Women?'

9 See the work of Catherine Clark Kroeger and Nancy Nason-Clark: *No Place for Abuse*, Downers Grove, IL, IVP, 2011; *Refuge from Abuse: Healing and Hope for Christian Women*, Downers Grove, IL, IVP, 2004; *Responding to Abuse in Christian Homes*, Eugene, OR, Wipf & Stock, 2011.

10 Nason-Clark, Nancy, Holtmann, Cathy, Fisher-Townsend, Barbara, McMullin, Steve and Ruff, Lanette, 'The RAVE Project: Developing Web-based Religious Resources for Social Action on Domestic Violence', *Critical Social Work* 10(1), 2009, pp. 151–68.

11 Nason-Clark, Nancy, *The Battered Wife: How Christians Confront Family Violence*, Louisville, KY, Westminster John Knox Press, 1997.

12 Kiara's story is on the Hidden Hurt website: <http://www.hiddenhurt. co.uk/kiara_domestic_abuse_story.html>. Many other stories are found there also, and a forum exists for exchanging comments.

13 See Holcomb, Justin S. and Holcomb, Lindsey, *Is It My Fault? Hope and Healing for Those Suffering Domestic Violence*, Chicago, Moody, 2014.

14 Carter, 'Losing My Religion'.

15 Van Beek, Joanne, 'What's the Problem in Our Homes Today?', PASCH (Peace and Safety in the Christian Home) newsletter, October 2009, p. 7.

16 Daly, Mary, *Gyn/Ecology: The Meta-ethics of Radical Feminism*, Boston, Beacon Press, 1978, p. 39.

17 Christ, Carol, 'Patriarchy as a System of Male Dominance', *Religion and Feminism*, 18 February 2013: <http://feminismandreligion.com/ 2013/03/04/patriarchy-as-an-integral-system-of-male-dominance-created-at-the-intersection-of-the-control-of-women-private-property-and-war>.

18 See Johnson, Elizabeth, 'Feminism in Faith: Challenge to the Vatican', *BuzzFeed News*, 6 March 2014.

19 Hampson, Daphne, Sea of Faith Conference, Leicester, 1997: <http:// www.sofn.org.uk/conferences/hamps97.html>.

20 Kwok Pui Lan, Re-Imagining Conference, Minneapolis, 1993.

21 Daly, Mary, *Beyond God the Father: Toward a Philosophy of Women's Liberation*, Boston, Beacon Press, 1973, p. 77.

22 Williams, Delores S., at the 1993 Minneapolis Re-Imagining Conference which attracted 2,200 participants; taken from tapes. For a critical review see: <http://brfwitness.freeservers.com/Articles/1994v29n3.htm>.

23 Trible, Phyllis, *Texts of Terror: Literary Feminist Readings of Biblical Narratives*, Philadelphia, Fortress Press, 1984.

24 Mollenkott, Virginia, *Women, Men and the Bible*, Nashville, Abingdon Press, 1977; Scanzoni, Letha and Hardesty, Nancy, *All We Were Meant to Be*, Waco, TX, Word Books, 1974.

25 Russell, Letty, 'Authority and the Challenge of Feminist Interpretation', in Russell, Letty (ed.), *Feminist Interpretation of the Bible*, Philadelphia, Westminster Press, 1985, p. 137.

26 Kroeger, Catherine Clark (with Richard Clark Kroeger), *I Suffer Not a Woman: Rethinking 1 Timothy 2:11–15 in Light of Ancient Evidence*, Grand Rapids, Baker Book House, 1992.

27 Ruether, Rosemary Radford, 'Feminist Interpretation: A Method of Correlation', in Russell (ed.), *Feminist Interpretation*.

28 Heyward, Carter, *Touching Our Strength: The Erotic as Power and the Love of God*, San Francisco, Harper & Row, 1989. See also: 'Is a Self-Respecting Christian Woman an Oxymoron?' in Thatcher, Adrian and Stuart, Elizabeth (eds), *Christian Perspectives on Sexuality and Gender*, Grand Rapids, Eerdmans, 1996, pp. 68–83; Chung Hyun Kyung, *Struggle to Be the Sun Again: Introducing Asian Women's Theology*, Maryknoll, NY, Orbis Books, 1990.

29 The 'divine patriarch [that] castrates women'. Daly, *Beyond God the Father*, p. 19.

30 Trible, Phyllis, in Russell (ed.), *Feminist Interpretation*, p. 147.

31 Quoted in Loades, Ann, 'Feminist Interpretation', in Barton, John (ed.), *The Cambridge Companion to Biblical Interpretation*, Cambridge, Cambridge University Press, 1998, pp. 81–94.

32 Oduyoye, Mercy, *Daughters of Anowa: African Women and Patriarchy*, New York, Orbis Books, 1995.

33 I have offered much more thorough contributions to Christian feminist analysis and critique elsewhere. Please see Storkey, Elaine, 'Who Is the Christ?' in Campbell, Douglas (ed.), *Gospel and Gender*, London, T&T Clark, 2004; Storkey, Elaine, *Created or Constructed? The Great Gender Debate*, Carlisle, Paternoster Press, 2001; *The Origins of Difference*, Grand Rapids, Baker Academic, 2001.

34 Figures from the Center for the Study of Global Christianity, Gordon Conwell College, Massachusetts, quoted in Allen, John L., 'The War on Christians', *The Spectator*, 5 October 2013: <http://www.spectator.co.uk/features/9041841/the-war-on-christians/>. In 1991 the Christian population in Iraq stood at over 1.5 million. By 2014 it had dropped to fewer than 400,000.

35 Center for the Study of Global Christianity, in Allen, 'War on Christians'.

36 Center for the Study of Global Christianity, in Allen, 'War on Christians'.

37 Fell, Margaret, 'Women's Speaking Justified', 1666: 'God has put no such difference between the Male and Female as men would make . . . If the Apostle would have had women's speaking stopped, and did not allow of them, why did he intreat his true yoke-Fellow to help those Women who laboured with him in the Gospel? (Phil. 4.3)'. The full text is available at: <http://www.qhpress.org/texts/fell.html>.

38 Jewish Encyclopedia: <www.jewishencyclopedia.com/articles/13194-sarah-sarai>.

39 See the work of Tamara Cohn Eskenazi, editor of *The Torah: A Women's Commentary*, and especially her article 'Women and Violence in the Hebrew Bible': <http://www.bibleodyssey.org/en/people/related-articles/women-and-violence-in-the-hebrew-bible.aspx>.

40 Exodus 15; Judges 4; 2 Kings 22 (2 Chronicles 34).

41 Exodus 1.15–22.

42 1 Samuel 25.32–33.

43 Esther.

44 Ruth.

45 Joel 2.28–29; Acts 2; 21.9.

46 Romans 12; 1 Corinthians 12; Ephesians 4.

47 Some people argue that because Paul does not specifically ask men to submit to their wives, this is a 'one-way' requirement. But Paul does not specifically ask women to love their husbands, yet no one argues that they should not!

48 1 Corinthians 7.1–4. 'The wife's body does not belong to her alone but also to her husband. In the same way, the husband's body does not belong to him alone but also to his wife.'

49 For a much fuller discussion of these and other passages, read Evans, Mary J., *Woman in the Bible*, Carlisle, Paternoster Press, 1984 and Evans, Mary J., Storkey, Elaine and Kroeger, Catherine Clark, *Study New Testament for Women*, London, Marshall Pickering, 1995.

50 See the summary by I. Howard Marshall, Emeritus Professor of Theology, University of Aberdeen, in: <http://www.cbeinternational.org/resources/how-i-changed-my-mind>.

51 The theme of many biblical passages, including 1 Corinthians 13; 1 John 4.7–21.

52 For a much fuller account, see Moltmann-Wendel, Elisabeth, *The Women around Jesus*, New York, Crossroad, 1982; Stagg, Evelyn and Stagg, Frank, *Woman in the World of Jesus*, Philadelphia, Westminster Press, 1978.

53 Storkey, Elaine and Hebblethwaite, Margaret, *Conversations on Christian Feminism*, London, HarperCollins, 1999.

Select bibliography

———————

Violence against women – global and general

Baksh, Rawwida and Harcourt, Wendy (eds), *The Oxford Book of Transnational Feminist Movements*, Oxford, Oxford University Press, 2015.

Bennett, Jane, *Feminist Africa 14: Rethinking Gender and Violence*, Cape Town, African Gender Institute, December 2010.

Edwards, Alice, *Violence against Women under International Human Rights Law*, Cambridge, Cambridge University Press, 2013.

Ertürk, Y, 'Violence against Women: From Victimization to Empowerment', presented at the forum, Where Is the Power in Women's Empowerment?, ESCAP, Bangkok, 4 August 2008.

Gordon, A., *Transforming Capitalism and Patriarchy: Gender and Development in Africa*, Boulder, CO, Lynne Rienner Publishers, 1996.

Heise, L. L., 'Violence against Women: Translating International Advocacy into Concrete Change', *American University Law Review* 44(1207), 1994–5.

Jarvinen, Justine, Kail, Angela and Miller, Iona, *Hard Knock Life: Violence against Women*, London, New Philanthropy Capital, 2008.

Johnson, Holly, Ollus, Natalia and Nevala, Sami, *Violence Against Women: An International Perspective*, New York, Springer, 2008.

Klot, Jennifer F. and Nguyen, Vinh-Kim, *The Fourth Wave: Violence, Gender, Culture & HIV in the 21st Century*, UNESCO, 2009.

Kristof, Nicholas D. and WuDunn, Sheryl, *Half the Sky: Turning Oppression into Opportunity for Women Worldwide*, London, Hachette, 2009.

Krug, Etienne G., Dahlberg, Linda L., Mercy, James A., Zwi, Anthony B. and Lozano, Rafael (eds), *World Report on Violence and Health*, Geneva, World Health Organization, 2002.

Lombard, Nancy, *Young People's Understandings of Men's Violence against Women*, Farnham, Ashgate, 2015.

Mitchell, Penny, *About Canada: Women's Rights*, Manitoba, Fernwood Publishing, 2015.

Ptacek, James (ed.), *Restorative Justice and Violence against Women*, New York, Oxford University Press, 2010.

Sheehy, E., 'Legal Responses to Violence against Women in Canada', in Webber, M. and Bezanson, K. (eds), *Rethinking Society in the*

21st Century: Critical Readings in Sociology, 2nd edn, Toronto, Canadian Scholars' Press, 2008.

Thiara, Ravi K. (ed.), *Violence against Women in South Asian Communities: Issues for Policy and Practice*, London, Jessica Kingsley Publishers, 2009.

True, Jacqui, *The Political Economy of Violence against Women*, New York, Oxford University Press, 2012.

Westmarland, Nicole, *Violence against Women: Criminological Perspectives on Men's Violence*, London, Routledge, 2015.

Selective abortion / female genital mutilation / child brides

Barnes, Virginia Lee and Boddy, Janice, *Aman: The Story of a Somali Girl*, London, Bloomsbury, 1995.

The Bristol Peer Review, Principal Researcher Dr Eiman Hussein, 'Women's Experiences, Perceptions and Attitudes of Female Genital Mutilation', Foundation for Women's Health Research and Development, 2010.

Cook, Kathy, *Stolen Angels: The Kidnapped Girls of Uganda*, Penguin Global, 2009.

Gill, Aisha K. and Sundari, Anitha (eds), *Forced Marriage: Introducing a Social Justice and Human Rights Perspective*, London: Zed Books, 2011.

Hudson, Valerie M. and den Boer, Andrea M., *Bare Branches: The Security Implications of Asia's Surplus Male Population*, Boston, MIT Press, 2005.

Klasen, Stephen and Wink, Claudia, '"Missing Women": Revisiting the Debate', *Feminist Economics*, 9 January 2003.

Kuruvilla, Moly, *Discrimination against Girl Child: The Trajectory of Missing Girls*, New Delhi, Gyan Publishing House, 2011.

Mufaka, Kenneth, 'Scottish Missionaries and the Circumcision Controversy in Kenya, 1900–1960', *International Review of Scottish Studies* 28, 2003.

Nashipae Nkadori, Evelyn, 'FGM: Maasai Women Speak Out', *Cultural Survival 40 Years 1972–2012*, Cambridge, MA, 2010.

Patel, Tultsi, *Sex Selective Abortion in India: Gender, Society and New Reproductive Technologies*, London, Sage, 2007.

Saeveras, Elin Finnseth, *Female Genital Mutilation, Understanding the Issues*, Oslo, Norwegian Church Aid, 2003.

Strayer, Robert W., *The Making of Mission Communities in East Africa*, London, Heinemann Educational, 1978.

Toubia, Nahid, *Female Genital Mutilation: A Call for Global Action*, New York, Women Ink, 1993.

UN Women, *Gender-Based Violence and Child Protection amongst Syrian Refugees in Jordan with a Focus on Early Marriage*, New York, 2014.

United Nations Population Fund (UNFPA), *Marrying Too Young: End Child Marriage*, New York, 2012.

Honour killings / domestic violence

Athwal, Sarbjit Kaur, *Shamed*, London, Virgin Books, 2013.

Barter, Christine, McCarry, Melanie, Berridge, David and Evans, Kathy, *Partner Exploitation and Violence in Teenage Intimate Relationships*, London, NSPCC, 2009.

Browne, Angela, *When Battered Women Kill*, New York, The Free Press, 1987.

Dobash, R. Emerson and Dobash, Russell P., *When Men Murder Women*, New York, Oxford University Press, 2015.

Gill, Aisha K. (author), Strange, Carolyn and Roberts, Karl (eds), *'Honour' Killing and Violence: Theory, Policy and Practice*, London, Palgrave Macmillan, 2014.

Harne, Lynne and Radford, Gill, *Tackling Domestic Violence: Theories, Policies and Practice*, Maidenhead, Open University, 2009.

Human Rights Watch, *'He Loves You, He Beats You': Family Violence in Turkey and Access to Protection*, 2011.

Herman, Judith Lewis, *Trauma and Recovery*, New York, Basic Books, 1997.

Holcomb, Justin S. and Holcomb, Lindsay, *Is It My Fault? Hope and Healing for Those Suffering Domestic Violence*, Chicago, Moody Publishers, 2014.

Jones, Ann, *Next Time She'll Be Dead: Battering and How to Stop It*, Boston, Beacon Press, 1995.

Manckton-Smith, Jane, *Murder, Gender and the Media: Narratives of Dangerous Love*, London, Palgrave Macmillan, 2013.

Salhi, Zahia Smail (ed.), *Gender and Violence in Islamic Societies: Patriarchy, Islamism and Politics in the Middle East and North Africa*, London, I. B. Tauris, 2013.

Walby, Sylvia, *The Cost of Domestic Violence*, London, Women and Equality Unit, 2004.

Walby, Sylvia and Allen, Jonathan, *Domestic Violence, Sexual Assault and Stalking: Findings from the British Crime Survey*, London, Home Office, 2004.

Trafficking and prostitution

Batstone, David, *Not for Sale*, New York, HarperCollins, 2007.

Brown, Louise, *The Dancing Girls of Lahore*, New York, HarperCollins, 2005.

Ekberg, Gunilla, 'The Swedish Law That Prohibits the Purchase of Sexual Services: Best Practices for Prevention of Prostitution and Trafficking in Human Beings', *Violence Against Women* 10(10), October 2004.

Farley, M. (ed.), *Prostitution, Trafficking and Traumatic Stress*, Binghamton, NY, Haworth Press, 2003.

Nag, Moni, *Sex Workers in India: Diversity of Practice and Ways of Life*, Mumbai, Allied Publishers, 2006.

Picoult, Jodi, *The Tenth Circle*, New York, Atria Books, Simon & Schuster, 2006.

Sage, Jesse and Kasten, Liora (eds), *Enslaved: True Stories of Modern Day Slavery*, London, Palgrave Macmillan, 2008.

Shelley, Louise, *Human Trafficking: A Global Perspective*, Cambridge, Cambridge University Press, 2010.

Siddarth, Kara, *Sex Trafficking: Inside the Business of Modern Slavery*, New York, Columbia University Press, 2009.

Tyler, Megan, *Selling Sex Short: The Pornographic and Sexological Construction of Women's Sexuality in the West*, Newcastle, Cambridge Scholars Publishing, 2011.

United Nations Office on Drugs and Crime, *Global Report on Trafficking in Persons 2014*, Vienna, 2014.

Rape / sexual violence in war

Arieff, A., 2009, *Sexual Violence in African Conflicts*: a Congressional Research Service report for Congress, 25 November 2009.

Ayiera, Eve, 'Sexual Violence in Conflict: A Problematic International Discourse', *Feminist Africa 14: Rethinking Gender and Violence*, Cape Town, African Gender Institute, December 2010.

Hirsch, Michele Lent and Wolfe, Lauren, 'Women under Siege: Democratic Republic of the Congo', The Women's Media Center, 8 February 2012.

Holmes, John, 'Congo's Rape War', *Los Angeles Times*, 11 October 2007.

Hussain, R., 'Rape for Ethnic Cleansing', in Altmuslimah, 2010. Available at: <http://www.altmuslimah.com/a/b/gva/3535/>.

Jones, Ann, *War Is Not Over When It's Over: Women Speak Out from the Ruins of War*, New York, Metropolitan Books, Henry Holt, 2010.

Lewis, S., 'Congo's Rape and Sexual Violence: UN's Delinquency', *Pambazuka* 364, 15 April 2008: <http://pambazuka.org/en/category/feature/47347>.

Lewis, S., 'Peace is a Mere Illusion When Rape Continues', *Pambazuka* 395, 10 September 2008: <http://pambazuka.org/en/category/feature/50445>.

Lwambo, Desiree, *'Before the War I Was a Man': Men and Masculinities in Eastern Congo*, Goma, Heal Africa Publication, 2011, in partnership with Harvard Humanitarian Initiative, Cambridge, MA, 2009.

Nduwimana, Françoise, *The Right to Survive: Sexual Violence, Women and HIV/AIDS*, Quebec, International Centre for Human Rights and Democratic Development, 2004.

Scott, N. R., 'Rape Warfare: Sexual Violence as a Systematic Weapon of War', *American Journal of Scientific Research* 9, 2010.

Seifert, R., 'The Second Front: The Logic of Sexual Violence in Wars', *Women's Studies International Forum* 19(1–2), 1996.

Shepherd, L. J., 'Women, Armed Conflict and Language: Gender, Violence and Discourse', *International Review of the Red Cross* 92(877), March 2010.

Skjelsbæk, I., 'The Elephant in the Room. An Overview of How Sexual Violence Came to Be Seen as a Weapon of War', *Report to the Norwegian Ministry of Foreign Affairs*, Oslo, Peace Research Institute, May 2010.

Stearns, J., 'Mass Rape in Walikale: What Happened?', *Congo Siasa*, 24 August 2010.

Storkey, Alan, *War or Peace?*, Cambridge, Christian Studies Press, 2015.

UN News Service, 'UN Voices Outrage at Mass Rape by Rebels in Eastern DR Congo', 24 August 2010. Available at: <http://www.un.org/apps/news/story.asp?NewsID=35706>.

United Nations Division for the Advancement of Women (UNDAW), *Sexual Violence and Armed Conflict: United Nations Response*, 1998.

Vivona, Paula, 'Impunity in the DRC: An Examination of the Patriarchal Society and the Military Establishment', PDF file, 2012: <www.researchgate.net>.

Evolutionary analyses of violence against women

Buss, D. M. and Malamuth, N. M., *Sex, Power, Conflict: Evolutionary and Feminist Perspectives*, New York, Oxford University Press, 1996.

Daly, M. and Wilson, M., *Homicide*, New York, Aldine De Gruyter, 1988.

Ellis, Lee, *Theories of Rape: Inquiries into the Causes of Sexual Aggression*, Washington, DC, Hemisphere Pub. Corp., 1989.

Hamilton, R., 'The Darwinian Cage: Evolutionary Psychology as Moral Science', *Theory, Culture and Society* 25(2), 2008.

Malik, Kenan, 'What Science Can and Cannot Tell Us about Human Nature', in Wells, Robin Headlam and McFadden, Johnjoe (eds), *Human Nature: Fact and Fiction: Literature, Science and Human Nature*, London, Bloomsbury Continuum, 2006.

Midgley, Mary, *Science and Poetry*, London, Routledge Classics, 2006.

Pinker, S., *The Blank Slate: The Modern Denial of Human Nature*, London, BCA, 2002.

Searle, John, 'Putting Consciousness Back into the Brain' – reply to Bennett and Hacker in Bennett, M., Dennett, D., Hacker, P. and Searle, J. (eds), *Neuroscience and Philosophy: Body, Mind and Language*, New York, Columbia University Press, 2007, pp. 97–126.

Tallis, Raymond, *The Explicit Animal: A Defence of Human Consciousness*, London, Macmillan, 1991.

Thornhill, Randy and Palmer, Craig T., *A Natural History of Rape: Biological Bases of Sexual Coercion*, Cambridge, MA, Bradford Books, MIT Press, 2001.

Wells, Robin Headlam and McFadden, Johnjoe (eds), *Human Nature: Fact and Fiction: Literature, Science and Human Nature*, London, Bloomsbury Continuum, 2006.

Wilson, Glenn, *The Great Sex Divide*, London, Peter Owen, 1989.

Feminist analyses

Brownmiller, Susan, *Against Our Will: Men, Women and Rape*, New York, Simon & Schuster, 1975.

Daly, Mary, *Gyn/Ecology: The Meta-ethics of Radical Feminism*, Boston, Beacon Press, 1978.

Fairstein, Linda, *Sexual Violence: Our War against Rape*, New York, Berkley Books, 1995.

Gay, Roxane, *Bad Feminist: Essays*, New York, Harper Perennial, 2014.

Hall, Rebecca Jane, 'Feminist Strategies to End Violence against Women', in Baksh, Rawwida and Harcourt, Wendy (eds), *The Oxford Book of Transnational Feminist Movements*, Oxford, Oxford University Press, 2015.

Hennessy, Rosemary, *Profit and Pleasure: Sexual Identities in Late Capitalism*, New York/London, Routledge, 2000.

hooks, bell, *The Will to Change: Men, Masculinity and Love*, New York, Simon & Schuster, 2004.

Laurie, Penny, *Meat Market: Female Flesh under Capitalism*, Alresford, Hants, Zero Books, 2011.

Laurie, Penny, *Unspeakable Things: Sex, Lies and Revolution*, New York, Bloomsbury USA, 2014.

Lerner, Gerder, *The Creation of Patriarchy*, Oxford, Oxford University Press, 1987.

Mackay, Finn, *Radical Feminism: Feminist Activism in Movement*, London, Palgrave Macmillan, 2015.

Miller, Alice, *Breaking Down the Wall of Silence*, New York, Plume, 1997.

Moi, T., *What Is a Woman? and Other Essays*, Oxford/New York, Oxford University Press, 1999.

Morgan, Robin, *Sisterhood Is Powerful*, New York, Random House, 1973.

Price, Lisa, *Feminist Frameworks: Building Theory on Violence against Women*, Manitoba, Fernwood Publishing, 2005.

Storkey, Elaine, *Created or Constructed? The Great Gender Debate*, Carlisle, Paternoster Press, 2000.

Storkey, Elaine, *What's Right with Feminism*, London, SPCK, 1985.

Van Leeuwen, Mary Stewart, *My Brother's Keeper: What the Social Sciences Do (and Don't) Tell Us about Masculinity*, Downers Grove, IL, IVP, 2002.

Walby, Sylvia, *Theorizing Patriarchy*, Cambridge, Polity Press, 1997.

Religion and violence against women

Cooey, Paula M., Eakin, William R. and McDaniel, John B., *After Patriarchy: Feminist Transformations of the World Religions*, New Delhi, Sri Satguru Publications, 1991.

Daly, Mary, *Beyond God the Father*, Boston, Beacon Press, 1973.

Darwish, Nonie, *The Devil We Don't Know: The Dark Side of Revolutions in the Middle East*, Hoboken, NJ, John Wiley and Sons, 2012.

El Saadawi, Nawal, *The Hidden Face of Eve: Women in the Arab World*, Boston, Beacon Press, 1980.

Goodwin, Jan, *Price of Honour: Muslim Women Lift the Veil of Silence on the Islamic World*, New York, Penguin, 2003.

Kyung, Chung Hyun, *Struggle to Be the Sun Again: Introducing Asian Women's Theology*, Maryknoll, NY, Orbis Books, 1990.

Salime, Zakia, *Between Feminism and Islam: Human Rights and Sharia Law in Morocco*, Minneapolis, University of Minnesota Press, 2011.

Schüssler Fiorenza, Elisabeth, *In Memory of Her: A Feminist Reconstruction of Christian Origins*, New York, Crossroad, 1985.

Wadud, Amina, *Inside the Gender Jihad*, London, Oneworld, 2007.

Webb, Gisela (ed.), *Windows of Faith: Muslim Women Scholar-Activists in North America*, Syracuse, NY, Syracuse University Press, 2000.

Christian analyses and responses

Atkinson, Sue, *Struggling to Forgive: Moving on from Trauma*, Oxford, Monarch, 2014.

Baker, Jenny, *Enjoying Gender Equality in All Areas of Life*, London, SPCK, 2014.

Select bibliography

Bilezikian, Gilbert, *Beyond Sex Roles*, Grand Rapids, Baker Academic, 2006.

Campbell, Douglas (ed.), *Gospel and Gender*, London, T&T Clark, 2004.

Carson, Marion, *Human Trafficking, the Bible and the Church*, Eugene, OR, Wipf & Stock, 2015.

Croft, Stephen and Gooder, Paula, *Women and Men in Scripture and the Church*, London, Canterbury Press, 2013.

Dawn, Maggie, *The Writing on the Wall: High Art, Popular Culture and the Bible*, London, Hodder Paperbacks, 2012.

Evans, Mary J., *Woman in the Bible*, Carlisle, Paternoster Press, 1984.

Evans, Mary J., Storkey, Elaine and Kroeger, Catherine Clark, *Study New Testament for Women*, London, Marshall Pickering, 1995.

Goddard, Lis and Hendry, Clare, *The Gender Agenda*, Nottingham, IVP, 2010.

Jenkins, Philip, *The New Faces of Christianity; Believing the Bible in the Global South*, New York, Oxford University Press, 2006.

Kroeger, Catherine Clark and Kroeger, Richard, *I Suffer Not a Woman: Rethinking 1 Timothy 2:11–15 in Light of Ancient Evidence*, Grand Rapids, Baker Book House, 1992.

Kroeger, Catherine Clark and Nason-Clark, Nancy, *No Place for Abuse*, Downers Grove, IL, IVP, 2011.

Kroeger, Catherine Clark and Nason-Clark, Nancy, *Refuge from Abuse: Healing and Hope for Christian Women*, Downers Grove, IL, IVP, 2004.

Loades, Ann, 'Feminist Interpretation', in Barton, John (ed.), *The Cambridge Companion to Biblical Interpretation*, Cambridge, Cambridge University Press, 1998.

Mills, Sue, *The Butterfly Train*, London, New Wine Press, 2012.

Mollenkott, Virginia, *Women, Men and the Bible*, Nashville, Abingdon Press, 1977.

Moltmann-Wendel, Elisabeth, *The Women around Jesus*, New York, Crossroad, 1982.

Mufaka, Kenneth, 'Scottish Missionaries and the Circumcision Controversy in Kenya, 1900–1960', *International Review of Scottish Studies* 28, 2003.

Nason-Clark, Nancy, *The Battered Wife: How Christians Confront Family Violence*, Louisville, KY, Westminster John Knox Press, 1997.

Nason-Clark, Nancy, Holtmann, Cathy, Fisher-Townsend, Barbara, McMullin, Steve and Ruff, Lanette, 'The RAVE Project: Developing Web-based Religious Resources for Social Action on Domestic Violence', *Critical Social Work* 10(1), 2009.

Paul, Ian, *Women and Authority: The Key Biblical Texts*, Cambridge, Grove Books, 2011.

Russell, Letty M., 'Authority and the Challenge of Feminist Interpretation', in Russell, Letty M. (ed.), *Feminist Interpretation of the Bible*, Philadelphia, Westminster Press, 1985.

Russell, Letty M. (ed.), *Feminist Interpretation of the Bible*, Philadelphia, Westminster Press, 1985.

Scanzoni, Letha and Hardesty, Nancy, *All We Were Meant to Be*, Waco, TX, Word Books, 1974.

Storkey, Alan, *Jesus and Politics*, Grand Rapids, Baker Books, 2005.

Storkey, Alan, *The Meanings of Love*, London, IVP, 1994.

Storkey, Elaine, *The Origins of Difference*, Grand Rapids, Baker Academic, 2001.

Storkey, Elaine, *The Search for Intimacy*, London, Hodder Headline, 1998.

Strayer, Robert W., *The Making of Mission Communities in East Africa*, London, Heinemann Educational, 1978.

Trible, Phyllis, *Texts of Terror: Literary Feminist Readings of Biblical Narratives*, Philadelphia, Fortress Press, 1984.

Index

Index

Index

Index

Index

273

Index

Index

Index

CPSIA information can be obtained
at www.ICGtesting.com
Printed in the USA
LVOW12s1636260117
522285LV00003B/673/P